CATHOLIC THEOLOGICAL FORMATION

General Editor: Kevin Zilverberg

The Catholic Theological Formation Series is sponsored by The Saint Paul Seminary School of Divinity, the graduate school of theological formation for Roman Catholic seminarians and laity enrolled at the University of St. Thomas in St. Paul, Minnesota. As a premier institution of theological formation for the region and beyond, The Saint Paul Seminary School of Divinity seeks to form men and women for the task of fulfilling the specific call God has for them, a call grounded in their common baptismal vocation to serve one another in Christ.

As an institution of the Archdiocese of St. Paul and Minneapolis, the school is intentional in its commitment to priestly formation for the archdiocese and the broader region. As an institution of graduate theological education, the school prepares the laity for the equally compelling task of making Christ known and loved in the world. Though distinct in their various ministries, the common goal of intense theological formation is shared across the curriculum.

It is this challenge of theological formation—the challenge to faithfully inform one's understanding—that serves as the focus of this series, with special attention given to the task of preparing priests, teachers, and leaders within the Roman Catholic tradition. Although the series is academic in tenor, it aims beyond mere academics in its intellectual approach. We seek to promote a form of discourse that is professional in its conduct and spiritual in its outcomes, for theological formation is more than an exercise in academic technique. It is rather about the perfecting of a spiritual capacity: the capacity on the part of the human person to discern what is true and good.

This series, then, aims to develop the habits of mind required of a sound intellect—a spiritual aptitude for the truth of God's living Word and his Church. Most often, it will draw from the more traditional specializations of historical, systematic, moral, and biblical scholarship. Homiletics and pastoral ministry are anticipated venues as well. There will be occasions, however, when a theme is examined across disciplines and periods, for the purposes of bringing to our common consideration a thesis yet undeveloped.

Despite the variety of methodologies and topics explored, the series' aim remains constant: to provide a sustained reflection upon the mission and ministry of Catholic theological formation of both priests and laity alike.

The general editor of the Catholic Theological Formation Series, Fr. Kevin Zilverberg, serves as assistant professor of Sacred Scripture and the founding director of Saint Paul Seminary Press at The Saint Paul Seminary School of Divinity.

In the School of the Word

*Biblical Interpretation
from the New to the Old Testament*

by Carlos Granados *and* Luis Sánchez-Navarro

Translated by Kristin Towle

With an introduction to the English edition by
Kevin Zilverberg

**SAINT PAUL
SEMINARY PRESS**

SAINT PAUL, MINNESOTA • 2021

Cover image: detail of Mary and the apostles at Pentecost; Holy Spirit Chapel,
House of Formation of the Disciples of the Hearts of Jesus and Mary, Madrid, Spain
Cover artwork and photo by Ioan Gotia, DCJM
Cover design by Willem Mineur

Original title:
En la escuela de la Palabra. Del Nuevo al Antiguo Testamento
© Carlos Granados García y Luis Sánchez Navarro
© Editorial Verbo Divino, 2016
original ISBN: 978-84-9073-261-8

Published 2021 by
Saint Paul Seminary Press
2260 Summit Ave., Saint Paul, Minnesota 55105

Library of Congress Control Number: 2021940318
LC record available at https://lccn.loc.gov/2021940318

Catholic Theological Formation Series
ISSN 2765-9283
ISBN 978-1-953936-06-6 (paperback)
ISBN 978-1-953936-56-1 (ebook)

www.spspress.com

Contents

Introduction to the English Edition

In the late 2010s I met Fathers Carlos Granados and Luis Sánchez-Navarro as I pursued doctoral studies in Madrid and Rome. These priests, members of the Catholic religious institute of the Disciples of the Hearts of Jesus and Mary (DCJM), impressed me by their human warmth, biblical erudition, fraternal living, and lively faith. The original Spanish edition of the present book convinced me of their keen perception of the role of the faith-filled biblical scholar and of biblical hermeneutics at once scientifically rigorous and ecclesial. Therefore, soon after I became the director of the nascent Saint Paul Seminary Press, I procured the book's English translation rights on the press's behalf.

The reader will perceive differences in style between chapters authored by Granados and Sánchez-Navarro, as well as different formative influences documented in their footnotes. Nevertheless, their years of shared prayer, study, conversation, and ministry have led to this unified literary production bearing witness to that ongoing unity that they live as confreres. Not surprisingly, they frequently reference the same theologians, especially Brevard Childs, Paul Beauchamp, SJ, and Pope Benedict XVI. Granados and Sánchez-Navarro's Spanish publisher, Editorial Verbo Divino, did well to accept this collection of essays ordered thematically into a coherent book;[1] by the present translation, Saint Paul Seminary Press now affirms that book's success.

"Part I: The Church, Living Subject of Sacred Scripture," takes up a

1. For the list of original publications, see 215–216.

foundational theme of the whole book: Sacred Scripture calls for a reading within the community of the People of God under the guidance of the Holy Spirit, and the same People constitutes the living subject of Scripture.[2] Within this context the testimonial character of the New Testament emerges clearly; the texts testify to Christ on behalf of the Church and lead to the Church's growth. The fact of Sacred Scripture's testimonial character constitutes a hermeneutical lynchpin for the authors, as does the precedence of the New Testament for the interpretation of the whole Bible. That is why Sánchez-Navarro has chosen as the topic and title of the book's first chapter "The Testimonial Character of Sacred Scripture" and has focused on the New Testament to make his case. Given the fundamentally testimonial orientation of the Scriptures, any interpretive approach that rejects or fails to take proper account of biblical testimony will lead to false or distorted results. The pretense of a neutrality that prescinds from faith when interpreting the Bible in the end is quite biased, and biased such that it fails even on scientific grounds, by failing to apply a method of inquiry fit to its object. Sánchez-Navarro continues to focus on the New Testament in the second chapter, "The Word of God and the Church in the New Testament." He shows the close relationship between the Word, Jesus, and the Church, as he brings to bear the categories established in the previous chapter. The Church is the subject of the Scriptures insofar as she produced them. Yet the Scriptures are the *locutio Dei* or "speaking of God" and have God as their deepest author, so the Church is also object of the Scriptures as she receives their divine message. Only because of the Church was Scripture composed and transmitted, and Scripture becomes incomprehensible when separated from the Church. This obtains not only when giving an account of how the Scriptures came to be, but even for their interpretation in the present: their meaning depends upon their ecclesial context.

Granados offers a reflection in chapter three, "From Scripture in the Body to Scripture in the Church," that complements what has been said so far. He begins by philosophizing about writing (*escritura*, "scripture," in Spanish) and its relationship to speaking. Although he considers the word to have a certain priority over writing, he appreciates the arguments proffered by those who prioritize writing. In fact, the two phenomena are so closely related that scripture, writing, represents the social body of the word. Granados leverages these philosophical tenets to draw profound conclusions about the nature of Sacred Scripture. Holy Writ always refers back to the originating Word of which it is

2. For Pope Benedict XVI's formulation of this principle, see the "Preface to the Spanish Edition" of the present volume, p. 10.

the body and which it expresses. Sacred Word and Scripture, therefore, remain always dynamically linked together in the Church. Hence, Tradition cannot be a mere supplement to Scripture, but rather the principle that ensures that Word and Scripture conserve their mutual union.

Part I culminates in Sánchez-Navarro's chapter four, "The Ecclesial Reading of Scripture." He resumes themes from the previous chapters to describe an approach to Scripture fitted to its content and nature: a reading within the Church. This reading puts down roots in history and approaches the Old Testament with reverence, even as it takes the Messiah of the New Testament as the interpretive key that unites the whole book that is the Bible. This Messiah, Christ, is alive, and the Bible continues to be a living book as believers read it. In the words of the Bible those believers, who are the Church and the bride, hear the voice of the bridegroom resounding from start to finish.

In Part II, "Christ, Exegete of the Fulfillment," the authors focus on the relationship between the two biblical testaments. They argue that the Christian can both respect and venerate the Old Testament on its own terms, even as they find in Jesus, as presented in the New Testament and encountered in faith, the key for unlocking the Old Testament's deepest meaning.

Granados opens Part II with his chapter "How Should We Read the Old Testament? With Christ, Exegete of the Fulfillment." He begins by pointing out those ways in which the Old Testament is an "open book" that admits of multiple interpretations. Although we Christians read it in the school of the New Testament, there is no warrant for reading all of the New in the Old. Rather, he proposes the model of fulfillment, which extends trajectories already present in the Old toward fulfillment in the New. The responsible use of typology can accomplish this, along with readings that elucidate from Old Testament texts the Christian moral (tropological) and theological (anagogical) meanings consistent with the texts' literal meanings.

Sánchez-Navarro's next chapter, "Old and New: Conflict or Fulfillment?" complements that of Granados just before it. The author recognizes that there are indeed discontinuities between the two testaments, yet he affirms their inseparability: "Jesus was incomprehensible without Scripture; now Scripture is incomprehensible without Jesus."[3] What Christians now call the Old Covenant was always open to fulfillment in a new one; Sánchez-Navarro shows how the New Testament supports his thesis that fulfillment, not conflict, best labels the dynamic relationship between Old and New. In the next chapter, "The Old-New Relationship, Hermeneutical Key to Scripture," Sánchez-Navarro

3. P. 117.

continues to show how a proper understanding of the two testaments' relationship is crucial for interpreting the Bible. He begins with examples from each Testament to show how they depend on one another, and then he highlights the approaches of Childs and Beauchamp, who each wrote creatively about the unity of the Bible. Sánchez-Navarro concludes that the Bible is a single, unified book. Whereas he focused on the testimonial character of the New Testament in the first two chapters, now he expands that category to speak of Old Testament testimony as well.

Sánchez-Navarro contributes his final chapter for Part II, in "Christians and the Old Testament: The Teaching of Vatican II (*DV* §§15–16)." By focusing on the changes made to the drafts preceding the dogmatic constitution *Dei verbum*, he highlights the document's theological progress. The Council Fathers unabashedly proposed a Christological reading of the whole Bible, yet they took care to adjust their language to show a respect for the Old Testament that became increasingly apparent from one draft to the next. Moreover, *Dei verbum*'s careful distinction between revelation itself and the biblical books as a written expression of that revelation remind one of the need for an ecclesial context for biblical interpretation; the Bible must be read in the same Spirit in which it was written in order to perceive the divine revelation to which they bear witness. A Christological reading, aided by the Spirit, does not collapse the Old Testament into the New but reveres it as a distinct expression of divine revelation within the unified whole of the Bible.

Granados concludes part two with a focused case study in chapter nine, "A Model for the Relationship between the Old and New Testaments: 1 Corinthians 9:9," followed by a chapter in which he takes a broad view of the Old Testament to ask whether it gives witness to Christ. 1 Corinthians 9:9 reads: "For it is written in the law of Moses, 'You shall not muzzle an ox when it is treading out the grain.' Is it for oxen that God is concerned?" Some scholars take issue with this Pauline interpretation of the Old Testament for contorting a text (Deut 25:4) concerning the treatment of animals, so that it concerns humans instead. Granados, however, shows through responsible exegesis that the literal meaning of the Old Testament passage does indeed have to do with humans. In fact, it is open to readings like Paul's, so that 1 Corinthians 9:9 is not an allegorical reading but rather gives Deuteronomy 25:4 "significance" flowing from the literal "meaning" of the text.

In the final chapter of Part II, "Does the Old Testament Give Testimony of Christ? Canonical Exegesis and Postmodern Exegesis," Granados answers his title's question from the perspectives of Childs's canonical exegesis and Walter Brueggemann's postmodern exegesis. Whereas Childs answers affirmatively, claiming that one must go deeper than the textual level in order to encounter its theological subject matter, Brueggemann focuses on the language of Old Testament discourse and shrinks from any reading that presupposes Christ from the outset. Although Granados appreciates Brueggemann's care to read the Old Testament on its own terms, he ultimately sides with Childs: the Christian cannot prescind from the extra-textual reality of Jesus Christ when seeking the meaning of the Old Testament.

The third and final part of this book, "The Teaching in Benedict XVI's *Verbum Domini*," examines Pope Benedict XVI's 2010 post-synodal apostolic exhortation on the word of God in the life and mission of the Church. In chapter 11, "Listening to the Word: On the Subject of *Verbum Domini*," Sánchez-Navarro examines the first part of the three-part document, the part dedicated to the theological study of the Word and its correct interpretation. He begins by recounting the pertinent aspects of preceding Church documents on Sacred Scripture, and some past teachings on Scripture by the author, Benedict XVI. The pope's own approach based on the *Logos* of the prologue of John's Gospel fits well with that of the present book: God speaks his *Logos* to humankind, and the sacred writings bear written witness to that revelatory Word that continues to elicit a response of faith. The hermeneutic of faith insisted upon all through this book finds here a magisterial validation, for the Bible belongs in the Church and makes sense in the ecclesial context in which it was formed. If it were otherwise, how would one explain the remarkable lives of so many saints nourished by Sacred Scripture, heroic witnesses to the Lord Jesus whom they encountered in the Bible? The pope (and Sánchez-Navarro) calls on all to hear the Word of God in all its freshness and vigor, in the manner of the saints.

In chapter 12, "The Fulfillment of the Scriptures according to *Verbum Domini*," Granados interprets the Binding of Isaac (Gen 22) according to Benedict XVI's document. He strives to respect the Old Testament text even as he affirms its openness to fulfillment in Jesus Christ, thereby applying principles that he laid out in previous chapters, especially his defense of typological interpretations in chapter 5. Granados defends the view that both Abraham and Isaac prefigure Christ, evoking Beauchamp's insight about the increasing concentration of figures that results in paroxysm as their definitive fulfillment draws near.

Sánchez-Navarro contributes the final chapter, "*Verbum Domini*: A Logocentric Vision of the Christian Faith," in which he draws out the magisterial document's implications for recognizing the divine *Logos* pervading every aspect of life. Benedict XVI's own emphasis on the prologue of John's Gospel leaves a logocentric imprint on the document *Verbum Domini*: God has spoken his incarnate *Logos* to enter into dialogue with humans, who are called to respond in faith. Doing so results in the Word pervading every aspect of their lives in the communion of the Church. Mary of Nazareth, who had the greatest familiarity with the Word, stands out as the model Christian believer who received the *Logos* in faith and joyfully lived out her ongoing obedience to the Word.

Every chapter of this book pertains to reading the Bible with Christian faith, not as one approach among many, but as a disposition demanded by the New Testament for proper interpretation of both the Old and the New. Even so, the authors' faith never leads them to dismiss history or to discard the tools of the historical-critical method. On the contrary, these sciences allow the faithful reader to take a holistic approach to biblical truth. When the reader also takes full account of the ecclesial reality in which the Bible was formed and transmitted, and in which it must be read still today, he or she encounters the word proclaimed by the text. Indeed, the words of Holy Writ ultimately proclaim *the* Word (*Logos*), Jesus Christ, in whose Spirit they were written.[4]

Fr. Kevin Zilverberg
April 10, 2021

4. I would like to thank all those who contributed to this book, beginning with Fathers Carlos Granados and Luis Sánchez-Navarro. Your dedication as priests and scholars inspires me to be a better priest and scholar. Thank you, Dr. Kristin Towle, for your hard work and dedication to making this volume known in a polished English translation. Finally, I would like to thank the rest of my editing and production team for their work: Erika Zabinski, copyeditor; David McEachron, indexer; Maggee Becker, proofreader; and Judy Gilats, typesetter. You carry out your roles with competence and professionality.

Translator's Foreword

In translating this book about reading Scripture within the Church, I have strived to follow the sentence structure and terminology of the authors as closely as possible, so that their voices could come through in English. I hope that I have made their message clear to English-speaking readers, for it is a crucial message about the truth of God's Word in the Bible.

In their explorations of how to read the Bible faithfully, the authors have included sundry quotations from other scholars. Tracking down the quotations of these scholars in published English editions of their works has proved to be rather arduous. I have felt like Sherlock Holmes at times with this task of locating quotations: the game was definitely afoot in the footnotes! Hence wherever possible, the quotations that appear in the text and the footnotes are from the published English versions of the works. Where no published English edition exists, I have translated from the language of the original publication, or failing that, from the Spanish translation quoted in the Spanish edition.

Scripture citations, unless otherwise indicated, are from the Revised Standard Version, Catholic Edition (RSVCE) of the Bible. Regarding the Dogmatic Constitution on Divine Revelation *Dei verbum*, which is cited and quoted frequently in this book, I have used the Gonzalez edition of the Vatican II documents (Boston: Daughters of St. Paul, [1967?]), which is published on the Vatican website. For Pope Benedict XVI's magisterial document *Verbum Domini*, which also appears many times in this work, I have used the translation that is found on the Vatican website and published by the United States Conference of Catholic Bishops. Occasionally the RSVCE or the English translations of magisterial texts do not capture what the authors are trying to highlight about wording, so I have followed the authors and their Spanish renditions instead of the RSVCE or the published English translations of magisterial documents.

Bracketed words and statements in this book are added by me as editorial notes.

I wish to offer a note of thanks to those who helped me in this endeavor of

7

translating *In the School of the Word*: my friend and colleague, Fr. Kevin Zilverberg, who is the editor-in-chief of SPS Press and who spurred on this translation; my copyeditor, Erika Zabinski; my husband, Michael, who cared for our children while I worked, and who helped me find many elusive quotations and citations; and my parents, Joe and Mary, and parents-in-law, Mike and Peggy, who offered our family much support as I labored over this work.

At the end of his tremendous book *De Trinitate*, St. Augustine, who had used so many words, images, and arguments to try to understand and explain the Divine Trinity, summed up his book by highlighting how his words fell far short of God. Whenever I finish a theological writing, I try to keep in mind the words from Scripture that St. Augustine cited to show our human limitations and God's grandeur:

> "We say many things, and fall short,
> and the sum of our words is, 'He is all.'"
> (Sirach 43:27).[5]

May this humble work of translation be all for the glory of God.

KRISTIN TOWLE, PhD
May 10, 2021

---

5. As cited in Augustine, *On the Trinity*, book 15, chapter 28, trans. Stephen McKenna, CSSR (Washington, DC: Catholic University of America Press, 1963), 524–525.

Preface to the Spanish Edition

This book has been written over years of reflection on hermeneutical and inter-pretive themes regarding the Bible, the Old and New Testaments. Taking a look back, we the authors recognize a common key that binds the texts together: Scripture can only be interpreted well when one is introduced "into the school of the Word," listening to the voice of God from within the group of Jesus' disciples. The biblical texts only let their meaning unfold in the framework of a threefold obedience: obedience to the received text, obedience to the community of faith that has transmitted it, and obedience to the God who speaks and reveals himself through the text.

The school thus becomes the "theological place" in which we wish to situate the contributions collected in this book. The exegesis of the laboratory has a pretension of sterile objectivity, so typical of modern science, which relegates to the place of "inappropriate prejudice" every consideration related to the faith of the investigator or the interpreter. The aim of the laboratory is that of a person who situates himself before the biblical texts with a microscope, treating the text as a dead tissue, separated from its living organism. The text is thus studied in light of an archaeology, sociology, or historical science that, liberated from their roles as auxiliary sciences, expect to be the ultimate criteria, and even expect to have the power to decide whether certain parts of the text should be cut out in order to adapt them to what the microscope cannot see.

Let us say also, in order not to fall into the other extreme, that the "school" is not the solitariness of the oratory. The scientific reading [of the Bible] conserves its autonomy; we speak specifically of the philological, literary, and historical sciences, and above all the retinue of the human sciences: anthropology, psychology, and sociology, to name a few. All of these sciences provide the framework in which this reading [of Scripture] becomes relevant and truly touches the experience of human beings.

But the "school" makes a singular reference to two elements that we want to illuminate briefly: a communal space shared by all the students (the Church), in which the Word instructs the reader by directing him or her to a necessary deepening; and a presupposition of an understanding that arises out of one's own human experience and illuminates it ([and thus we speak of] the hermeneutic of faith). We therefore distinguish two elements belonging to the person who situates himself in the "school of the Word."

1. *The ecclesial mark.* The first part of the book is titled "The Church, Living Subject of Sacred Scripture." This part treats the true *leitmotiv*, the central theme of the book. These words of Joseph Ratzinger sum up well the nucleus of what is treated here: "Scripture can become the foundation of life only when it is entrusted to *a living subject*, the same from which it came. Scripture was formed in the People of God guided by the Holy Spirit, and this people, this subject, has not ceased to exist."[1] The Church is the subject that makes Scripture truly alive when it is read.

Let us take note that the sacred author speaks not of what *he saw*, but rather about what *we have seen* (1 John 1:1); he does not present his testimony as something individual, but rather he speaks as a member of a believing community; hence the "we" that we encounter at the end of the gospel of John (21:24). The New Testament is written from a "we" and for an "us." This can also be said about the Christian reading of the Old Testament. And so we also achieve an understanding of the concept of "tradition," which is no more than Scripture read within the Church (*Scriptura in Ecclesia*, as Tertullian said), in other words, Scripture read within the framework that is appropriate to it.

2. *The hermeneutic of faith.* The reader will observe that the whole third part of this book is dedicated to the post-synodal apostolic exhortation *Verbum Domini.* This magisterial text contains within it a whole program of renewal for biblical science and pastoral care. It should be, without a doubt, a point of reference for any Christian interested in going deeper into the interpretation of the Bible. In *Verbum Domini*, Pope Benedict XVI calls attention to "the danger of dualism" and a "secularized hermeneutic" (§35). He says the following: if the hermeneutic of faith, the obedience of faith, is disregarded, the interpreter does not stay within strict objectivity, something that is otherwise impossible. On the contrary, the ecclesial hermeneutic is replaced by "another

---

1. Joseph Ratzinger, "Grenzen kirchlicher Vollmacht: Einführung zum Apostolischen Schreiben 'Ordinatio sacerdotalis,'" 139–153 in Benedict XVI and Gerhard Ludwig Müller, *Künder des Wortes und Diener eurer Freude: Theologie und Spiritualität des Weihesakramentes*, Gesammelte Schriften 12 (Freiburg: Herder, 1994), 146, emphasis added.

hermeneutic, a positivistic and secularized hermeneutic ultimately based on the conviction that the Divine does not intervene in human history. According to this hermeneutic, whenever a divine element seems present, it has to be explained in some other way, reducing everything to the human element. This leads to interpretations that deny the historicity of the divine elements" (§35).[2]

We see here another axis that has guided the composition of these texts: the necessity of generating a "hermeneutic of faith" that begins with the faith. Faith does not distort the interpretation of Scripture; on the contrary, it adapts its eyes, which are suited to recognize the ultimate meaning of the texts. This "hermeneutic of faith," which is, therefore, conformed to the text, can unite itself also with a historical hermeneutic that is conscious of its own limits, in such a way that it approaches a methodological whole, a concept of the "science of faith" that permits one to read the biblical text more profoundly.

The subtitle of our book permits us to add yet a third key for reading the texts that follow. The subtitle reads, "Biblical Interpretation from the New to the Old Testament." The reader will perhaps think it a mistake: would it not be better to say "From the Old to the New Testament"? The formulation of the title, which is certainly provocative, aims to emphasize what is theologically primary, without devaluing the chronological element. The succession "Old Testament-New Testament" continues to be valuable; the importance of historical development is not lessened; but we recognize the primacy of one moment in history (the action of Christ) that gives a new meaning to the whole set [of biblical texts] and allows one to say that in the plan of the "meaning" of the texts, one must go "from the New to the Old Testament." The collected essays in the second part of the book ("Christ, Exegete of the Fulfillment") respond to this intuition: it is he who opens up and gives meaning to the Old Testament in light of what is new.

With the subtitle of this book, we are emphasizing the aspect of fulfillment, whose point of departure is the *telos*, the end to which everything is directed. The "final cause" is the explanation that permits us to access the beginning. Looking at the final unfolding of the second creation, we can comprehend the roads that have been taken since the first creation.

Some say that this point of view "reduces the potential of the text to only one meaning" by imposing a Christological principle on texts that in themselves are open-ended. Some say also that this reading makes us incapable of

---

2. Benedict XVI, *Verbum Domini* (September 30, 2010); *The Word of the Lord: Verbum Domini* (Washington, DC: United States Conference of Catholic Bishops, 2010).

dialogue, since we are redirecting all meaning of the Old Testament to the New Testament. In reality, beginning with the end is the only way of drawing all the text's possibilities out into the light, for only in this way can one see the forest without losing oneself in the trees; only in this way does one have the panoramic view of the whole, which permits one to discern the value of each Old Testament figure. Beginning with the end is also the only way to be able to dialogue with our brothers and sisters who have stayed at the doors of the fulfillment, still seeing from afar the promises, having within their hands a Scripture (our Old Testament) that is on its own open to many channels of fulfillment, and yet remains without a resolution for the enigma of the figures that come to light in it. Dialogue is carried out from the truth, not from a fiction. Dialogue is constructed in the place in which each person recognizes the gift that he has received from God.

And now it only remains for us to thank all those who are behind these pages. Exegesis in the Church is carried out thanks to a great many people who have made it possible. Placed in the "school of the Word," we cannot but remember our parents, our superiors who sent us to study, our teachers at the Pontifical Biblical Institute of Rome, the friends with whom we have gone deep into these enthralling topics . . . and last but not least, our students at the San Dámaso Ecclesiastical University, with whom we currently carry on this adventure of listening to the Word.

CARLOS GRANADOS *and* LUIS SÁNCHEZ-NAVARRO
Madrid, June 3, 2016
Solemnity of the Sacred Heart of Jesus

"The phrase 'heart of Christ' can refer to Sacred Scripture,
which makes known his heart, closed before the Passion, as the
Scripture was obscure. But the Scripture has been opened since
the Passion; since those who from then on have understood it,
consider and discern in what way the prophecies must be interpreted."

(St. Thomas Aquinas, *Expositio in Psalmos,*
chapter 21, paragraph 11; CCC §112)

Abbreviations

AAS	*Acta Apostolicae Sedis*
ABE	Asociación Bíblica Española
AnBib	Analecta Biblica
AncB	Anchor Bible
BAC	Biblioteca de Autores Cristianos
BACh	Bible in Ancient Christianity
BEB	Baker Encyclopedia of the Bible
BHBib	Bibliotheca Hispana Biblica
BibL	Biblia y Lenguaje
BibMid	Biblioteca Midrásica
BKAT	Biblischer Kommentar Altes Testament
BRFT	Biblioteca Razón y Fe de Teología
CBJer NT	Comentarios a la Nueva Biblia de Jerusalén / Nuevo Testamento
CCC	Catechism of the Catholic Church, 2nd ed. (Vatican City: Libreria Editrice Vaticana, 2019)
CMat	Collectanea Matritensia
CSEL	Corpus Scriptorum Ecclesiasticorum Latinorum
DV	*Dei verbum*
EstBib	Estudios Bíblicos
GS	*Gaudium et spes*
IBO	Instituto Bíblico y Oriental
IEB	Introducción al Estudio de la Biblia
JSOTS	*Journal for the Study of the Old Testament*, Supplement Series
LeDiv	Lectio Divina
LG	*Lumen gentium*
LoB	Leggere oggi la Bibbia
LP	Libros Palabra
NICNT	New International Commentary on the New Testament

NPNF	A Select Library of Nicene and Post-Nicene Fathers of the Christian Church, ed. Philip Schaff and Henry Wace (Edinburgh: T&T Clark, 1991)
OBO	Orbis Biblicus et Orientalis
PL	Patrologia Latina, ed. Jean-Paul Migne (Paris: J.-P. Migne, 1857–1866)
PreDi	Presencia y Diálogo
QD	Quaestiones Disputatae
RSVCE	Revised Standard Version, Catholic Edition
SC	*Sacrosanctum Concilium*
SIT	Simposios Internacionales de Teología
StBi	Studi Biblici (Brescia)
SubBi	Subsidia Biblica
SVal	Series Valentina
TECC	Textos y Estudios "Cardenal Cisneros"
TG.T	Tesi Gregoriana, Serie Teologia
VD	*Verbum Domini*
VeIm	Verdad e Imagen
WBC	Word Biblical Commentary
WUNT	Wissenschaftliche Untersuchungen zum Neuen Testament
YJS	Yale Judaica Series

The Church, Living Subject of Sacred Scripture

1

The Testimonial Character of Sacred Scripture

Luis Sánchez-Navarro

The writings that form the biblical canon appear before the reader with an entirely singular claim: they present themselves as a point of access to God's revelation, to which they truthfully bear witness in a binding and definitive manner. The testimonial nature of these books is therefore relevant to their internal structure.[1] Taking "listening to the word" as the point of departure, we find a reflection on the category of "testimony" to seem, therefore, very opportune. It is this reflection that we present in this first chapter; despite its limited character, we think that it can offer elements of hermeneutical interest.

Our exposition develops in two phases. The first and fundamental one centers on *Scripture as written testimony of revelation*, after which we present synthetically the *relation between the Church and this testimony*. The factor that integrates the two phases is the action of the Holy Spirit, which is at the origin of the scriptural testimony (2 Pet 1:21) and makes possible the ecclesial experience of it (cf. Rom 8:14–15).

1.1. Testimony and Scripture

In order to understand the testimonial dimension of biblical writings, we begin with the fact of revelation and, after a reflection on the nature of testimony and its personal and communal character, we will offer the hermeneutical implications.

---

1. Cf. Javier Prades López, *Dar testimonio: La presencia de los cristianos en la sociedad plural*, Estudios y Ensayos BAC, Teología 184 (Madrid: Biblioteca de Autores Cristianos, 2015), 109–152: "El testimonio en la Sagrada Escritura."

a) Scripture and revelation

What is the relationship between Scripture and revelation? Can they simply be identified with each other, as often happens in the language of believers, or do they need to be distinguished?

Revelation, an event of dialogue

God's revelation, from its first manifestations in the period of the patriarchs to its plenitude in Jesus Christ, does not constitute a unilateral activity. God has not limited himself to manifesting his mystery in the form of a monologue: the response of human beings is an integral part of this phenomenon. Revelation only occurs when human beings enter into dialogue with God and, with a posture of faith, receive his mystery: revelation is a dynamic process between God and human beings, which is realized anew only in the encounter.[2] Revelation is not, therefore, a static reality: it is an event of dialogue; through it "the invisible God . . . speaks to men as friends" (*DV* §2).[3]

The depositum fidei, *testimony of revelation*

The history of the relationship between YHWH and the people of Israel has been demonstrated in the Old Testament; this finds its culmination in the salvific event of Jesus Christ, of which both the Old Testament and the New give differentiated testimony.[4] The resurrection of the Lord has not remained buried in the vicissitudes of history; through its own internal dynamics it has perdured by means of witnesses, the men and women who had the immediate and unmistakable experience of the Risen One. Outstanding among them are the Apostles, to whom the Lord entrusts in a special way the care of the Church. The apostolic testimony constitutes the *depositum fidei*, that treasury of faith which contains the supreme manifestation, in Jesus Christ, of the being of God and the vocation of human beings. As the Acts of the Apostles testifies, the activity of the nascent Church is synthesized in the universal transmission of

2. Joseph Ratzinger, "Biblical Interpretation in Conflict," trans. Adrian Walker, 1–29 in *Opening Up the Scriptures: Joseph Ratzinger and the Foundations of Biblical Interpretation*, ed. José Granados, Carlos Granados, and Luis Sánchez-Navarro (Grand Rapids: Eerdmans, 2008), 26.

3. Translator's note: The English translation of *Dei verbum* that I use throughout this book is published in [J. L. Gonzalez, ed.,] *The Sixteen Documents of Vatican II*, trans. National Catholic Welfare Council (Boston: Daughters of St. Paul, [1967?]), 373–394. This translation is used on the Vatican website: http://www.vatican.va/archive/hist_councils/ii_vatican_council /documents/vat-ii_const_19651118_dei-verbum_en.html

4. Brevard S. Childs, *Biblical Theology of the Old and New Testaments: Theological Reflection on the Christian Bible* (Minneapolis, MN: Fortress, 1993), 78.

this testimony[5] so that, by means of it, people gain access to a new life, joining themselves to Christ through baptism.[6] Writing to Timothy, Paul will exhort him to "guard the deposit."[7] This deposit is a dynamic reality, because it is vivified by the Holy Spirit (2 Tim 1:14). By participating in it, we human beings enter into dialogue with God.

Sacred Scripture, written testimony of revelation
This transmission (*traditio*) was produced first in an oral form; but soon, by divine inspiration, it was deemed appropriate to put it into writing as well. Thus is born what we know as the "New Testament," which, inseparably united to the oral tradition, constitutes the written testimony of God's revelation in Jesus Christ. The writings of the New Testament therefore show, from their very origin, a testimonial structure; over and above the diversity of literary genres, this structure intimately unites them in their intention: to give witness that Jesus is the Messiah and the Son of God (cf. *DV* §§17–18).[8]

The fact that this testimony is realized through a process of writing confers on it a singular quality; not only because it acquires the characteristics of the written word as opposed to the oral word,[9] but also because with it the author shows his conviction that the modality of written testimony offers a specific and irreplaceable opportunity to access the truth of the "thing" known in its revelation and experienced in faith. In this form, the literary activity of the author is destined from its very origin to transmit a testimony for the memory of future generations.[10]

---

5. Acts 1:8, 22; 2:32; 3:15; 4:33; 5:32; 10:39, 41, 42; 13:31; 18:5; 20:21, 24; 22:15, 18, 20; 23:11; 26:16, 22; 28:23.

6. See Acts 2:37–41; 8:14–17, 36–39; 9:18; 10:44–48; 16:14–15, 33–34; 18:8, 24–28; 19:1–7; 22:16.

7. Translator's note: I translated from the Spanish version here to keep the same wording.

8. "The books of the New Testament testified, in the Spirit, to the unique gospel of God and of Jesus Christ (and there is no other) which includes in itself the gospel of the kingdom, preached and brought by Jesus of Nazareth, prepared for since the covenant between God and Israel, and pre-announced by the Prophets of Sacred Scripture, in particular Isaiah 52:3–7 and 61:1–3." Giuseppe Segalla, "La testimonianza dei libri del Nuovo Testamento ad un unico kerygma/evangelo, buon annuncio dell'evento originario," 304–319 in *L'interpretazione della Bibbia nella Chiesa*, Atti del Simposio promosso dalla Congregazione per la Dottrina della Fede (Rome: September 1999), Atti e Documenti 11 (Vatican City: Libreria Editrice Vaticana, 2001), 316.

9. Pierangelo Sequeri, *Il Dio affidabile: Saggio di teologia fondamentale*, 2nd ed. (Brescia: Queriniana, 1996), 615.

10. Cf. Pierangelo Sequeri, "La struttura testimoniale delle scritture sacre: teologia del testo," 3–27 in *La rivelazione attestata: La Bibblia fra testo e teologia*, ed. Giuseppe Angelini (Milan: Glossa, 1998), 15.

b) Testimony, between history and meaning

As Paul Ricœur has shown, a testimony of the absolute is a complex reality; on the one hand, it affirms a fact, and on the other—inseparably—it manifests the transcendent meaning of this fact. It is, simultaneously, a narration of facts and a confession of faith.[11]

Narrative aspect: testimony and history

The biblical testimony presents itself to us as a narration of historical events.[12] Focusing our attention on the New Testament: if faith in Jesus Christ saves, it is because he truly rose from the dead (cf. 1 Cor 15:14). The form in which these facts are narrated deserves serious study, given that one of the evangelists' principal theological methods consists in applying Old Testament schemas to the narration of the events of Christ's life. But this does not necessarily affect its historicity, since it is precisely a matter of methods employed to communicate an event; moreover it is possible that Jesus himself acted on occasion in accordance with biblical models: an open possibility, if we keep in mind the consciousness that Jesus has of bringing the Old Testament promises to fulfillment.[13] On the other hand, the authors' intention to reflect faithfully the events that really happened cannot be ignored without thereby depriving their very work of literary composition of its meaning.[14] The historicity of the evangelical accounts,[15] which is not characterized by the detailed precision proper to the modern science of history, is demanded, moreover, by the very nature of testimony:

---

11. Cf. Paul Ricœur, "The Hermeneutics of Testimony," trans. David Stewart and Charles E. Reagan, *Religion Online*, at https://www.religion-online.org/book-chapter/chapter-3-the-hermeneutics-of-testimony/ (originally "L'herméneutique du témoignage," *Archivio de Filosofia* 42 [1972]: 35–61).

12. In this it is different from a symbol, which lacks—or can lack—historical "depth": its meaning is more important than its historicity (Ricœur, "Hermeneutics," I).

13. A paradigmatic episode in this regard is the preaching of Jesus in the synagogue of Nazareth according to Luke: "Today this scripture has been fulfilled in your hearing" (Luke 4:21, RSVCE). But all four evangelists testify to this consciousness of Jesus: cf. Matt 5:17, Mark 14:49; John 5:39.

14. Cf. Luke 1:1–4: "Inasmuch as many have undertaken to compile a narrative of the things which have been accomplished among us . . . it seemed good to me also, having followed all things closely for some time past, to write an orderly account for you, most excellent Theophilus, that you may know the truth concerning the things of which you have been informed."

15. Cf. *DV* §19.

a true testimony can never be based on fictitious events.[16] This basic historicity is, furthermore, presupposed by Christian theology.[17]

Confessional aspect: testimony and meaning

The biblical testimony, nevertheless, is not limited to affirming certain historical facts: its ultimate end consists in declaring the salvific meaning of those events in which the Transcendent has intervened in a direct way. This aspect is so profoundly intertwined with the foregoing, that they cannot be separated. We can recognize it in 1 John 1:1, where the affirmation of those things of which the author has had an immediate sensible experience—historical realities—is indissolubly united to the confession of their salvific value: it is "concerning the Word of life."[18] The entire narration of the life, passion, death, and resurrection of the Lord is guided by the desire to show that he is the Messiah, the Son of God (cf. Mark 1:1), with the purpose of giving rise to faith in him (cf. John 20:31).

Tension between history and meaning

The evangelical testimony, therefore, narrates facts and affirms their revelatory and salvific meaning. This is the principal end of the sacred writer: if one has made the effort to narrate the life, passion, death, and resurrection of Jesus of Nazareth, and not of another person, it is because in him one has discovered a meaning that makes him absolutely distinct from all other men of his time.[19]

This can end up causing a tension between the mere facticity of the events and the affirmation of their transcendent meaning. In order that the latter may be shown, the inspired author—in virtue of his mission at the service of revelation—treats those events in the manner most suitable to this end. This

---

16. "It is not possible to testify for a meaning without testifying *that* something has happened which signifies this meaning." Ricœur, "Hermeneutics," III.

17. "Today it continues to be strictly necessary for theology to be able to affirm the historical veracity of the apostolic testimony, which is the way of accessing the event of Revelation; the meaning of the Scriptures and, more radically, of Revelation itself and its permanence in history is at stake in it." Alfonso Carrasco Rouco, "La puesta en cuestión histórico-crítica del testimonio apostólico sobre Jesucristo," *Revista Española de Teología* 61 (2001): 207–231, at 212.

18. 1 John 1:1: "That which was from the beginning, which we have heard, which we have seen with our eyes, which we have looked upon and touched with our hands, concerning the word of life."

19. "The 'confessional' kernel of testimony is certainly the center around which the rest gravitates. The confession that Jesus is the Christ constitutes testimony par excellence." Ricœur, "Hermeneutics," III.

leads him to reorder them, regroup them, shape them according to determined narrative schemas, and enrich them with references (implicit or explicit) to the Old Testament, etc. (cf. *DV* §19). In this way one can explain the redactional work that a mere "synopsis" of the gospels reveals. In this sense, the pole of confession affects (by "modifying" it) the pole of narration. But this narration does not lose its reference to the reality: without the reality, the confessed meaning would disappear.

The truth, an essential quality of testimony

Testimony is a category of the juridical discipline.[20] A journalistic news story that does not fit with the truth does not necessarily carry with it a penal responsibility; nevertheless, in a trial the testimony that is not true constitutes a crime ("false testimony"), given that it intends to cause an unjust sentence by the court.[21] A testimony is never a neutral narration: it intends to induce in the listener a judgment about a reality;[22] for this reason, reference to the truth is characteristic of testimony.[23] Veracity, a quality inherent to every testimony,[24] affects the evangelical testimony,[25] as much in its narrative dimension as in its confessional aspect. The truth of the latter is not enough: the meaning depends on the historical authenticity of the facts. When John affirms that "his testimony

20. "The action of testifying has an intimate relation to an institution—the judiciary; a place—the court; a social function—the lawyer, the judge; an action—to plead, that is, to be plaintiff or defendant in a trial." Ricœur, "Hermeneutics," III.

21. Ricœur says that "false testimony is a lie in the heart of the witness." "Hermeneutics," II.

22. "Even in the case of the so-called 'testimony of the senses,' this counts as 'testimony' only if it is used to support a judgment which goes beyond the mere recording of facts." Ricœur, "Hermeneutics," II.

23. "It should be clear what the horizon within which that specific information which is legal testimony is. It is testimony about a truth that, although it is of a mundane and particular order, is not for that reason less existentially vital for those who have been divided by the dispute." Sergio Cotta, "La testimonianza giuridica: sui generis o humani generis?," 15–24 in *Informazione e testimonianza* (*Archivio de filosofia* 3 [1972]), 18. Translator's note: my translation from the Italian, here and in the following citations from Italian articles.

24. Cf. Klaus Hemmerle, "Verità e testimonianza," in *Testimonianza e verità: Un approccio interdisciplinare*, ed. Piero Ciardella and Maurizio Gronchi (Rome: Città Nuova, 2000), 307–323. "Testimony has essentially a double origin: the testimony and the truth itself, *in* its origination before the testimony" (315).

25. "'The testimony of the books of the NT' imply that such books are not considered simply as 'neutral documents of a past history,' but rather as 'testimony about a person and the salvific truth of that person in relation to human beings, their history, and the history of the world.'" Segalla, "La testimonianza," 304.

is true" (John 19:35; cf. 21:24), he argues for this quality as much in the narrated events as in their transcendent significance.[26]

c) Personal and communal dimension of testimony

The evangelical testimony has a marked procedural character: it assumes opposition or resistance to the message that is proclaimed, and in favor of which it advocates. In this context the figure of the author gains importance. He is not a mere chronicler guaranteeing the exactness of what he narrates: he is a witness who, being in and from the Church, affirms the transcendent truth of his account.

The witness, guarantor of truthfulness
A testimony is accepted, in the end, by the credibility (*pistis*) of the witness; its logical or factual coherence is not enough. This also happens with the testimony of what is transcendent: whether or not to accept it depends in great measure on who maintains it. If the witness is a person marked by a special authority, his testimony is qualitatively superior. This confers primacy on the apostolic testimony, since the apostles, designated by Jesus at the beginning of his public life to live in a greater degree of intimacy with him ("to be with him" [Mark 3:14]), have been constituted as witnesses by the same resurrected Christ (cf. Luke 24:48; Acts 1:8); this explains the interest of the primitive Church in recognizing the genuine apostolic testimony, transmitted by the apostles or by persons close to them. Each writing of the New Testament is the fruit of an apostolic witness;[27] this fact makes these books canonical, and therefore linked to divine inspiration.[28]

---

26. "Absolute testimony, on the contrary, in concrete singularity gives a caution to the truth without which its authority remains in suspense. Testimony, each time singular, confers the sanction of reality on ideas, ideals, and modes of being." Ricœur, "Hermeneutics," I.

27. We do not intend here to enter into the question about the author of each New Testament writing, work which would go beyond the limits of this reflection. Regarding the authorship of the gospels, see *DV* §18b.

28. Cf. Bruce M. Metzger, *Il Canone del Nuovo Testamento* (Brescia: Paideia, 1997), 223; Giustino Borgonovo, "Una proposta di rilettura dell'ispirazione biblica dopo gli apporti della Form- e Redaktions-geschichte," 41–63 in *L'interpretazione della Bibbia*, 55–59 ("Ispirazione e testimonianza dell'evento originario").

Testimony, theologies and theology

In the New Testament each author offers *his* testimony of Jesus Christ; that is to say, he presents the salvific event from his particular point of view, with insistence on some point that is central in his opinion or on an aspect that he has experienced in a stronger way.[29] In this way the testimony flows into "theology," a faithful understanding of the unique event of Christ; and we can speak of the Christology of Matthew, of Mark, etc.[30] Each perspective thus permits us to approach the mystery while discovering in it an aspect that reflects its inexhaustible richness. Nevertheless, these diverse ways of understanding are complementary,[31] and they converge in the reality to which they testify, which one accesses by faith, and which constitutes the object of Christian theology.[32] Faith in Christ is, therefore, the presupposed hermeneutic that allows one to integrate the diverse presentations of the mystery of Christ contained in the New Testament. One does not try to harmonize them (they are already harmonious),[33] but to allow them to ring out in all the richness of their polyphony.

Testimony and the Church

The sacred author does not present his testimony as something individual, but rather he speaks as a member of a believing community; this illuminates, for example, the striking absence of any mention of the author in the texts of the gospels.[34] Even the fourth gospel, which mentions the author (John 21:24),

29. "The books of the NT testify to the one gospel, but they also contain the testimony of the witnesses who handed down [their testimony of] the original salvific event, and who thought about, developed, and lived it." Segalla, "La testimonianza," 319.

30. Regarding the relationship between "biblical theologies" and "biblical theology," cf. Paul Beauchamp, "Es posible una teología bíblica?," 99–115 in Carlos Granados and Luis Sánchez Navarro, eds., *Escritura e interpretación bíblica*, LP 42 (Madrid: Palabra, 2003), 100–101.

31. "This unitary structure of the gospel is expressed in various ways in the theologies of the NT in relation to diverse situations, diverse cultural milieus, and diverse addressees, but it is always the one gospel of God and of Jesus Christ, which includes the kingdom of God." Segalla, "La testimonianza," 318.

32. "The most profound unity is given by the original event which took place in the person of Jesus Christ, from the super-abundance of meaning that explains the possibility for originating diverse models, which reflect in a varied and homogeneous way the original salvific event and the gospel which announces and contains it." Segalla, "La testimonianza," 319.

33. Harmony: "Union and combination of sounds that are simultaneous and different, but in accord with each other." *Diccionario de la lengua española* [*Dictionary of the Spanish Language*] (Madrid: Real Academia Española, 2014), 201. Harmony is not uniformity; it necessarily assumes a difference.

34. The titles "According to Matthew," etc., appear in manuscripts beginning in the second century.

does it in an anonymous way. For that reason, his testimony is at the same time singular and plural, something that one can appreciate in the evangelical writings, particularly at the end of John ("we": John 21:24). The believing community, the Church, is at the origin of the New Testament, and its authority recognizes the validity of the Old Testament. One can thus say that the Church (in the person of the hagiographer) testifies to her faith in these blessed writings, and at the same time this very Church (in her practice of liturgy, prayer, etc., and posteriorly in doctrinal decisions) authoritatively recognizes them as a testimony of her faith.

d) Hermeneutical consequences

First and foremost, something obvious: biblical exegesis has to keep in mind the testimonial character of Scripture, adapting to this reality the variety of methods that it uses.[35] History and meaning are inseparable.

The meaning depends on history
The salvific meaning of the evangelical testimony, without the historical event, vanishes. The affirmation of the "Christ of faith" loses all its force if it prescinds from reference to the "historical Jesus." The transcendent significance of testimony is true *only* if the event is real. To affirm that the Gospels contain a true testimony implies not only the transcendent truth of the confession but also the historical truth of the narration. One cannot bracket the historicity of the evangelical accounts in order to concentrate on their religious message; we cannot forget that their primary religious message is, precisely, the message of the salvific intervention of God in history.

History, rescued by its meaning
In a certain sense, history "depends" on its meaning; not so much on the facticity of the events, but on their importance and survival. To say that meaning creates history would be an aberration; but if these historical events were not filled with salvific value, they would be irremediably lost, like so many other events, in the shadows of oblivion. On the contrary, their transcendent meaning rescues them from this sad fate and converts them into a locus of permanent interest for human beings of all times and all cultures.

35. A synthesis of the principal methods of which exegesis makes use today: Albert Vanhoye, "Exégesis bíblica y teología: la cuestión de los métodos," 114–128 in *Biblia y ciencia de la fe*, ed. Carlos Granados and Agustín Giménez, Ensayos 311 (Madrid: Encuentro, 2007), 121–123 (originally published in *Seminarium* 31 [1991]: 267–278).

The critical challenge: access to history through testimony
Biblical exegesis cannot prescind from historical criticism: measuring the historicity of the events witnessed by Scripture is legitimate, and even obligatory.[36] But one must respect its testimonial character, adapting the methods to this object and maintaining full consciousness of the limits inherent to historical science.[37] One must keep in mind, moreover, that testimony is to history what empirical demonstration is to the natural sciences.[38]

If exegesis were to neglect history, Scripture would lose its roots in human reality and would dilute the central fact: the history of the Incarnation. But neither can exegesis prescind from faith:[39] only the cordial acceptance of the biblical testimony permits sure access to the history that it maintains. *The faith of the witness* does not detract from the credibility of his testimony.[40] On the contrary: the solemn character of this testimony manifests the witness's certainty about its veracity. In his testimonial word he is promising all of his being; the witness knows himself to be specially obligated to tell the truth before God. "How could a believer himself dare to falsify the testimonial memory of the word of God?"[41]

In the same way, *the faith of the interpreter* is not an obstacle, but rather a

36. "Historical investigation is a discipline that . . . has great importance for many other disciplines, among which are exegesis and theology. But neither exegesis nor theology can be confused with historical investigation. . . . In order to interpret correctly the biblical texts it is necessary, therefore, to situate them in their historical context. Nevertheless, the fundamental point of reference should be the Word of God, not a reconstruction of history." Vanhoye, "Exégesis bíblica," 121.

37. "The teachers from the past dreamed of an ideal objectivity established on the criticism of documents; the historian has learned to be wary of himself, at least as much as he is of his witnesses. While systematically trying to purify the texts from the additions he believes he detects, he knows well that he risks above all interpolating his own prejudices." Charles Pietri, "Alcuni paralogismi della critica biblica: domande d'uno storico," 87–134 in *Letture attuali della Bibbia*, ed. Paul Beauchamp, StBi 48 (Brescia: Paideia, 1979), 97.

38. "Testimony is one of the proofs that the prosecution or the defense advances with a view to influencing the decision of the judge." Ricœur, "Hermeneutics," II.

39. As Jean-Marie Sevrin ("L'exégèse critique comme discipline théologique," *Revue théologique de Louvain* 21 [1990]: 146–162) has postulated, from the Catholic camp, distinguishing radically between "critical exegesis" and "faithful hermeneutics"; see an evaluation of this proposal in Vanhoye, "Exégesis bíblica," 124–127.

40. With respect to the "philology of suspicion" and the positivist historiography of the nineteenth century, see Pietri, "Alcuni paralogismi della critica biblica," 91–94. "The scholar accepts the document with apprehension, deeming the witness to be guilty, necessarily deceptive, if he does not bring proofs of his innocence, which are his sources" (93).

41. Sequeri, "La struttura testimoniale delle scritture sacre," 5–6.

necessary interpretive key. In order to understand the Bible, a pre-understanding is necessary: that which comes from faith in the events witnessed by it.[42] Only then can historical criticism offer any guarantee of credibility.

Thus prevails an exegetical method with a solid hermeneutical foundation, which unites the critical requirements with the appropriate character of these writings:[43] a "testimony criticism."[44]

Distinct testimonies, one reality

As we have indicated above, each witness presents the mystery of Christ in conformity with his personal vision of Jesus, according to his experience. It would be absurd to try to make uniform the testimony of Paul and that of John, just as it would lack meaning to reduce these two persons to a single model of being Christian. On this point the "redaction criticism," which culminates in the description of the diverse "theologies" present in the New Testament, manifests its full validity. However, the exegete cannot stop there: he must go deep into the *truth* of these salvific events, that truth of which each sacred book offers us a personal understanding. Only when he penetrates the witnessed reality, to this end making use—when necessary—of other biblical testimonies about the same reality, can the exegete consider his labor concluded.

The exegete, "interpreted interpreter": exegesis and faith

This task requires of the exegete an openness to the truth witnessed by Scripture; only someone disposed to let himself be "criticized" by the word of God

---

42. We distinguish between "pre-understanding" and "prejudice"; the latter implies an inadequate idea of the reality in question, while pre-understanding has a positive connotation. "In order to interpret the Bible, the most valid point of departure is the experience of faith, transmitted in the same Tradition that has created the biblical texts." Vanhoye, "Exégesis bíblica," 126. A pre-understanding of faith is necessary, which has to be at the same time carefully differentiated from theological conceptions belonging to a phase posterior to the production of the biblical texts (Vanhoye, "Exégesis bíblica," 127-128). "If [exegesis] wishes to be theology, it must take a further step: it must acknowledge that the faith of the Church is precisely the sort of sym-pathy without which the text remains closed." Ratzinger, "Biblical Interpretation in Conflict," 29.

43. Pierangelo Sequeri highlights the critical requirement of faith regarding the testimony of Scripture, as something that corresponds to the original intention of the text ("La struttura testimoniale delle scritture sacre," 9).

44. For this one has to keep in mind the original structure of revelation; cf. Borgonovo, "Una proposta di rilettura dell'ispirazione biblica," 55-56. See also Carlos Jódar Estrella, "La búsqueda del evento en la estructura testimonial de la Revelación Bíblica," *RevAg* 43 (2002): 371-390.

is in a condition to tackle a critical exegetical study with any possibility of success. Interpretation presents itself now, not as a cold academic exercise, but as an impassioned mission whose exercise requires purity of heart,[45] and from which the exegete is called to emerge transformed.[46] Authentic scientific rigor requires this openness of faith to the evangelical testimony, because only in faith can it be comprehended and accepted; the exegete can thus penetrate the reality that he interprets, to "participate" in the reality witnessed by the text.[47]

In summary

The fact that the biblical writings show a testimonial structure has a notable relevance, and it should be reflected in the scientific study of them: every method has to adapt itself to its object and not vice versa. Affirming the existential validity (the meaning) of biblical revelation requires the acceptance of its historical veracity;[48] the exegetical labor reaches its end when the interpreter can affirm with the evangelist that "we know that his testimony is true" (John 21:24).

1.2. The testimonial word and the Church

The testimony that God offers of himself in Scripture[49] does not affect the believer in an isolated way, but rather it takes place in the Church. This refers as much to the transmission of this testimony as to its internal dynamics.

a) The transmission of the testimony

The evangelical testimony is not reduced to a moment in the past; on the contrary, it lives on in the believing community. The Church lives by this testimony preserved in her heart.

---

45. Cf. Beauchamp, "Es posible una teología bíblica?," 111–112.

46. "The word 'inter-pretation' itself furnishes a clue to the reality: every interpretation requires from the interpreter an 'inter,' a going into the middle, a being with. Pure objectivity is an absurd abstraction. One does not come to know by standing apart uninvolved; rather, involvement is the antecedent condition of knowing. The only question is how to get involved in such a way that, instead of your ego shouting down the voice of the others, you achieve an inner 'accord' with the reality of the past, an accord that purifies your ears for the word those others have to speak." Ratzinger, "Biblical Interpretation in Conflict," 9.

47. See the quotation from Ratzinger in the previous footnote.

48. This relies on many internal and external signs whose treatment would exceed the limits of this reflection. Regarding the historical application of credibility, see Salvador Pié-Ninot, *La teología fundamental* (Salamanca: Secretariado Trinitario, 2001), 223–224.

49. Cf. Sequeri, *Il Dio affidabile*, 622.

Closed deposit, open reality

The written deposit of revelation is concluded, since the biblical canon was closed with the apostolic writings.[50] But the event to which these writings bear witness is something alive: the resurrected Christ transcends time; he lives while offering himself to the Father in a constant present.[51] In that clay vessel, which is the biblical writings, is enclosed a treasure, a living reality.

Christ alive, constant origin of new witnesses

Through faith in Christ, human beings enter into personal communion with him. This immediate experience of the divine action, which is a direct experience of Christ, makes the Christian his witness.[52] People of all ages can thus be incorporated into this spring of life which is the apostolic testimony, and which extends into the mighty river of Christian testimony; the history of the Church is, in its nucleus, the history of the transmission of that testimony. As the Christ who raises up witnesses, he is also the one who throughout history guides the People of God.

b) Interior testimony: the action of the Paraclete

The resurrected Christ carries out this work through his Spirit, who acts constantly in the Church through "interior testimony."

The Holy Spirit, guarantor of Christian testimony in the Church

The Holy Spirit is the invisible teacher who—according to the words of Jesus— "will guide you into all truth" (John 16:13); he does this by testifying on behalf of Jesus: "He will bear witness to me" (John 15:26). In this way the interior testimony of the Holy Spirit arouses in human beings the adherence of faith that introduces us into friendship with Christ. This Spirit of sanctity not only guarantees the conformity of the ecclesial magisterium to the teaching of Jesus (cf. John 14:26: "But the Counselor . . . will teach you all things, and bring to

---

50. Cf. *DV* §20. For the process of formation of the New Testament canon, see the Pontifical Biblical Commission's document *The Jewish People and Their Sacred Scriptures in the Christian Bible* (Vatican City: Libreria Editrice Vaticana, 2001), §§16–18.

51. "But when Christ had offered for all time a single sacrifice for sins, he sat down at the right hand of God" (Heb 10:12).

52. "There is no intrinsic difference between the facts and gestures of Jesus of Nazareth, or between the appearances of the resurrected Lord and the manifestations of the Spirit in the Pentecostal communities. On the contrary, the continuity of the same manifestation justifies a corresponding extension of testimony given of things seen and heard." Ricœur, "Hermeneutics," III. See the note on 1 Cor 15:8 in the *Biblia de Jerusalén* (Bilbao: Desclée de Brouwer, 1998).

your remembrance all that I have said to you"), but he also acts in the heart of the listener, inclining him to accept in faith the evangelical testimony.[53] He is the defense attorney (*Paraclete*)[54] of the evangelical truth, who acts within human beings through the interior exhortation that is consolation.[55] Preaching is thus accompanied by the action of the Spirit, who with his presence marks that human testimonial word with the seal of transcendent truth: "And we are witnesses of these things, and so is the Holy Spirit whom God has given to those who obey him" (Acts 5:32).

Scripture, witness of "what is within human beings":
Scripture and human experience
The words that the Gospel of John (2:25) predicates of Jesus[56] can be applied in an analogous way to Sacred Scripture. The testimonial action of the Holy Spirit within human beings, supporting the evangelical kerygma, is strongly linked to the desire for happiness hidden in our heart. The Spirit does not act in an inhuman way, eliminating the profound inclinations that drive the life of the person. On the contrary, when we open ourselves up to the evangelical message, we discover that this Word of salvation responds to our most intimate human aspirations: happiness, truth, goodness, friendship. For its part, the Word of God purifies those aspirations, conforming them more and more to our own interior truth. In this way, the Lord, through his written Word, bears witness to the truth of every authentic human experience. And at the same time, the Spirit moves the whole person (in reason and in affect) to a more fully human life, which the Spirit himself makes possible through grace.

Scripture and Christian experience
Scripture, finally, nourishes and strengthens Christian testimony. The believer who, through faith, has united himself to Christ discovers in the sacred books a reflection and an illustration of his own spiritual experience, which leads him to deepen his faith. Guided by the Holy Spirit, he finds in the pages of Scripture

53. The words of Peter in the "Council of Jerusalem," with which—alluding to the baptism of the centurion Cornelius (Acts 10:44-48)—he affirms the divine plan to accept the Gentiles into the Church, are significant in this respect: "And God who knows the heart *bore witness to them*, giving them the Holy Spirit, just as he did to us" (Acts 15:8; emphasis added).

54. Cf. Ricœur, "Hermeneutics," III.

55. The Greek word *parakaleō*, from which *paraklētos* derives, means "to exhort" and "to console," in addition to its original meaning ("to call next to oneself," from which we get "advocate").

56. "He himself knew what was in man" (John 2:25b).

a testimony of his interior life. The Beatitudes (Matt 5:3–10) are a good example: the faithful one who inspects them with his heart sees reflected in them his experience, or at least his aspirations, of Christian life. In turn, this experience induces him to go deeper into the sapiential knowledge of the Word of God. In this way, *Sacred Scripture and Christian experience mutually nourish each other.* Scripture testifies objectively to the authenticity of Christian life, and the very living out of faith attests in a subjective way to the perennial truth contained in the canonical writings. At the origin of both testimonies, objective and subjective, is the Spirit of holiness.

1.3. Conclusion: dimensions of the testimonial character of Sacred Scripture

In light of what we have said, it is possible to distinguish diverse levels in the testimonial quality of Scripture:

1. *Historical dimension.* Scripture attests to historical events; in the end, all of its truth depends on them. The testimonial character does not nullify this dimension, but rather is founded on it. The believer who approaches the Bible accesses the knowledge of God's salvific intervention in human history; but the exceptional character of these "actions of God" requires an interpretation, so that they do not remain "silent wonders."

2. *Confessional dimension.* The very purpose of Scripture is manifested in the conclusion of chapter 20 of the Gospel of John: "These are written that you may believe that Jesus is the Christ, the Son of God" (John 20:31). From this point of view, the biblical testimony transcends history and acquires a value that is universal throughout time and space. When the believer accepts through faith the transcendent meaning of the historical event, he discovers in the scriptural texts a permanent reality: they are capable of illuminating people of every age, authoritatively demonstrating to them the truth about God, about human beings, and about the world.

3. *Existential dimension.* By connecting with the desire for happiness written on every human heart, Scripture attests to the truth of everyone's aspiration for a life lived to the full, while at the same time showing us the path for reaching that goal. On the other hand, the believer who approaches the Word of God with the openness of faith realizes how this Word judges with authority the evangelical authenticity of one's own life, testifying to one's adaptation or unconformity to the will of God.

2

The Word of God and the Church in the New Testament

Luis Sánchez-Navarro

The previous chapter, in which we saw the communal dimension of the evangelical testimony, has allowed us to intuit a reality: the Church and the Word of God mutually require each other. The Church is the place where the Word vitally resonates, and in its turn this Word belongs to the essential elements of the Church. In the New Testament writings the relationship between both realities is so profound and varied that it cannot be described easily; but because of this fact it is no less necessary to do so, or at least to try, if we want to understand the place that the Word of God occupies in the life of the Christian.[1]

Above all we intend to specify what is contained in the expression "Word of God"; as we continue, we will deal with its relationship to the Church, to this end adopting the double perspective of the Christian community as subject and as object of the Word.

---

1. "Exegetes have also to explain the relationship that exists between the Bible and the *church*. The Bible came into existence within believing communities. In it the faith of Israel found expression, later that of the early Christian communities. United to the living tradition which preceded it, which accompanies it and is nourished by it (cf. *Dei Verbum*, 21), the Bible is the privileged means which God uses yet again in our own day to shape the building up and the growth of the church as the people of God. This ecclesial dimension necessarily involves an openness to ecumenism." Pontifical Biblical Commission, *The Interpretation of the Bible in the Church* (Washington, DC: United States Catholic Conference, 1993), III.C.1.

2.1. The Word of God: Scripture in the Tradition

It is well known that "Word of God," a concept of transcendental importance in the Old Testament,[2] has in Christian theology a gamut of analogous meanings, the first of which is the personal order: Jesus, the Son of God, is called in the Johannine tradition "the Logos of God," that is to say, his Word (Rev 19:13; cf. John 1:1, 14—"the Logos"; 1 John 1:2—"the Logos of life"). This first sense merits our attention, since it shows us to what extent the Word of God is central in the Christian faith. God himself is Word: we return to the prologue of the fourth gospel, "the Word" is "God" (John 1:1), "the only-begotten God" (John 1:18).[3] The Son of God, whose being consists in revealing the Father (John 1:18; cf. Matt 11:27), is by that very fact the exhaustive expression of the mystery of God. It is not possible to conceive of a Word that is more semantically complete. Therefore the Gospels attribute his words directly to God as the subject: "And the word which you hear is not mine but the Father's who sent me" (John 14:24); the words of Jesus are a faithful expression of the will of the Father (Matt 7:21–27).

Therefore it is not strange to us that the apostolic testimony of this Word— both oral and written—would be designated with this same term: the apostolic word about the Logos of God, which communicates it or makes it accessible, is also in an analogous sense the Word of God. As the Second Vatican Council will say, "Sacred Tradition transmits the Word of God with integrity" (*DV* §9).[4] Paul expresses this conviction in the first of his letters, which allows us to access the moment in which the word becomes written, in such a way that the message announced orally to the Christians of Thessalonica is proposed to them, again and without any break in continuity, by a letter: "And we also thank God constantly for this, that when you received the word of God which you heard from us, you accepted it not as the word of men but as what it really is, the word of God, which is at work in you believers" (1 Thess 2:13). In his preaching, Paul announced to them the Word of God, that very same one which is now contained in his writing.[5]

---

2. See Ignacio Carbajosa, "La progresiva condescendencia de la Palabra de Dios en Israel," in *Palabra encarnada: La Palabra de Dios en la Iglesia*, ed. Ignacio Carbajosa and Luis Sánchez Navarro, PreDi 20 (Madrid: Universidad Eclesiástica San Dámaso, 2008), 15–66.

3. Translator's note: this translation is from the Spanish version.

4. Translator's note: Latin: *transmittit integre*; I translated from the Spanish, since the English translation in the Gonzalez edition is less concise.

5. In fact this letter will serve Paul in completing his face-to-face teaching and undoing any misconception; see 1 Thess 4:13–18.

The New Testament Scripture appears, then, in its very genesis as a modality of the Apostolic Tradition.[6] "Sacred Tradition and Sacred Scripture form one sacred deposit of the word of God, committed to the Church" (*DV* §10).[7] It is a matter of a modality through which God speaks in the present moment; we know the expression that the Council uses to define Scripture, *locutio Dei*, which—paradoxically—designates an action and not a static reality: "Sacred Scripture is the *speaking of God* inasmuch as it is consigned to writing under the inspiration of the Holy Spirit" (*DV* §9).[8] The phrase thus reflects a reality present in the New Testament, where on various occasions it is affirmed that Scripture "says."[9] By adopting this perspective, *Dei verbum* coincides with the letter to the Hebrews, which in referring to Psalm 95—a written word—describes the Word of God as "living" and "active" (Heb 4:12). It is a written and immutable word, but not inactive or dead; this peculiar nature makes *Scripture* a *locutio*. "The result is that Sacred Scripture is not defined in its final form, as a text already separated from its author, but in the moment of its being put into writing, as a 'living act.'"[10] This corresponds to the nature of its subject, God, who is activity without end: "My Father is working still, and I am working" (John 5:17).

Scripture is thus the Word of God; a word whose highest dignity is expressed theologically, since the apostolic age, by means of the doctrine of biblical inspiration (*theopneustos*, 2 Tim 3:16; cf. 2 Pet 1:21).[11] But this Scripture

6. Something similar should also be affirmed about the books of the Old Covenant, that they were oral traditions before acquiring their definitive written form.

7. Regarding the relationship between Scripture and Tradition, see Luis Sánchez Navarro, "La Escritura y el *Compendio* del *Catecismo de la Iglesia Católica*," *TeolCat* 99 (2006): 11–24, at 12–15.

8. Translator's note: the English translation in the Gonzalez edition of the Vatican II documents has "word of God," but the Latin is *locutio Dei* and the Spanish is *hablar de Dios*.

9. John 7:38, 42; 10:35; 19:37; Rom 4:3; 9:17; 10:11; 11:2; Gal 4:30; 1 Tim 5:18; James 2:23; 4:5. "In the Hellenic use of the word *legein* (to say), it is never used in relation to the expression *written* in thought; its use is always limited to the spoken expression. The neologism of the Greek of the New Testament . . . combines two antithetical concepts: the oral word and the written word." Valerio Mannucci, *La Biblia como Palabra de Dios* (Bilbao: Desclée de Brouwer, 1997), 114–115.

10. Albert Vanhoye, "The Reception in the Church of the Dogmatic Constitution *Dei Verbum*," 104–125 in *Opening Up the Scriptures: Joseph Ratzinger and the Foundations of Biblical Interpretation*, ed. José Granados, Carlos Granados, and Luis Sánchez (Grand Rapids, MI: Eerdmans, 2008), 106 (originally "La recepción en la Iglesia de la Constitución dogmática *Dei Verbum*," 147–173 in *Escritura e interpretación: Los fundamentos de la interpretación bíblica*, ed. Carlos Granados and Luis Sánchez-Navarro, LP 42 [Madrid: Palabra, 2003], 149–150).

11. See on this subject Antonio Izquierdo, ed., *Scrittura ispirata: Atti del Simposio internazionale sull'ispirazione promosso dall'Ateneo Pontificio "Regina Apostolorum,"* Atti e Documenti

is not manifested as the Word of God if it is isolated from its vital context: only when read in the Church, in that great current of life that is the Apostolic Tradition, does it reveal its interior dynamism and its efficacy.[12] Therefore when speaking in these pages of the Word of God, we will refer to Scripture—the written form of the apostolic testimony—not as if isolated from, but rather as being *in*, the Tradition.

2.2. The Church, subject of the Word of God

By "subject" we understand the human community that produced the writings of the New Testament in history and that appears as their bearer and their guarantor; that is to say, we are moving on a historical plane. There are many signs that indicate its importance, as is revealed by the consideration of some fundamental aspects of Scripture in which that subject [the Church] is, simply speaking, essential. The situation varies according to the nature of the writings; what is evident for the epistolary literature (an ecclesial context that is as much about the authors as about the recipients), ends up being more complex for the Gospels, Acts, and Revelation. But in all of them we perceive the importance of the ecclesial subject.[13] In order to prove this, it will suffice to spend some time pondering the fundamental stages of the formation, transmission, and reception of the writings.

a) Configuration of the evangelical traditions

The task of compiling the sayings and actions of Jesus and giving them a form that would favor their transmission (first oral, and then written) had its beginning, very probably, at the time of Jesus' earthly mission through the work of his disciples;[14] this activity, made fruitful and invigorated by the pascal event

16 (Vatican City: Libreria Editrice Vaticana, 2002); and the recent document of the Pontifical Biblical Commission: *Ispirazione e verità della Sacra Scrittura: La parola che viene da Dio e parla di Dio per salvare il mondo* (Vatican City: Libreria Editrice Vaticana, 2014).

12. "Tradition is not the transmission of things or words, a collection of dead things. Tradition is the living river that links us to the origins, the living river in which the origins are ever present." Benedict XVI, General Audience "Communion in Time: Tradition" (April 26, 2006); English trans. in *L'Osservatore Romano* 39, no. 18 (May 3, 2006): 11.

13. This reality is the premise of a publication that, although not free of a polemical tone, is interested in openly posing the question of the ecclesiality of Scripture: Carl E. Braaten and Robert W. Jenson, eds., *Reclaiming the Bible for the Church* (Grand Rapids: Eerdmans, 1995).

14. James D. G. Dunn, *A New Perspective on Jesus: What the Quest for the Historical Jesus Missed* (Grand Rapids: Eerdmans, 2005), ch. 1: "The First Faith: When Did Faith Become a Factor in the Jesus Tradition?"

and enriched by its light, reached its definitive form in the heart of the Christian community. Studies about the methods of biblical interpretation in Judaism make ever more obvious the importance of these ways of proceeding in the context of the diverse New Testament traditions.[15] It is practically impossible to define the concrete outlines of this process, or rather these processes;[16] they are thus an object of continual hypotheses on the part of scholars.[17] But that does not take away their importance: it remains beyond doubt that thanks to the initial labor of the communities (and, it is reasonable to think, of their most qualified or authoritative members) the "deposit" (cf. 1 Tim 6:20; 2 Tim 1:14) of Revelation has been communicated, including its written testimony. In the very genesis of the New Testament is the believing memory of the Christian communities; the Church appears therefore as the decisive subject from the beginning.[18]

15. Agustín del Agua, *El método midrásico y la exegesis del Nuevo Testamento*, BibMid 4 (Valencia: Artes Gráficas Soler, 1985), 265–272: "Deráš sobre dichos de Jesús"; 273–290: "El papel de la 'escuela midrásica' en la configuración del Nuevo Testamento"; Domingo Muñoz León, *Derás: Los caminos y sentidos de la palabra divina en la Escritura, Parte I: Derás targúmico y Derás neotestamentario*, BHBib 12 (Madrid: Consejo Superior de Investigaciones Científicas, 1987), 541–606: "Derás intraneotestamentario."

16. We refer here principally to the two great evangelical traditions (synoptic and Johannine), which go back to the same origin—the history of Jesus—but which probably developed in parallel form. Cf. Rafael Aguirre Monasterio and Antonio Rodríguez Carmona, *Evangelios sinópticos y Hechos de los Apóstoles*, IEB 6 (Estella: Verbo Divino, 2012), 35–60; Raymond E. Brown, *An Introduction to the New Testament* (New York: Doubleday, 2016), chs. 6 and 11; Francis J. Maloney, *The Gospel of John*, in Sacra Pagina, ed. Daniel J. Harrington, SJ (Collegeville, MN: 1998), "Introduction."

17. Xavier Léon-Dufour, *I vangeli a la storia di Gesú* (Cinisello Balsamo: Edizioni Paoline, 1973), 411–446: "Alla fonte della tradizione." James D. G. Dunn, *Jesus Remembered*, Christianity in the Making 1 (Grand Rapids: Eerdmans, 2003), 173–254: "The Tradition." David Laird Dungan and John S. Kloppenborg, "The Synoptic Problem," 1231–1240 in *The International Bible Commentary*, ed. William R. Farmer (Collegeville, MN: Liturgical Press, 1998); Frans Neirynck, "Synoptic Problem," 587–595 in *The New Jerome Biblical Commentary*, ed. Raymond E. Brown, Joseph A. Fitzmyer, and Roland E. Murphy (Englewood Cliffs, NJ: Prentice Hall, 1990).

18. Joseph Ratzinger/Benedict XVI shows the close dependence between this believing memory and the charism of inspiration. "The Church's remembering is not merely a private affair; it transcends the sphere of our own human understanding and knowing. It is a being-led by the Holy Spirit, who shows us the connectedness of Scripture, the connection between word and reality, and, in doing that, leads us 'into all truth.' This also has some fundamental implications for the concept of inspiration. The Gospel emerges from human remembering and presupposes the communion of those who remember.'" *Jesus of Nazareth, I: From the Baptism in the Jordan to the Transfiguration*, trans. from the German by Adrian J. Walker (New York: Doubleday, 2007), 234.

b) Literary composition of the New Testament writings

The gospels and Acts, according to the schema of *Dei verbum* §19, have undergone a process in whose phases ecclesiality continues to be a determining factor; we focus now on the third phase, the literary composition.[19] The authors draw on traditions already existing in the Church, of which they thus appear to be active members. And their work is conditioned by "the condition of the churches": this is therefore about an intra-ecclesial labor, which springs forth from the Church and is directed toward the Church. Again, and even though the comparison of the evangelical texts permits one to arrive at hypotheses more or less probable, we have to say—as we did in the earlier section—that the concrete outlines of this work of literary composition are uncertain. But, even amidst the very ignorance about the sources that the evangelists used to compose their work, the intrinsic ecclesiality of these writings is commonly accepted. The conclusion of the fourth evangelist, with that "we" which attests to the truth of all that the beloved disciple has written (John 21:24), shows that the authorship of this book is at once singular and plural. The individual author does not exist at the margin of the community, but instead only within it. And at the same time, his work is directed to this community: "So that you all may believe" (John 19:35, 20:31).

We can affirm something analogous about the other books of the New Testament. Most of the *letters of Paul* are explicitly directed to concrete ecclesial communities (Rome, Corinth, Galatia, Ephesus, Philippi, Colossae, Thessalonica) or their leaders (Timothy: Ephesus; Titus: Crete).[20] The fact that Paul's epistolary writings frequently have a "collegial" sender is significant;[21] by presenting himself along with another brother, or brothers, at the same time that he reinforces the value of his testimony (cf. Deut 19:15), he also reveals that the letter's contents do not respond to an individual initiative only, but that they

---

19. *DV* §19: "The sacred authors wrote the four Gospels, selecting some things from the many which had been handed on by word of mouth or in writing, reducing some of them to a synthesis, explaining some things in view of the situation of their churches and preserving the form of proclamation but always in such fashion that they told us the honest truth about Jesus." Cf. Brown, *An Introduction to the New Testament*, 35–36: "The Three Stages of Gospel Formation."

20. Only the very short Letter to Philemon is addressed to a particular member of the church of Colossae.

21. Paul, Sylvanus, and Timothy (1–2 Thess); Paul and Sosthenes (1 Cor); Paul and Timothy (2 Cor, Phil, Col, Phlm). The exceptions are Romans and Ephesians, as well as the pastoral letters. In Galatians Paul represents himself "and all the brethren who are with me" (Gal 1:2) as the senders.

also involve the community. The letter to the Hebrews, which has no known addressee, is a Christian homily (*logos parakléseos*, Heb 13:22; cf. Acts 13:15) that is thus born in a clearly ecclesial context. All in all, the "catholic letters" (James, Peter, Jude, John), which lack a concrete addressee (but cf. 2 and 3 John), are not thereby less "ecclesial" than the letters of Paul; on the contrary, they reflect in a clearer way the catholicity (that is, universality) of the Church of the Lord, which, like the historical Israel, is disseminated throughout the Roman Empire (*diaspora*, Jas 1:1 and 1 Pet 1:1). Finally, let us note that also the Book of Revelation is directed to "the seven churches of [the Roman province of] Asia" (Rev 1:4). But seven, a number of plenitude, suggests to us that the addressees are not only the churches enumerated (Rev 1:11); Revelation is ultimately directed to all Christian communities, which journey toward their consummation in the one celestial Jerusalem (cf. Rev 21–22).[22]

c) Transmission of the biblical writings: textual criticism and translations

We cannot enter even summarily into the description of the process of transmission of the biblical writings within the Church, which is the object of textual criticism.[23] But it is enough to consult the list of Greek and Latin codices used in the 28th edition of Nestle-Aland (pp. 792–819) in order to give ourselves an idea of the enormous cultural work carried out over centuries by the Christian communities in order to be able to access the biblical text.[24] It concerns a task similar to the one carried out in the Jewish communities between the fourth and tenth centuries by the *soferim* (scribes: AD 135–500) and the Masoretes (AD 500–1000), in order to conserve and transmit the text of the Hebrew Bible;[25] the manuscripts of Qumran testify to every religious Jewish group's

22. "The seven churches . . . in some manner represent the universal Church." Domingo Muñoz León, *Apocalipsis*, CBJer NT 8 (Bilbao: Desclée De Brouwer, 2007), 45. Cf. Ugo Vanni, *Lectura del Apocalipsis: Hermenéutica, exegesis, teología* (Estella: Verbo Divino, 2005), 61 (originally *L'apocalisse: Ermeneutica, esegesi, teologia* [Bologna: Dehoniane, 1988]). In fact, the vision that constitutes this sacred book has an evident intention of universality, as is shown in the enormous multitude of the saved "from every nation, from all tribes and peoples and tongues" (Rev 7:9).

23. Mannucci, *La Biblia como Palabra de Dios*, 93–105: "The text of the Bible"; Raymond E. Brown, D. W. Johnson, Kevin G. O'Connell, and Xabier Pikaza, "Texts and Versions," 561–589 in *New Jerome Biblical Commentary*.

24. We find an ample description of this process in Giovanni Maria Vian, *La biblioteca de Dios: Historia de los textos cristianos* (Madrid: Ediciones Cristiandad, 2006).

25. Cf. Ellis R. Brotzman, *Old Testament Textual Criticism: A Practical Introduction* (Grand Rapids: Baker Books, 1994), 47–55.

need to have the biblical text.[26] By its great quantity of textual testimonies, many of them close in time to the composition of the texts, Christian Scripture contrasts with other works of antiquity that have reached us almost always in more scarce and more recent manuscripts:

> No other text of antiquity has been as widely read, transcribed, cited, and translated as the Bible. This explains why its manuscript tradition (the testimonies that transmit it) is very ancient and abundant, above all with regards to what is referred to as the Greek Bible and, in particular, the New Testament. On the contrary, the tradition of classical Greek and Latin texts is confined in general to a few testimonial manuscripts. To the Septuagint version of the Old Testament diverse papyrus scrolls testify, and these are fragmentary but of great importance because of their antiquity (between the end of the 3rd century BCE and the 3rd century CE): some 30 codices in parchment and written in capital letters (between the 9th and the 10th centuries), and almost 1600 written in lowercase letters (between the 9th and the 16th centuries). The Greek New Testament manuscripts, however, approach 6000: some 100 papyrus scrolls (mostly between the 2nd and 4th centuries), more than 300 codices in parchment and written in capital letters, almost 3000 in lowercase letters, and around 2500 lectionaries. . . . To these truly impressive statistics . . . we must add tens of thousands of citations by the Christian authors of the first centuries . . . and the ancient translations into Eastern languages.[27]

This is due to the churches' permanent need to make use of the Word of God in their daily life. All this allows us to understand that textual criticism, a science that is supremely technical and specialized, at the same time turns out to be an open window to the concrete situation of the Christian communities in which each volume or codex that attests to the biblical text lived.

Within textual criticism, the *translations* of the Bible merit particular mention. Already in the 3rd century BC, the Jewish community of Alexandria had commenced the translation of the Pentateuch into Greek, thus originating one of the greatest cultural undertakings in human history, which would reach its culmination some centuries later (the Septuagint Bible).[28] The Chris-

---

26. "The collection of materials coming out of each cave presents the same general profile: biblical works, related religious literature, sectarian works." Fiorentino García Martínez, *Textos de Qumrán* (Madrid: Editorial Trotta, 1993), 37.

27. Vian, *La biblioteca de Dios*, 58–59.

28. Cf. Natalio Fernández Marcos, *Introducción a las versiones griegas de la Biblia*, TECC 64 (Madrid: Consejo Superior de Investigaciones Científicas, 1998). "The Septuagint, the first biblical translation, constituted a singular phenomenon in antiquity. . . . The translation of the Jewish Pentateuch into Greek in the 3rd century AD can be considered as a phenomenon without precedents . . . , of capital importance for the history of our civilization" (31).

tian churches prolonged this practice, which was necessarily required by the universal call of the Gospel.[29] So already in the first centuries we have numerous translations into Latin, Syriac, and Coptic; Armenian, Georgian, Ethiopian, and Ancient Slavic would follow them.[30] The Latin version completed by Jerome at the end of the 4th century, which through its diffusion would be known as the Vulgate, has had immense religious and cultural influence in the West. Let us point out the obvious: the translation of Scripture has been historically an intra-ecclesial task; the complexity that the ancient versions confer on the art of textual criticism of the Old and New Testaments expresses the vigorous strength of Scripture in the Christian communities. The continuous translations into modern languages only confirm this strength.[31]

We should note that the Christian scribes do not copy only the New Testament but rather the whole Christian Bible, already unified by the Greek language. This fact shows an essential theological detail: the internal unity of Scripture, perceived as an exigency of faith in Christ. The principal ancient codices (4th century: Vatican, Sinaitic; 5th century: Alexandrian), which "bind" into a united whole the books of the Old and the New Covenant, thus become a theological phase of primary magnitude.

In summary: the transmission of the great treasure of the Tradition that is Scripture, in its original versions and in its diverse translations, has been possible only in the heart of the People of God, that is, the Church. Without the Church there would be no Scripture.

d) Reception of the New Testament writings: the biblical canon

We have already indicated that the literary composition of the New Testament ends up being, in many cases, impossible to know as far as its concrete process goes. Something similar happens with the process of acceptance of these books as canonical, that is, normative for the faith and life of the Church; the fluctuations experienced by some biblical books, whose canonicity was disputed

---

29. Cf. Matt 24:14 ("in all the *oikoumenē*"); Matt 26:13 and Mark 13:9 ("in the whole *kosmos*"; Matt 28:19 and Luke 24:47 ("to all the nations"); Mark 16:15 ("to the whole creation"); Acts 1:8 ("to the end of the earth"); John 12:32 ("all men").

30. Brown, Johnson, O'Connell, and Pikaza, "Texts and Versions." Cf. Carlos Jódar Estrella, "El texto de la Biblia," 83–87 in *Diccionario de Teología*, ed. César Izquierdo, Jutta Burggraf, and Félix María Arocena Solano (Pamplona: EUNSA, 2006), 86.

31. Carlo Buzzetti, *La Bibbia e le sue trasformazioni*, LoB 3.4 (Brescia: Queriniana, 1984); Jean-Claude Margot, *Traducir sin traicionar: Teoría de la traducción aplicada a los textos bíblicos*, BibL 8 (Madrid: Cristiandad, 1987).

in some circles, are well known.[32] We distinguish between the fixing of the Old Testament canon (which must be considered in light of the biblical canon existing in Judaism, although this is not free from difficulties either) and that of the New Testament, which—obviously—was produced *ex novo*.[33] But what is beyond all doubt is the ecclesial character of that process, and this applies to both parts of the biblical canon.[34] In fact, historians of the canon recognize the *ecclesial use* of the books as decisive criteria for canonicity, even more than apostolic authorship and doctrinal orthodoxy; as the great Augustine said, *ego vero Evangelio non crederem, nisi me catholicae Ecclesiae commoveret auctoritas*.[35] The writings that have been read in the churches, and therefore in the Church, are canonical.[36] Few themes show so clearly the ecclesiality of the Church as the formation of the Christian biblical canon; it has even been said that "the definition of the Canon is an act of self-consciousness, the first in the true sense of

32. Raymond E. Brown and James C. Turro, "Canonicity," 515–534 in *New Jerome Biblical Commentary*.

33. The question of the Hebrew canon and the Christian canon of Scripture is synthesized in the Pontifical Biblical Commission's document *The Jewish People and Their Sacred Scriptures in the Christian Bible* (Vatican City: 2001), §§16–18.

34. Thomas Söding, "Il canone biblico: Storia e teologia," 231–260 in *Rivisitare il compimento: Le Scritture di Israele e la loro normatività secondo il Nuovo Testamento*, ed. Stefano Romanello and Roberto Vignolo, Biblica 3 (Milan: Glossa, 2006). For the Christian Old Testament, see E. Earle Ellis, *The Old Testament in Early Christianity*, WUNT 54 (Tübingen: Mohr Siebeck, 1991), 3–50. "The community of Jesus, then, did not differ from other groups in Judaism in the Old Testament canon that it received, but it continued a hermeneutical process that inevitably brought into being a further supplement to the ancient canon. That hermeneutical process also brought about a radically new perception of the Old Testament itself" (Ellis, *Old Testament*, 50). See also Agustín del Agua, "El 'Antiguo' Testamento, primera parte de la Biblia Cristiana," in *Biblia, literatura e Iglesia*, ed. Félix García López and Ángel Galindo García (Salamanca: Universidad Pontificia de Salamanca, 1995), 155–193.

35. "In fact I would not believe the gospel if the authority of the Catholic Church did not move me." Augustine, *Contra epistulum Manichaei quam uocant fundamenti*, chapter 5, section 6 (CSEL 25:197; PL 42:176); trans. "Answer to the Letter of Mani known as *The Foundation*," 234–267 in *The Manichean Debate*, ed. Boniface Ramsey (Hyde Park, NY: New City Press, 2006), 236. Cf. Carlos Jódar Estrella, "La relación Antiguo-Nuevo Testamento y la configuración de la Biblia como texto," 69–84 in *Entrar en lo Antiguo: Acerca de la relación entre Antiguo y Nuevo Testamento*, ed. Ignacio Carbajosa and Luis Sánchez Navarro, PreDi 16 (Madrid: Universidad Eclesiástica San Dámaso, 2007), 78–79.

36. "Through the same tradition the Church's full canon of the sacred books is known" (*DV* §8). "Here there is affirmed not only a *datum of fact* . . . but a *datum of faith*, even though *Dei Verbum* does not say how or through what arguments or criteria the Tradition provided the Church with the certainty about the Sacred and Canonical Books." Mannucci, *La Biblia como Palabra*, 199. Regarding the criteria for canonicity, see pp. 199–204.

the word, on the part of the Church."[37] Canonical criticism, a method recently developed in the exegesis of the Old and New Testament, shows the theological dimension of the canon, and the necessity of taking it into consideration for the sake of a correct interpretation of the books of Scripture.[38]

e) Understanding of the New Testament writings: Christian theology

Finally, we want to add some considerations about the relationship between Scripture and the Church. Ever since the time of Paul, reflection on Christ has revolved around Scripture; the very first Christian theology emerges, therefore, from a reading of Scripture in light of Christ, and always in a concrete historical and cultural context. The first heresies (Gnosticism, Marcionism), just as much as the theology of the apostolic Fathers and apologists, were constantly centered on the Bible;[39] and later theological controversies would be imbued with recourse to Scripture.[40] We can also remember here the great biblical commentaries, in which the Fathers and later the medieval and more recent authors have expressed a theology that emerges from a faithful and contextualized reading of the Bible. But also the great systematic works emerge from the scriptural data, which they continually confront and in which they find the foundation of their affirmations.[41] All of these initiatives throughout history demonstrate the immense potentiality of the Word of God expressed in Scripture and its capacity to illuminate people in all ages.[42] But at the same time, they cause us to recognize that Christian theology has been possible because the Church has conserved, transmitted, read, and lived out Sacred Scripture.

37. Mannucci, *La Biblia como Palabra*, 204.

38. Brevard S. Childs, *Biblical Theology of the Old and New Testaments: Theological Reflection on the Christian Bible* (Minneapolis, MN: Fortress, 1993); James A. Sanders, *From Sacred Story to Sacred Text: Canon as Paradigm* (Philadelphia: Fortress, 1987). Cf. Pontifical Biblical Commission, *The Interpretation of the Bible in the Church*, I.C.1: "Canonical Approach"; Benedict XVI, *Jesus of Nazareth*, I, 14–16.

39. Ramón Trevijano Etcheverría, *La Biblia en el cristianismo antiguo: Premicenos, Gnósticos, Apócrifos*, IEB 10 (Estella: Verbo Divino, 2001), especially 31–175 ("Exégesis prenicena") and 313–340 ("Exégesis gnósticas").

40. On the use of Scripture by the Fathers of the Church, see Charles Kannengiesser, *Handbook of Patristic Exegesis: The Bible in Ancient Christianity*, 2 vols., BACh 1 (Leiden: Brill, 2004).

41. Cf. Ceslas Spicq, *Esquisse d'une histoire de l'exégèse latine au moyen âge* (Paris: J. Vrin, 1944); Henri de Lubac, *Exégèse médiévale: Les quatre sens de l'Écriture*, 4 vols. (Paris: Aubier, 1959–1964).

42. Josep M. Rovira Belloso, "Lectura teológica de la Biblia," in *Biblia, literatura e Iglesia*, 195–214.

f) In summary

The aspects that we have just distinguished are related to each other. The formation of the biblical canon decisively influenced the reproduction and the diffusion of the biblical books, which is necessarily reflected in textual criticism. As for the influence of theological investigation on the transmission of Scripture, it is enough for us to pause before a figure like Origen, who in order to be able to read the Bible and compose his great commentaries, as well as to make possible a dialogue with the Jews of his time about a biblical text accepted by them, found that he needed to start by focusing on the Greek text of the Old Testament. This led him to complete the monumental undertaking of the *Hexapla*, by reason of which he is justifiably considered the father of Christian textual criticism.[43] In all these aspects, finally, we discover how the community of Christian believers, in its diverse local concretizations and in its universal dimension, constitutes the subject without which the Word of God could not be born, be transmitted, and persist in human history. "The People of God—the Church—is the living subject of Scripture; it is in the Church that the words of the Bible are always in the present."[44]

2.3. The Church, object of the Word of God

But in spite of the situation that we have just described, the Church does not exercise her dominion over the Word of God. The Church is not a despotic owner of the Word. On the contrary: she comes to know herself, she discovers her own identity, in the Word of God that she lives out and transmits. For that Word expressed in Scripture is not an "ecclesial product"; its origin is situated, precisely through the mediation of the ecclesial community, in transcendence:

> One could say that the books of Scripture refer to three subjects that interact among themselves. First of all, there is the individual author or group of authors to whom we owe a particular text. But these authors are not autonomous writers in the modern sense; they form part of a collective subject, the "People of God," from within whose heart and to whom they speak. Hence, this subject is actually the deeper "author" of the Scriptures. And yet likewise, this people does not exist alone; rather, it knows that it is led, and spoken to, by God himself, who—through men and their humanity—is at the deepest level the one speaking.[45]

---

43. According to calculations, it must have filled at least some fifty codices (!) in papyrus. See Vian, *La biblioteca de Dios*, 109–114: "Los *Hexapla* y su historia."
44. Benedict XVI, *Jesus of Nazareth, I*, xxi.
45. Benedict XVI, *Jesus of Nazareth, I*, xx–xxi.

Therefore the Word of God transmitted in the Church and expressed in Scripture becomes the objective measurement that shows to the same Church the principal features of her identity and that manifests her vocation to her. The one who is rightly considered the subject of Scripture turns out to be its object (the content of its teaching) at the same time. This we can verify from several perspectives.

a) A Church prepared by the Word of Scripture

A characteristic feature of the community of disciples that Jesus created around himself is its continuity with the people of Israel; despite the elements of discontinuity in the new thing, it does not presuppose Israel's rupture, but rather its fulfillment. This intention of Jesus is manifested in the constitution of the group of the Twelve, the number that is relates directly to the twelve tribes of Israel (cf. Matt 19:28; Luke 22:30). The importance of this feature should not be sidestepped, since it situates that new community in continuity with the people of the Covenant.[46] The *ekklēsia* of Jesus (cf. Matt 16:18; 18:17) is not an absolute innovation: it has been prefigured, prophesied, prepared for, and anticipated by the Church of the Lord (*ekklēsia Kuriou*), about which Scripture testifies (cf. *LG* §2).[47] It is the same intuition that guides Peter when, in his discourse on the first Christian Pentecost, he explains the outpouring of the Spirit: the miracle just witnessed by all the Jews present in Jerusalem fulfills the prophecy of Joel that refers to the sons of Israel (Acts 2:16–21, citing Joel 3:1–5a). Furthermore the openness to the Gentiles, an important trajectory of the Acts of the Apostles, is presented in the mouth of Paul as the fulfillment of the word: "For so the Lord has commanded us, saying, 'I have set you to be a light for the Gentiles, that you may bring salvation to the uttermost parts of the earth'" (Acts 13:47, citing Isa 49:6). The vision of the celestial Jerusalem in which the Book of

---

46. "It is often said that Jesus established the Twelve as the representatives of the new Israel, that with them he founded the new People of God. . . . The expression 'new People of God' is unfortunate; it does not appear in Sacred Scripture, which only speaks about the 'new Covenant.' The constitution of the Twelve is thus not directed to a new Israel, but rather to a new Covenant with Israel. In no way should this constitution be understood in the sense that Jesus founds a new Israel because of the rejection he experienced in Israel. The action of Jesus is totally positive . . . . With it he affirms that the restoration of Israel is beginning." Klemens von Stock, *Boten aus dem Mit-Ihm-Sein: Das Verhältnis zwischen Jesus und den Zwölf nach Markus*, AnBib 70 (Rome: Gregorian & Biblical Press, 1975), 36.

47. The expression (Hebrew: *q^ehal yhwh*) appears in Deut 23:2, 3, 4, 9; 1 Chron 28:8; 29:20; Mic 2:5. Cf. also *ekklēsia theou* in Neh 13:1 (Hebrew: *q^ehal hā'ělōhîm*); we find an identical Greek expression in 1 Tim 3:5, 15.

Revelation culminates, and with it the whole biblical canon, presents to us this city surrounded by a wall whose twelve gates are the tribes of Israel, and whose twelve foundations are the apostles of the Lamb (Rev 21:12–14). All of these data point in the same direction: in the Church is realized that community of the redeemed that has its most notable announcement and prefiguration in the people liberated from Egypt.[48] The Word of Scripture, read every Saturday in the synagogues (cf. Acts 15:21), constitutes the necessary soil that allows the community of believers in Jesus to be able to understand itself and to be recognized by everyone else as the realization of God's plan.

b) A Church that is born of the Word of Jesus

The Church receives its existence from the authoritative word of Jesus: "On this rock I will build my church" (Matt 16:18). With good reason we have discovered in this declaration of Jesus his will to configure the community of believers as a stable structure; it thus turns out to be a prophecy of the community's future constitution. But one must see the origin of this new assembly in the formation of the initial group of disciples (Matt 4:18–22 || Mark 1:16–20; cf. Luke 5:1–11). The original community is born out of the call to follow Jesus: "Follow me, and I will make you fishers of men" (Matt 4:19). That powerful word, whose efficacy is shown in the immediate reaction of his interlocutors ("Immediately they left their nets and followed him" [Matt 4:20]), is therefore the reality in which the community is founded. All of Jesus' instruction to his disciples, of which we find a complete expression in the great discourses of the Gospel of Matthew (Matt 5–7; 10; 13; 18; 24–25) and of John (the farewell discourse: John 13–16), as well as in the parables of Luke (especially Luke 10–19) and in the rest of the evangelical teachings, is oriented toward building up the future community, illuminating its life. Particularly notable is Matthew 18, called precisely the "ecclesial discourse" for its reference to the relationship among the members of the *ekklēsia* of Jesus (cf. 18:17). The Church, which emerges from the word of Jesus and is constructed by it, finds certainty about her future maturity in this same word.

c) A Church centered on service to the Word

When the Risen Christ bids farewell to his disciples, he commends to them a specific mission: "And you shall be my witnesses in Jerusalem and in all Judea and Samaria and to the end of the earth" (Acts 1:8). The Book of Acts, the

48. Filippo Belli, Ignacio Carbajosa, Carlos Jódar Estrella, and Luis Sánchez Navarro, eds., *Vetus in Novo: El recurso a la Escritura en el Nuevo Testamento*, Ensayos 290 (Madrid: Encuentro, 2006), 63: "La Iglesia del cumplimiento."

second part of the great Lucan work, fulfills what we could call a "testimonial concentration" of the ecclesial mission: the task of the Christian community is concentrated in the testimony about Christ.[49] This testimony includes the works (cf. Acts 4:32–35) but is manifested particularly in the word that reveals the meaning of those works. The abundance of discourses in Acts is a consequence of this reality. But the gospels also reveal the importance of the word in the ecclesial mission: "Go, therefore, and make disciples of all nations . . . teaching them to observe all that I have commanded you" (Matt 28:19–20a); "Go into all the world and preach the gospel to the whole creation" (Mark 16:15); "And that repentance and forgiveness of sins should be preached in his name to all nations" (Luke 24:47); at the origin of that testimony will be the action of the Holy Spirit (John 14:26). The testimonial word of Christians is, in the end, decisive for salvation: "So every one who acknowledges me before men, I also will acknowledge before my Father who is in heaven; but whoever denies me before men, I also will deny before my Father who is in heaven" (Matt 10:32–33). Jesus himself describes the ecclesial mission in terms of the proclamation of the gospel (Matt 24:14). The rapid production of New Testament writings in the second half of the first century is clear proof of the importance attributed to the word as a form of communicating the Christian event. In every moment of history the Church has made herself present via the announcement of the Word of God revealed in Jesus.

d) A Church that believes, and is identified with, the Word

We know about the "summaries" of Acts;[50] among them are three, very brief, summaries in which we encounter a singular expression: "The Word of God increased" (*ho logos tou theou ēuxanen*: Acts 6:7; 12:24; 19:20).[51] In the medieval period a similar phrase would refer to Scripture;[52] but in the Book of Acts the "Word of God" designates the oral testimony of the apostles.[53] The first text

---

49. Cf. Acts 1:22; 2:32; 4:33; 8:25; 18:5; 20:24; 22:15.

50. Joseph A. Fitzmyer, *The Acts of the Apostles*, AncB 31 (New York: Doubleday, 1998), 97.

51. In Acts 19:20 only "the Word" is mentioned. Cf. Jerome Kodell, "'The Word of God Grew': The Ecclesial Tendency of Logos in Acts 1:7; 12:24; 19:20," *Biblica* 55 (1975): 505–519.

52. *Sacra Scriptura aliquo modo cum legentibus crescit*: Gregory the Great, *Moralia in Job*, book 20, paragraph 1 (PL 76:135 B–D). See the commentary on this text in Pier Cesare Bori, *L'interpretazione infinita: L'ermeneutica cristiana antica e le sue trasformazioni* (Bologna: Il Mulino, 1987), 27–41.

53. In direct continuity with the word of Jesus, which Luke also designates as the Word of God. Regarding this expression, typical of Luke in the New Testament, see Joseph A. Fitzmyer, *The Gospel According to Luke I–IX*, AncB 28 (New York: Doubleday, 1981), 565.

reveals to us the meaning of the expression: "And the Word of God increased, and the number of disciples multiplied greatly in Jerusalem" (Acts 6:7); the parallelism shows that the Word of God is here equivalent to the "number of disciples"; that is, to the Christian community, to the Church.[54] In fact in Acts 12:24 it will simply say that "the word of God grew and multiplied": what multiplies is no longer the disciples, but the Word itself. This growth implies at the same time a strengthening.[55] In an audacious way, Luke implicitly identifies the Church with the Word of God; it is possible to see in this a development of the parable of the sower, which speaks to us of "the mysteries of the Kingdom of God" as of a "seed" that grows, and that is "the Word of God" (Luke 8:10–11).[56] This is confirmed by the rest of the Lucan work, in which "the Word of God" appears as the content of Jesus' preaching[57] and as the principal ministry of the apostolic Church.[58] That the "growth" was applied early on to the Church is demonstrated also by the Pauline letters, which use the verb "to grow" within the metaphors of the Church as the field of God (1 Cor 3:6–7), the Body of Christ (Eph 4:15; Col 2:19), or the building of God (Eph 2:21). The New Testament, therefore, shows us a Church that not only announces and transmits the Word of God, but also—in a certain way—is herself that Word.

e) A Church that suffers persecution for the Word

The ministry of the Word does not always lead to positive consequences; on the contrary, it is often a cause of persecution. Jesus, according to the evangelical testimony, had already predicted "tribulation or persecution on account of the Word" (Matt 13:21; Mark 4:17), as the prophets had been persecuted in the

54. This interpretation is confirmed by the only time in Acts that the verb "to grow" (*auxanō*) appears apart from this phrase, and also next to the verb "to be multiplied" (*plēthunō*): "But as the time of the promise drew near, which God had granted to Abraham, the people grew and multiplied in Egypt" (Acts 7:17). In his discourse, Stephen thus refers to the growth of the people (*laos*) of Israel. When the verbs *auxanō* and *plēthunō* appear together in the Old Testament, they always refer either to humanity created by God (Gen 1:22, 28; 8:17; 9:1, 7) or to the people of Israel (Gen 17:20 [Ishmael]; 28:3; 35:11; 47:27; 48:4; Exod 1:7; Lev 26:9; Jer 3:16; 23:3).
55. Acts 19:20: "So the word of the Lord grew and prevailed mightily" (the verb is *ischuō*).
56. In Luke 8:8 the verb *auxanō* does not appear without its synonym *phuō*. But *auxanō* appears in the parable of the mustard seed (Luke 13:19). In Col 1:5–6 it is "the Gospel" that " is bearing fruit and growing."
57. Luke 5:1; 8:21; 11:28.
58. Acts 4:31: "and they were all filled with the Holy Spirit and spoke the word of God with boldness"; 6:2: "It is not right that we should give up preaching the word of God to serve tables"; 8:14: "when the apostles at Jerusalem heard that Samaria had accepted the word of God" (cf. 11:1). See also 12:24; 13:5, 7, 46; 17:13; 18:11.

past (Matt 5:12). This consequence is verified from the beginning: again and again Acts presents us with the apostles imprisoned because of their testimony (Acts 4:1–3; 5:17–18; 12:3–10; 16:22–24).[59] In a similar situation we discover the seer John, imprisoned on the island of Patmos "on account of the Word of God and the testimony of Jesus" (Rev 1:9).[60] In his first letter, Paul, formerly a persecutor of the Church of God (1 Cor 15:9; Gal 1:13; Phil 3:6), recalls how the Christians of Thessalonica received "the word in much affliction" (1 Thess 1:6); and in several of his writings he presents himself as a prisoner (Eph 3:1, 4:1; Col 4:18; 2 Tim 1:8, 2:9; Phil 1:13–14; Phlm 1:1, 9).[61] But persecution is not the last word, as Paul affirms in his exaltation of the love of God (Rom 8:35–39). The response of the Christian in the face of persecution over the Word of God is, according to this very Word of God, a blessing (Rom 12:14) and a prayer for the persecutors (Matt 5:44).[62]

Persecution on account of Jesus is a constant theme in the New Testament;[63] in essence it fully coincides with "persecution on account of the Word."[64] So, if in the earlier section we discovered an implicit equivalence of the Word of God with the Church, now it is possible to demonstrate a fundamental identification between the Word and Jesus himself, an identification that we have already examined (cf. John 1:1; Rev 19:13). Jesus, Church, Word of God: we find ourselves before realities essentially united with each other, and even to a certain point identifiable with each another.

---

59. From Acts 21:27 to the end of the book (Acts 28:31), Paul is a prisoner, first in Jerusalem, later in Caesarea, and lastly—after appealing to Caesar—on the road to Rome.

60. It is about a present, current fact: Vanni, *Lectura del Apocalipsis*, 129.

61. We will not here enter into the debate about the authenticity of the writings traditionally ascribed to Paul, about which we are far from a basic consensus that goes beyond the determination of the "seven undisputed letters"; cf. Jordi Sánchez Bosch, *Escritos paulinos*, IEB 7 (Estella: Verbo Divino, 1998), 16–18. On 2 Thess, cf. 183–190; on Eph and Col, 422 and Heinrich Schlier, *Carta a los Efesios: Comentario*, BEB 71 (Salamanca: Sígueme, 1991), 31. Regarding the "pastoral letters" (1–2 Tim, Tit), see Luke Timothy Johnson, *The Writings of the New Testament: An Interpretation* (Minneapolis, MN: Fortress, 1999), 424–428; Philip Towner, *The Letters to Timothy and Titus*, NICNT (Grand Rapids: Eerdmans, 2006).

62. Cf. Joseph A. Fitzmyer, *Romans*, AncB 33 (New York: Doubleday, 1993), 655; Luis Sánchez Navarro, *La Enseñanza de la Montaña: Comentario contextual a Mateo 5–7*, EstBib 27 (Estella: Verbo Divino, 2005), 90–91.

63. Matt 5:11; Luke 21:12; John 15:20; Acts 9:5; 22:4; 2 Cor 4:7–10; 12–10; 1 Pet 4:14–15; Rev 6:9.

64. This is evident from Rev 1:9, a text already cited. "The two phrases, in progressive synonymous parallelism, signal that God's own message reaches us through the mediatory action of Jesus, in this regard called 'reliable testimony' ([Rev] 1:5a; 3:14). In effect, he is personally the 'Word of God' ([Rev] 19:13)." Vanni, *Lectura del Apocalipsis*, 132.

f) A Church that expresses and discovers its being in the Word

In its preaching and its testimony, the Christian community not only announces Jesus: it also expresses itself. Already the redactional work of the Gospels reveals the self-comprehension of the communities that are at their origin;[65] this will become explicit in Acts and above all in the apostolic letters. Thus is born the ecclesiology of the New Testament. This theme is very broad; right now we will focus principally on two ways of elaborating on this New Testament ecclesiology, which are based on the metaphors of a body and a building. They are two images intimately connected with each other in the Semitic mind, which understands the body as something that is "constructed" (Gen 2:22) and the "house" as a reality that is living;[66] this is seen in passages like 1 Corinthians 6:19, where the Christian's body is spoken about as a "temple."[67]

The Church as a body appears first and foremost in 1 Corinthians 12:12–30 and Romans 12:4–8. This image allows one to express two things: unity within diversity (many members, one body), which allows for the complementarity of the members based on their unity; and the life that animates that body (the Spirit: cf. 1 Cor 12:4). In Ephesians and Colossians we find a development of this notion, when Christ is presented to us as "the head of the body, the Church," which is fundamentally considered a universal reality (Col 1:18; cf. Eph 1:22; 4:15–16; 5:23).[68] On the other hand, the image of the Church as a building also appears in 1 Corinthians (3:9) and in Ephesians (2:21); we should note that in this latter text it culminates in a spontaneous way in the notion of the "temple." And the reality is that the Church cannot be understood as a "house" except insofar as she is a temple, since she is penetrated by the presence of the Lord. Hence the two images allow the Church to be presented as a reality firmly and deeply rooted in the transcendent.

This self-presentation of the Church, her own production, acquires a normative character precisely as an expression of the apostolic word. So the Church that has expressed her nature in the New Testament writings discovers her identity in them. We thus encounter a circularity that we have previously been able to detect between the Word of God and the Church.

---

65. A classical presentation of the method of redaction history: Heinrich Zimmermann, *Los métodos históricos-críticos en el Nuevo Testamento*, BAC 295, Spanish trans. Gumersindo Bravo (Madrid: Editorial Católica, 1969), 233–284.

66. Thus, for example, the "house of David" (2 Sam 7:16) is not a palace without its family, its descendants. In Hebrew the word "son" (*bēn*) derives from the root of the verb *bānāh* "to construct."

67. Cf. John 2:21: "But he spoke of the temple of his body"; 1 Pet 2:5: "and like living stones be yourselves built into a spiritual house, to be a holy priesthood."

68. Cf. Sánchez Bosch, *Escritos paulinos*, 416–417.

g) A Church that will be consummated in the Word

In the synoptic Gospels the eschatological discourse of Jesus reaches its zenith when he affirms: "Heaven and earth will pass away, but my words will not pass away" (Matt 24:35; Mark 13:31; Luke 21:33). The Word of Jesus—the Word of God—enjoys the same perennial nature as its Author.[69] In the Book of Revelation, the vision of the New Jerusalem is characterized in a similar way because "the first heaven and the first earth had passed away" (Rev 21:1); but that does not imply the disappearance of the words of God: on the contrary, we hear God himself saying, "Write this, for these words are trustworthy and true" (Rev 21:5, cf. 22:6). The definitive new thing is characterized by the presence of God, who is "the Alpha and the Omega" (Rev 21:6), in other words, who reunites in himself all words, and is an infinite wealth of signification.[70] The eschatological consummation of the Church, which as the new Jerusalem descends from heaven as a bride prepared to be married (Rev 21:2; cf. Eph. 5:25–27), will thus represent the definitive manifestation of the Word of God. To such an extent Scripture is about two inseparable realities: the Church does not exist without the Word of God.

h) In summary

The Church is the daughter of the Word of God: she has been prepared and begotten by it. Her mission and her growth are centered on the Word, and in it she also finds the expression of her own reality. Therefore she listens to it religiously (*DV* §1): given that it plunges its roots into the transcendence of God, that Word is a light, it is a rule, it is an objective measurement which has to be constantly confronted. And given that it proceeds from the Most High, that Word enjoys a permanence that makes it a precious reality for Christians, whose mission consists in making it fruitful within themselves and thus transmitting it to all nations.

---

69. "The genitive μου acquires . . . a certain epi-exegetical nuance, being able to be paraphrased with 'the words *that I am*' . . . . In 'his words,' Jesus himself is established in contraposition to that one who is said to be over heaven and earth." Salvador Villota Herrerro, *Palabras sin ocaso: Función interpretative de Mc 13,28–37 en el discurso escatológico de Marcos*, IBO 1 (Estella: Verbo Divino, 2006), 81.

70. "The alpha and the omega are the first and the last letters of the Greek alphabet. In them are understood all the rest of the letters and all that is expressed in their diverse combinations, that is to say, all of them in their totality." Klemens von Stock, *La última palabra es de Dios: El Apocalipsis como Buena Noticia*, Sicar 3 (Madrid: San Pablo, 2005), 187.

2.4. Conclusion

We have tried to delineate the complex relationship existing between the Church and the Word of God in the New Testament; a relationship that goes from the real distinction (subject/object) to the greatest identification. All of the New Testament writings are a product of the Church; and yet the Word precedes them. By means of the charism of inspiration it is the Lord who is acting. This fact does not imply any lessening of the human author, who is the author completely; but it gives to this Word—Sacred Scripture in the Tradition—an authority that in practice is identified with that of its Author. Therefore Scripture occupies a preeminent position in the Church, so that in her life she does not cease to recognize it, proclaim it, and listen to it as the Word of God.

To conclude these reflections, we should note, finally, that in what we have said we do not intend to relegate the Word of God to a group (the Church) closed in on itself, as a sort of exclusive and mysterious instruction for initiates. The facts would suffice to refute this idea, as today the Bible is studied from the widest range of perspectives (literary, historical, social, psychological, etc.). But this would bring us to a theme whose scope permits us to mention it only. Let us limit ourselves, therefore, to remember that just as the Church exists for all people, so also Scripture remains a reality that is accessible to anyone who feels attracted by this Word of truth and beauty. Moreover, the universal call is intrinsic to the Word of him who commanded the Church to "make disciples of all nations" (Matt 28:19).

3

From Scripture in the Body to Scripture in the Church

Carlos Granados

Our body is a book in which we recognize the pen strokes of writing, or scripture.[1] The "social body" (the structured society) is equally a text, a fabric, ordered by a law, by a certain scripture, or writing. The Church is also a body, that of Christ, in which exists, finally, a Scripture. It frequently happens that the theologian has more affinity with these latter realities (the Church and Scripture) and less with the former. Our thesis is that the "scripture in the body" offers us an indispensable key for understanding the intimate relationship between Sacred Scripture and the Church, that is, the community of faith which, as a body, reads it. The "earthly things" are necessary for understanding the "heavenly things" (cf. John 3:12).

This reflection is understood to be complementary to what was said in the previous chapter about the Word of God, Scripture, and the Church. The fundamental question is, what is the "place" of Scripture in the life of the Church? It is well known that this issue was one of the nuclear points of the controversy with Luther and subsequent Protestantism. Also, many other theological debates, before and after Luther, have revolved around this question: Does the Church measure Scripture, or is she measured by it? How can the two things be compatible?

---

1. Translator's note: The Spanish word is *escritura*, which means writing, or scripture, and is related to the verb *escribir* (to write). In English, we use the word "scripture" to mean the sacred writing of the Bible or perhaps the sacred writings of other religions, but not to refer to writing in general. In this chapter, however, we will follow the author's lead in using "scripture" more generally to refer to something that is written.

In order to respond to this question, I propose to the reader, as I said before, a road that begins with "earthly things." We will thus first consult philosophy, which has thought about what is appropriate to "scripture."[2] Scripture, we can conclude, is that which, in the form of law or a constitution, gives shape to the social body, structures it, and defines it. Understanding what is characteristic of "scripture" in general will offer us a new point of departure for grasping the place of "Scripture" in the faith of the Church, and also illuminating to some degree the classical theme of the relationship between Scripture and Tradition. It is evident that the Bible is a "singular case" in the general framework of scripture, but the Bible occupies a special place with respect to literature in general not because it does not fit within literary categories, but because *it manifests them in an exemplary way.*[3] For that reason a brief reflection on what "writing" means in general will help us to understand what "reading Scripture" in the Church means.

At a later time, we will go directly into the dogmatic principle that speaks to us about what Sacred Scripture is. We will refer above all to the truths taught by Vatican II. It will then be evident to us how the dogmatic principle is enriched with the previous reflection, which, in turn, is brought to fulfillment.

3.1. Scripture and word in a social body

I propose, then, three steps. In the first place, I will try to illustrate the problematic relationship that occurs between word and scripture, attempting to bring to light some prejudices that could impede us from advancing. In the second place, I would like to propose a thesis: scripture is the body of the word. Finally, I would like to draw out the consequences of this thesis in its application to the body of society: scripture is the social body of the word, which structures, differentiates, and gives form to a society.

---

2. Carlo Sini's introduction to *Etica della scrittura* (Milan: Mimesis, 1992) offers a general vision of this process. Of particular interest are the reflections of Paul Beauchamp, *El uno y el otro Testamento: Cumplir las Escrituras*, BAC (Madrid: Biblioteca de Autores Cristianos, 2015), 51–104 (originally in French: *L'un et l'autre Testament*, vol. 2, *Accomplir les Écritures* [Paris: Éditions du Seuil, 1990]); and Paul Ricœur, especially in his compilation *Du texte à l'action: Essais d'herméneutique, II* (Paris: Éditions du Seuil, 1986). There are many important studies; we recall here only the following: Eric A. Havelock, *Preface to Plato* (Cambridge, MA: Harvard University Press, 1963); *Origins of Western Literacy* (Toronto: Ontario Institute for Studies in Education, 1976); *The Muse Learns to Write: Reflections on Orality and Literacy from Antiquity to the Present* (New Haven, CT: Yale University Press, 1986); Walter J. Ong, *Orality and Literacy* (London: Methuen, 1982); Clarisse Herrenschmidt, *Les Trois écritures: Langue, nombre, code* (Paris: Gallimard, 2007).

3. Beauchamp, *El uno y el otro Testamento*, 71.

a) Word and scripture

Can scripture be reduced to a pure "instrument of the word"? There are some who have thought so. On the other hand, we can also say that words are carried away by the wind, while what is written down remains: can the word, then, be purely reduced to something that expires? And if we think about the laws that structure social life, or about the texts that organize the life of religious communities, could we not also say that the spoken word is an instrument that serves to disseminate and make known what is written down? In sum, generally speaking, how are oral tradition and scripture related to each other? And more concretely: how are they related to each other within the framework of a culture? One will immediately perceive that these questions are of interest for whoever searches out a response to the great questions posed at the beginning of this chapter.

Paul Beauchamp sees the union of word and scripture in a sentence of Saint Paul: "Born of a woman, born under the law" (Gal 4:4). Human beings have been born under the sign of a "maternal language" and under that of a "paternal scripture" (law); we have been born within the framework of a pair (word–scripture) that are as inseparable as a mother and a father.[4] We shall see that this explanation contains a profound truth.

How are word and scripture related to each other? Claude Lévi-Strauss, Ferdinand de Saussure, and Jean-Jacques Rousseau figure among those who have most extolled the value of oral transmission in opposition to scripture. For Rousseau, scripture is reduced to a mere "supplement of the spoken word." He thinks that in the first place there was a "purely oral" culture and only later did scripture appear as a supplement. Lévi-Strauss denies even that this supplement was good, and he sees it as the result of social violence (we will soon return to his thesis). Perhaps this idea of Rousseau about scripture as something secondary and posterior remains in the collective imagination.

Jacques Derrida, in his *Gramatology*, represents the other extreme of the pendulum, in opposition to the authors just cited. The others were "logophiles" [word-lovers]; Derrida represents the "graphophiles" [writing-lovers]. He gives a strong critique of this widespread "myth" of a primitive "society without scripture." For him such a thing has never existed:

> If one stops understanding writing in its narrow sense of linear and phonetic notation, one should be able to say that all societies capable of producing, that is to say of obliterating, their proper names, and of playing classificatory difference, practice writing in general. No reality or concept would therefore

4. Beauchamp, *El uno y el otro Testamento*, 51.

correspond to the expression "society without writing." . . . The scorn for writing, let us note in passing, accords quite happily with this ethnocentrism.[5]

Derrida denies the existence of a "purely oral" primitive culture: from which human beings have the spoken word, and has also, in one way or another, according to the diverse possibilities of each epoch, the capacity of "representing" the spoken word. The figures of animals painted in the caverns of prehistoric people are already a "legend" (that is, they were made to be read). Scripture forms an inalienable part of our origins.[6]

In the "graphophile" current we also find the Italian philosopher Giambattista Vico. He tells us in the *New Science*: "Philosophers have very mistakenly believed that languages were born first and scripture later; but on the contrary, they were born as twins and walked in parallel."[7] He believes, as we see, in the contemporaneity of word and scripture. Both were born as twins and have always walked in parallel.

How then are oral tradition and scripture, word and written text, related to each other? Are they "twins," or must we acknowledge that the spoken word has the primary place of "first-born daughter"? In my opinion, as I will presently explain in more detail, it is necessary to acknowledge that the word has a more original position. It is what was "in the beginning" (cf. John 1:1). But, in any case, Vico's affirmation helps us to understand that the commencement of scripture is not traceable; that in some way it is lost in the night of times past. Paul Beauchamp introduces here a distinction that is very useful for my understanding. The word is in the "origin"; scripture is in the "beginning." "Origin" is spoken regarding the primordial and gratuitous font, in the sense that it is continually current and present; "beginning" refers to that which "always" has existed in relation to the origin.[8]

---

5. Jacques Derrida, *Of Grammatology*, trans. Gayatri Chakravorty Spivak (Baltimore: Johns Hopkins University Press, 2016), 118 (originally *De la Grammatologie* [Paris: Éditions de Minuit, 1967]).

6. "The origin of the human language is lost in prehistory; the moment of the appearance of writing is also unknown and mysterious. . . . In a certain way writing qualifies a civilization: social evolution in fact advances together with variations in writing, which demonstrates a prodigious capacity for adaptation, both in its expressive forms and in the records with which it is passed on to posterity." Pietro Bovati and Pasquale Basta, *"Ci ha parlato per mezzo dei profeti": Ermeneutica biblica* (Milan: San Paolo Edizioni, 2012), 141n1.

7. Giambattista Vico, *Ciencia nueva*, Spanish trans. Rocío de la Villa (Madrid: Tecnos, 1995), section 3.1.

8. See Beauchamp, *El uno y el otro Testamento*, 61.

In any case, the affirmations of the "graphophiles," such as Derrida or Vico, oblige us to expand our framework of understanding regarding the concept of "scripture." For them scripture is not reduced to a pure linear and phonetic notation: it should not be understood, therefore, as a "recent accident" in the history of humanity. In reality, a book already exists in the human body itself, in which a human person writes his or her history. The "name" that the parents imprint on the body of the child, even before his or her birth, is the first word written on the person.

Without developing these ideas yet, let us draw the conclusion from this first introduction that to reduce scripture, or writing, to a mere "supplement of the spoken word" is to take away its *virtus*, that is, its virtue or power.[9]

b) Scripture, body of the word

After having shaken off some prejudices, I will now try to argue for the following thesis: "scripture represents the social body of the word," almost like its "incarnation" in social life. Here we will already anticipate some elements that touch more directly on our theme of reference, the relationship between Scripture and the Church. At the moment, in this part I will argue only for the fact that the concept of "body" is useful for understanding the relationship between word and scripture. In the next part we will see the application to the social body.

We begin with the following question: what is writing? Could we say that it means "representing" the word, understanding the verb "to represent" in its densest meaning? With this meaning, the definition that we could give to "scripture" would have to make continual reference to the word. Therefore, the first thing that we could say is that scripture provides an element of *distancing* with respect to the word; scripture "distances" the message from its speaker, from its initial situation and from its primitive addressee. "With written discourse," says Paul Ricœur, "the intention of the author and the intention of the text cease to coincide."[10] Thanks to scripture, the word is extended to us and reaches us through its "meaning" and through what it is about, and no longer only through the voice of the one who proclaims it. This *distancing* is one of the characteristics belonging to scripture: the author ceases to be the "owner" of what is said, and the receiver will no longer be his immediate circle

9. Translator's note: The Spanish is "desvirtuarla (en sentido literal: quitarse su virtus)." The author instructs us to take the Spanish "desvirtuar" literally, which means "to take away its virtue."

10. Ricoeur, *Du texte à l'action*, 187 [translated from the author's Spanish translation].

of listeners, but rather, in principle, whoever wants to read [what is written down].[11]

This *distancing* of which we have just spoken can be understood better by applying to scripture, or writing, the concept of "body." This is the explanation that Paul Beauchamp offers us regarding the relationship of both terms: "Word and scripture are linked as word and body. The latter term should be understood as the social body and also the body of humanity."[12] Word and scripture are not confused with each other. As we have said before, the word is in the "origin," as what is original and what originates; scripture is in the "beginning," being "from always" the place of representation of the act of the word. And now we have heard Beauchamp say that scripture is "like the social body" of the word. It is a way of trying to understand it better. In reality, in order to understand this last expression, it is necessary to remember how Beauchamp defines the body. For him, the body is the human person's mode of presence in the world and the permanence of his "beginning" in the "now."[13] If we apply this definition to scripture, then the result is that this is the (spatiotemporal) place in which the word continues to exist permanently; it is the mode in which the word becomes, in a way, permanent in a space and in a time within the world. Words "fly"; they certainly drift into the temporality of the people who are listening, but they do not "continue to perdure." Writing gives that permanence which is proper to the body. This signifies two things: that scripture without the word would be but a scribble, it would lack content, it would be reduced to a cadaver; and that, in its turn, the word without scripture would lack history and presence in the world. Let us recall that we are speaking here of scripture in the sense already defined, that is to say, in the sense which Derrida can affirm:

> Historicity itself is linked to the possibility of writing: to the possibility of writing in general, beyond those particular forms of writing in the name of which one has long spoken of peoples without writing and without history. Before being the object of a history—of an historical science—writing opens up the field of history—of historical becoming. And the former (*Historie*, one would say in German) [pre]supposes the latter (*Geschichte*).[14]

11. Ricoueur, *Du texte à l'action*, 125 [translated from the author's Spanish translation].

12. Beauchamp, *El uno y el otro Testamento*, 57.

13. Beauchamp, *El uno y el otro Testamento*, 8: "In the body are joined together space and time.... The body is the 'still being here' of the beginning, its permanence in the now. It is not a space like the rest but one that is known; not a time like the rest but one that continues in existence . . . it is the only space-time that we could name."

14. Derrida, *Of Grammatology*, 30.

Scripture can be understood, then, within the framework of this notion of the "body." In this respect an observation that Paul Ricœur makes can also be illuminating. It is certain that with scripture/writing one loses the usual force of the facial expressions and gestures that come from the body of the speaker. With scripture, the author loses the support of his body, that is, his gestures, which would accompany what he is saying.[15] His body, in reality, is "substituted," in a way, by the body of text in which his word is now incarnated in a certain manner. Ricœur speaks simply about a parallelism that can be useful for recognizing the proximity of the concepts of "body" and "text."[16]

Let us pause here for a moment to draw out a concrete application of our theme.

These reflections help us to understand the insufficiency of the famous search for the *ipsissima verba Iesu* in the gospels, that is, the attempt to distill from the gospels the authentic words of Jesus.[17] This intention cannot ever arrive at convincing results. Not only because one cannot demonstrate that certain words are *ipsissima verba Iesu*, but also because the very intention to get a writing back to its pure orality is mistaken as an interpretive act. The "body" of the word is not an instrument that can be taken away as one pleases, but rather it is an integral and inseparable part of the meaning. To say the contrary would be to say that the writing is a container of the words, which are impoverished, moreover, by the admixture of spurious elements that we could now eliminate, like dross, in order to restore the pure metal. It arises out of a conception of scripture as "a supplement of the spoken word," not as "the body of the word."

We can glimpse here also the meaning of tradition and the mistake that results when talking about a writing without an interpretive oral tradition, that is, "scripture alone," which the reader also finds himself facing alone. The writing is not understood to be marginal to the word that accompanies it and transmits it. Here we can already anticipate the elements of the polar tension that exists between what is written and the tradition:

The writing helps to renew the tradition. In order to illustrate this aspect one can remember what 2 Kings 22 narrates to us. It happened in the reign of Josiah that the king "found" a book in the Temple, the book of the law. This book contained a message of reform and started a renewal of the religious tradition

---

15. Bovati and Basta, *Ci ha parlato*, 169, speak of the "silent" character of writing, that is to say, being less expressive than the oral message, because it lacks the paralinguistic elements of that latter (tone of voice, pauses, rhythm of diction, gesturing, etc.).

16. Ricœur, *Du texte à l'action*, 186.

17. The author to whom we refer, who pursues this search, is Joachim Jeremias; see, among other titles, *Palabras desconocidas de Jesús* (Salamanca: Sígueme, 1976).

of the people. The writing renews the tradition. So it happens also with many religious orders, which look for renewal in a return to the "rule," the written document in which the freshness of the origin is contained. The oral transmission has been contaminated and a "return to the letter" turns out to be purifying and beneficial.

But at the same time, the tradition helps to renew what is written. A writing without a word that transmits it, that explains it, that makes it comprehensible and actualizes it, is nothing. Even the book encountered by Josiah would be nothing without the religious tradition that receives it (deformed, certainly, in some aspects, but indispensable for understanding the meaning of the written document) and without the mediation of the persons who put it into action. The writing would remain petrified in an unreachable past without the help of the word.

c) Scripture and the social body

I would like to recall here the explanation that Lévi-Strauss presents in his *Tristes topiques* about the origin of "scripture." The French ethnologist maintains that written language was born of the desire for dominion of some classes over others; that is, it was born of the violence exercised in society. "If my hypothesis is exact," he affirms, "it is necessary to admit that the primary function of written communication is to facilitate servile dominion."[18] The wealthy classes, which knew how to write, reinforced their dominion over the dominated classes, making use of a knowledge that had been forbidden for the rest: scripture. Only they knew how to record, document, and give an account. Scripture was in its origin above all, according to Lévi-Strauss, a medium of dominion that was absent in the primitive societies without scripture.

This explanation of the origin of scripture has its originality, but we can at least recognize its marked Marxist roots and its clear dependence on an ideology. It is possible that scripture/writing has served as a medium for dominion over the masses; but it is improper to deduce from this that it is essentially so from its origin. In any case, Lévi-Strauss's hypothesis puts us on the trail toward solving the issue of scripture's close relationship with culture and society.

Lévi-Strauss certainly gives us an important key for relating *scripture* to the constitution of the *social body*. Scripture engenders a structured people,

---

18. Claude Lévi-Strauss, *Tristes topiques* (Paris: Librairie Plou, 1955), 354: "Si mon hypothèse est exacte, il faut admettre que la function primaire de la communication écrite est de faciliter l'asservissement." And earlier: "[la communication écrite] paraît favoriser l'explotation des hommes avant leur illumination."

a people in which differences are instituted. Scripture marks the difference: the priests read the law, and the people listen to it. Scripture has an effect of differentiating the social body: the king, according to Deuteronomy, should conserve a written copy of the law, as the representative of the people (cf. Deut 17:18). It is not that scripture was reserved for priests and magi, but that it is indeed linked with a structured form of the social body. Only Moses receives the tablets of the law, written with the finger of God, in order to transmit them to the people. In a later period it is only the *pater familias* who should write upon the doorposts the words of the law (Deut 11:18, 20). In the present time, to point out another element also, the reading of the Gospel in the Eucharistic celebration is reserved for the ordained minister only. Scripture structures, differentiates, and gives form to the social body.

Within this social body we can also point out two processes, apparently opposed to each other, which set scripture in motion: one as a "centripetal" sign and the other as a "centrifugal" sign. Let's begin with the first, the centripetal dynamic. Eric Havelock points out that each social group has a radical, passionate, almost irrational attachment to its own scripture.[19] For him this attachment becomes incomprehensible. It is the case, for example, with the Slavic alphabet: the scandal of those who do not want to be controlled by the universal framework that would make communication easier for them. There is in scripture, effectively, an element of "social identity." Scripture wants to continue being particular, continue symbolizing a wound and a scar on the universal; we thus recognize its centripetal force and the "cohesion" of a determinate social body.

At the same time, scripture is the place in which we can best perceive the dialogue among diverse cultures. This is what is called the "intercultural force of scripture," and it begins with a simple fact: the possibility of "translation."[20] The phenomenon of translation is without a doubt the transcultural act *par excellence*, the most significant act of communication among cultures. This is the centrifugal force of scripture. The alphabet opens up a bridge between languages and heterogeneous cultures. Scripture is the place where diverse cultures can dialogue, each one with its singularity and, nevertheless, all related by a series of elements; elements that pass undetected by the majority and that are accessible to just a few erudite people; elements that thus refer to a "beginning" that is forgotten, unconscious, and yet very active and present as

19. Eric. A. Havelock, *Aux origines de la civilisation écrite* (Paris: François Maspero, 1981), 92.

20. See above all Beauchamp, *L'uno e l'altro Testamento 2*, 67.

an "intercultural force." Scripture is the place where the Canaanite and the Jew dialogue, the Jew and the Greek, the Greek and the Roman, the Roman and the barbarian, etc. This is its centrifugal force.

3.2. Word, Scripture, and Tradition

Up until now we have been able to reflect on the phenomenon of scripture, or writing. Its singularity and importance have come to light: it is distinct from the word; it is not originating, as the word is, but it has always existed as the social body of the word; it presupposes a certain distancing that produces a universalization with respect to the dialogic framework of the word; it has a series of precise functions in the social body: it structures it, gives it cohesion, opens it up.

Let us turn our attention now to a "scripture" that is very singular: Sacred Scripture. In it, as we suggested at the beginning, is fully realized what we have just pointed out about the general phenomenon of writing.

The development of this essay will now be the following. We will begin with the distinction between Word (*Verbum Dei*) and Scripture (part a). From here we will then focus on the distinction between Scripture (*Verbum Dei scriptum . . .*) and Tradition (. . . *vel traditum*) (part b). In order to understand it, precisely what was said before about the link between word and scripture will be useful for us. Finally, in part c we will apply what we have just explained, about scripture as the body of the word, in order to understand the function of Scripture, its place in the Church, and, in this way, its position in God's historical plan of salvation.

a) Verbum Domini–Sacra Scriptura

Our point of departure will be precisely the *incipit* of the Apostolic Constitution *Dei verbum*. This beginning immediately attracts our attention regarding the "Word of God." It is already well known that the apostolic constitution does not confuse *Verbum Dei* with *Sacred Scripture*, but rather it carefully distinguishes both terms.[21] Strictly speaking, it is a mistake, according to the constitution's own terminology, to say that Sacred Scripture is *the* Word of God. Let us recall that *Dei verbum* §10 uses the expression *verbum Dei scriptum vel*

---

21. On this point I follow the detailed analysis of Albert Vanhoye, "The Reception in the Church of the Dogmatic Constitution 'Dei Verbum,'" 104–125 in *Opening Up the Scriptures: Joseph Ratzinger and the Foundations of Biblical Interpretation*, ed. José Granados, Carlos Granados, and Luis Sánchez-Navarro (Grand Rapids: Eerdmans, 2008).

traditum: the Word of God written or transmitted. The "Word of God," identi-fied with Revelation, has therefore an anterior place to Scripture.

Equally clear in this respect is *Dei verbum* §9, where Scripture is defined with these words: *Sacra Scriptura est locutio Dei, quatenus, divino afflante Spiritu, scripto consignatur.* Note well that the text says *locutio* (speaking) not *Verbum* (word); it reserves the term *Verbum* as a reference to Revelation, and avoids using the term as an equivalent for "Sacred Scripture." Sacred Scripture is "the speaking of God inasmuch as, by the Holy Spirit's inspiration, it is con-signed to writing."[22]

Finally, *Dei verbum* §24 says that the Sacred Scriptures contain (*continent*) the Word of God, and, since they are inspired, they are truly the Word of God (*quia inspiratae, vere verbum Dei sunt*). In light of the other passages of the con-stitution, one can understand that here it is not said that Sacred Scripture is *the* Word of God, in a simple equation between the two, but rather that Scripture is the Word of God, in the sense that it contains the Word, not that it exhausts it.[23]

Christianity is certainly not a "religion of the book."[24] Scripture is not the only font of revelation and is not confused with the divine Word. The word is in the category of "origin" (original, originating), as we said earlier; scripture is in the category of "beginning." This distinction now finds a new support, consid-ering the testimony of what happens in the case of Sacred Scripture.

b) *Scripture and Tradition:* Verbum Dei scriptum vel traditum

We know that in the Second Vatican Council's discussions around the docu-ment that finally took the name of *Dei verbum*, the first schema that spoke of the "fonts" (plural) of revelation was rejected. With this rejection the Council did

22. Translator's note: Here I have translated from the Spanish and Latin, as the English translation in the Gonzalez edition of the Vatican II documents renders "locutio" simply as "word," and does not get at the distinction that the author is here trying to make.

23. Karl Barth ("Conciliorum tridentini et Vaticani I inhaerens vestigiis?" in *La revelación divina*, ed. Bernard-Dominique Dupuy et al., 2 vols. [Madrid: Taurus, 1970]; originally *La rev-elation divine* [Paris: Cerf, 1968], 2:229–242) affirms, starting with *DV* §24, that "only to Scrip-ture is the character of *verbum Dei* attributed" (232). But this affirmation does not keep in mind that reference to the *traditum* of *DV* §10. The solution that we propose for this text, that §24 should be translated as "[the Scriptures] are truly a Word of God," and not "are truly *the* Word of God," resolves this problem.

24. In this regard, cf. Henri de Lubac, *Scripture in the Tradition*, trans. Luke O'Neill (New York: Herder & Herder, 2001), 193–194: "Thus, the law of the Gospels is in no way a *lex scripta*. Properly speaking, Christianity is not a 'religion of the Book,' but the religion of the Word—but neither solely nor principally of the Word in its written form."

not want to say that the only font of revelation is Scripture, but rather to insist on the unity of origin and the symbiosis that occurs between "Scripture" and "Tradition," between *Verbum Dei scriptum* and *Verbum Dei traditum* (*DV* §10).

How are Scripture and Tradition related to each other?
The Council here faced a thorny problem. In those years, the theologian J. R. Geiselmann, from Tübingen, had developed a theory about the interpretation of the Tridentine formulas referring to the relationship between Tradition and Scripture. His work had great influence on the conciliar discussion. Up until then, it was affirmed that, according to Trent, the apostolic doctrine was contained *in part* in Scripture and *in part* in the oral Tradition (*partim–partim*). Geiselmann maintained, however, another interpretation: the apostolic doctrine is contained totally in Scripture and totally in the oral Tradition (*totum–totum*). The first position would result in saying Sacred Scripture does not give us complete knowledge of revelation. The second leads us to affirm that the Tradition is nothing more than a progressive exegesis of Sacred Scripture. The latter clearly presented difficulties in the case of explaining certain dogmas (such as the Assumption of the Virgin Mary) that do not seem to be founded on the literal sense of any text of Sacred Scripture.

The Council did not want to resolve definitively this question, but in *Dei verbum* §9 (added by the express desire of the pope) it gave some light: "Quo fit ut Ecclesia certitudinem suam de omnibus revelatis non per solam sacram Scripturam hauriat [Consequently it is not from Sacred Scripture alone that the Church draws her certainty about everything which has been revealed]" (*DV* §9). Thus was eliminated the possibility of understanding the Tradition as a simple history of exegesis of Scripture.[25]

What light do our previous reflections give us regarding scripture and the word in order to understand the relationship between Scripture and Tradition?

Before all else, it is important to say that the conciliar constitution *Dei verbum* uses a very rich concept of "word." By defining revelation as *Verbum Dei* it is saying that it understands the term "word" in reference to the Greek term *logos* (which is also "meaning") and to the Hebrew term *dabar* (which also includes "things done"; it is a performative word). In this same framework, the Council also wanted to avoid a definition of the Tradition that would reduce

---

25. This sentence of *DV* §9 was called "the modus of the pope." On the history of its introduction into the schema, see the commentary "Tres enmiendas al esquema sobre la revelación: Estudio histórico del R.P. Giovanni Caprile, S.J.," in *La revelación divina*, 2:421–441, at 424–434.

it merely to a doctrine transmitted orally. What is "transmitted" is the praxis and life of the Church (*DV* §8), the oral preaching, examples, institutions (*DV* §7).[26] It would be incomplete, consequently, to think that the Tradition is only the oral transmission of Scripture; rather we can say that the written book is understood within the framework of a complete ecclesial life (a sacramental and liturgical life, prayer, the sense of faith, magisterial doctrine, etc.) which is called "Tradition."

What then is Tradition? How is it related to Scripture?
There are those who refer here to a primacy of Tradition over Scripture. To this end, they refer above all to the fact that Christ did not hand down to us any written document, and also to the certain fact that it is the Church in her Tradition who finally fixes the canon of the sacred books.

There are those, on the contrary, who defend a primacy of Scripture. They point out in this regard that the charism of inspiration refers only to Scripture, and furthermore, that the special veneration that implies parallelism with the Body of Christ (to which *Dei verbum* §21 refers) applies only to Scripture. For Joseph Fitzmyer, for example, the Bible is *norma normans non normata* [the rule that rules and is not ruled], whereas the Tradition is *norma normans normata* [the rule that rules and is ruled].[27] But how does one explain, then, those key moments—such as the fixing of the canon—in which the Bible has been *normata* by the Tradition?

It seems that the solution to this conflict cannot be found in a search for "primacies," but rather in the co-presence of both principles from the logic of the "hermeneutical circle" or the "polar relationship" in which the affirmation of one extreme reinforces the other. The Tradition makes known the canon, and where tradition is negated, the canon is negated, and the scriptures never pass as being "Scripture." And furthermore it is the Tradition which makes the *Litterae* pass as *Colloquium*, animated by the Word.[28] But at the same time, and without falling into any "scripturalism," the Council has extolled the place of

26. See the speech of Monsignor Florit in the conciliar aula: "Even though the tradition extends over Scripture in a certain way, it is not exclusively understood in the sense of oral preaching," in *La revelación divina*, 2:379.

27. See Joseph A. Fitzmyer, *The Biblical Commission's Document "The Interpretation of the Bible in the Church": Text and Commentary*, SubBi 18 (Rome: Pontifical Biblical Institute, 1995), 145.

28. In the Council the speech of Andrei Scrima is also of interest. He asks: "Would a Scripture exist without Tradition? In that case it would exist and be understood outside of its own condition for existence and intelligibility," in *La revelación divina*, 2:252.

Scripture and its specificity as *Verbum Dei scriptum*. What is written down cannot be emptied of its contents by any oral interpretation; it also continues to be *regula* and *norma* with an "authority" of its own. In his commentary on *Dei verbum* §21, Joseph Ratzinger laments not only that in the final text the reference to Scripture as *norma* and *auctoritas* of the whole Christian religion is lost, but also that its character as *regula*, by which it is always necessary to measure true Christianity, is not signaled.[29] In any case, the final formulation does not cease to clearly point out the fact that Scripture measures the tradition.

In the first part, we referred to the relationship between the "Word of Revelation" (*Verbum Dei*) and "Scripture" (*Sacra Scriptura*); and there we spoke of the "original" character of the word in relation to scripture. Now we are referring to the relationship between a "transmitted Word" (*Verbum Dei traditum*) and a "written Word" (*Verbum Dei scriptum*). Hence there is not a primacy. To this purpose it is interesting to recall the expression *pari pietatis affectu*, with which *Dei verbum* §9 refers to the fact that Scripture and Tradition must be received and venerated "with the same attachment of piety."[30] The Second Vatican Council includes here a citation from Trent, which intended above all to defend the reverence with which one ought to receive also the words of the Mass (which are not strictly from Scripture). In the case of the Second Vatican Council, it seems clear that with this expression it does not intend to defend a generic equation of Tradition and Scripture, but to reaffirm the dogma of the ecclesial form of the faith. In any case, the expression clearly points us to the equal dignity of both things.

With this we understand better that the certainty about what Scripture says to us cannot come from Scripture alone or from a supposedly autonomous interpretation, a purely historicist one, that would renounce the ecclesial form. This is what the same Joseph Ratzinger points out:

> From where do we acquire the certainty about what Sacred Scripture wants to say? If only a purely historicist interpretation is given, and nothing more, then Scripture cannot give us any definitive certainty. The certainty of the

---

29. Joseph Ratzinger, "Einleitung und Kommentar zum Prooemium, zu Kapitel I, II und IV der Offenbarungskonstitution 'Dei Verbum,'" 715–793 in Joseph Ratzinger, ed., *Zur Lehre des Zweiten Vatikanischen Konzils*, Gesammelte Schriften 7 (Freiburg: Herder, 2012), 779. English trans. "Dogmatic Constitution on Divine Revelation," 3:155–272 in *Commentary on the Documents of Vatican II*, trans. and ed. Herbert Vorgrimler, 5 vols. (New York: Crossroad, 1989), 3:264.

30. Translator's note: I have translated from the Latin here, taking my cue from the Spanish translation. Author's note: See Karl Barth's fierce critique of this number, which he considers to be a "dizzy spell" of Vatican II (cf. "Conciliorum trindentini et Vaticani I").

historical investigation is, by its nature, always and only hypothetical: none of us were present. Scripture can become a foundation of life only when it is entrusted to *a living subject*, the same from which it came. Scripture was formed within the People of God by the Holy Spirit, and this people, this subject, has not ceased to exist.[31]

Within the context of the Second Vatican Council, we know that there was a speech by the theologian Oscar Cullmann regarding this matter. Cullmann thought that history and historical studies about the Bible gave us precisely the reliability we need to interpret the text. Joseph Ratzinger responds to him by returning to what Ernst Kässeman said, for his part, in responding to Joachim Jeremias some years earlier: "Is it possible to forget for a second that we are daily concerned with a flood of doubtful, even abstruse ideas in the fields of exegesis, history and theology, and that our scholarship has gradually degenerated into a world-wide guerilla warfare?"[32] Faced with this state of things, how do we believe those who want to make us believe that historical-critical science gives us certainty in the interpretation of Scripture? The Tradition is precisely the principle that ensures that Word and Scripture conserve their mutual union, and it is that which can provide, therefore, certainty in the interpretation of Scripture.

c) Scripture: body of the Word

The Church has always venerated the divine Scriptures just as she venerates the body of the Lord, since, especially in the sacred liturgy, she unceasingly receives and offers to the faithful the bread of life from the table both of God's word and of Christ's body (*DV* §21).

In this passage, the Second Vatican Council takes up again a traditional formula coming from Jerome and Augustine, among others.[33] Some conciliar Fathers feared that this thought would destroy faith in transubstantiation, by putting on the same level the true body of Christ and the written body of the biblical texts. In place of *velut* the Council therefore introduced *sicut et*, in order to

---

31. Joseph Ratzinger, "Grenzen kirchlicher Vollmacht: Einführung zum Apostolischen Schreiben 'Ordinatio sacerdotalis' (1994)," 139–153 in Gerhard Ludwig Müller, ed., *Künder des Wortes und Diener eurer Freude: Theologie und Spiritualität des Weihesakramentes*, Gesammelte Schriften 12 (Freiburg: Herder), 146, emphasis added.

32. Joseph Ratzinger, "Dogmatic Constitution on Divine Revelation," 3:193, quoting Ernst Käsemann, *Exgetische Versuche und Besinnungen*, 2 vols. (Göttingen: Vandenhoeck & Ruprecht, 1964), 2:36.

33. Ratzinger, "Dogmatic Constitution on Divine Revelation," 3:262.

slightly emphasize that it treats of a comparison, which must be understood *mutatis mutandis*, not in the sense of a synonymous parallelism. The document *Sacrosanctum Concilium* had already dealt with this theme by saying that the Liturgy of the Word and the Liturgy of the Eucharist constitute "one single act of worship" (*SC* §56).

But what exactly does this idea of divine Scripture being in parallel with the body of the Lord signify? Karl Rahner helps us to understand better the terms of the comparison:

> From here it follows that the Word of God is not presented to us in the Sacred Scriptures in its bareness and its immediate clarity, but rather enveloped in a veil of flesh, although in both forms it always continues to be one without confusion and in an inseparable way. This authentic humanity of the Word of God, far from reducing the dignity of Sacred Scripture, elevates it: in effect, the more that God deigns to descend from on high down into the abyss of our misery, the more splendidly the mystery of his infinite goodness and mercy toward us shines forth.[34]

Scripture is understood in the abasement belonging to the Incarnation, within the context of the "condescension" of God toward human beings. We said earlier that understanding scripture as a body implies that we understand it as that (spatiotemporal) place in which the word abides. In light of the Incarnation, thanks to which the Word has "made his dwelling" and "abides" among men (cf. John 1:14; 15:7), we understand that Scripture will also be that place in which the Word abides. "For the Sacred Scriptures contain the word of God and, since they are inspired, really are the Word of God" (*DV* §24).

This comparison of Scripture with the Eucharistic body also helps us to understand two dimensions of scripture in its relation to the social body, dimensions to which we alluded earlier and which now reach their full reality.

Sacred Scripture is *the principle of cohesion* of the People of God. The comparison of Scripture with the Eucharist helps us to understand that the Sacred Scriptures are a centripetal principle, of identity, within the ecclesial body. If "the Eucharist makes the Church," something similar could be said of the Sacred Scriptures, insofar as they are the rule, nourishment, and light of the Church. In them the ecclesial body finds its principle of cohesion. We know that the early Church had to protect herself from the gnostic idea of a series of "unwritten traditions" (*paradosis agraphos*), recognizing in Scripture (the Old Testament) a principle of cohesion and a point of reference. The process that

---

34. The quiet contribution of Rahner is treated in *La revelación divina*, 2:322. Translator's note: I have translated from the author's Spanish.

led to the establishing of a New Testament canon is related, more generally, to anti-heresy polemics (for example, against Marcion, who rejected the Old Testament; and against Montanus, who claimed to introduce his own revelations).[35] Christianity had to establish a canon in order to reaffirm its identity in the midst of the confusion that the heresies generated. The definition of Scripture thus became the principle of cohesion, by way of distinguishing those who were within the Church from those who were without.

Sacred Scripture is, at the same time, a *centrifugal principle* within the ecclesial body, that is to say, a principle that puts the Church in relationship with humanity in general. What we earlier called the "intercultural force of scripture" can be recognized now in a complete way in Sacred Scripture. The fact that the Bible is the translated book *par excellence* is very significant. *Dei verbum* specifically dedicates a section to translations (§22). It is a section of great theological significance.[36] The pragmatic declarations that appear here are in reality important theological affirmations. A comparison with what Trent says in this respect shows us how Vatican II has expanded the field of tradition by not only mentioning the Latin tradition, but along with it the Greek translation and the Eastern translations. Along with the esteem for these venerable translations, which honor the Tradition, *Dei verbum* opens up the way to interconfessional translations, which were inconceivable for Trent. In the invitation for new translations, in the openness to other ecclesial traditions and to dialogue with other confessions, we recognize the "intercultural force" of Scripture, which is called to "be accessible at all times" [*DV* §22] and in all cultures and thus asks for a process of translation.

We would like, however, to introduce a caveat here. People think at times that the Bible can be without further ado a good place for dialogue with our Protestant, Anglican, or Orthodox brethren—as if it were a type of neutral playing field in which the prejudices of each church no longer apply and which thus permits a greater understanding. This concept has led, in fact, to erroneous consequences. It has led to people saying that a detached use of the Bible, within the framework of a historical-critical exegesis, is advisable for ecumenical motives. What is advisable, however, is to read the Bible within a religious community, within an ecclesial life. Only in this way is dialogue possible: not in a "no-man's land," but rather in a land rooted in a life of Christian faith and Christian traditions, and animated by the presence of Christ and his

---

35. Julio Trebolle Barrera, *La Biblia judía y la Biblia Cristiana: Introducción a la historia de la Biblia* (Madrid: Trotta, 1993), 165.
36. Ratzinger, "Dogmatic Constitution on Divine Revelation," 3:266.

Spirit. It is not a "neutral" playing field but rather a playing field well defined by interpretation.

From Scripture as the "body of the Word" ensue two themes that we now want to develop briefly, which refer to the relationship of Scripture with the "Tradition" and with the "Magisterium."

Scriptura in Ecclesia

With the formula *Scriptura in Ecclesia*, coming from Tertullian, Joseph Ratzinger defines what the Tradition is: it is Scripture read within the Church. The affirmation is situated within the framework of a critique by Ratzinger of the formula *partim–partim* (to which we referred earlier), that is to say, of the intention to understand the relationship between Tradition and Scripture starting from their material contents ("part in the Tradition, part in Scripture"). The German theologian responds that neither the Fathers nor the pre-Tridentine Scholastics understood the *paradosis* as "individual propositions juxtaposed with Scripture," but rather they actually refuted the existence of such propositions. They understood by tradition the immersion of Scripture in the living organism of the Church and the Church's right of ownership over Scripture. This is what Tertullian formulates in his *Praescriptio haereticorum* with the phrase cited above. "Scripture lives by its living adoption on the part of the Church filled with the Holy Spirit, and only in this way is it the very same. Conversely, the majority of the fathers rejected as gnostic the idea of the *paradosis* of doctrinal propositions juxtaposed with Scripture."[37]

I believe that this clarifies that the concepts of Scripture and Tradition do not refer so much to a series of diverse contents; but rather the Tradition refers to the alliance between *Ecclesia* and *Scriptura*, giving us to understand that only in the Church is Scripture the Word of God; only thanks to the Tradition does *Scriptura* contain the *Verbum Dei*.

The Magisterium: a structured body

The classical distinction between the "learning Church" and the "teaching Church," or between the Church that "listens" to Scripture and the one that "teaches" Scripture, tells us something about the "structuring" that Scripture brings about in the ecclesial body. We spoke earlier about scripture's capacity to give order and structure to the social body. Now we recognize how our earlier reflection is demonstrated also in the ecclesial body.

Evidently, before this distinction between the "Church that teaches"

---

37. Ratzinger, "Einleitung und Kommentar Dei Verbum," 781 [translated from the author's Spanish].

and the "Church that listens" to Scripture, we have to introduce an important caveat. The Second Vatican Council dedicates a section in *Dei verbum* to speaking about the Magisterial–Scriptural relationship (§10). If one compares the affirmations of the Council with those that years earlier were made in *Humani generis*, one perceives an innovation. In the encyclical it was said that "This deposit of faith [of Sacred Scripture] our Divine Redeemer has given for authentic interpretation not to each of the faithful, not even to theologians, but only to the Teaching Authority [*soli magisterio*] of the Church" (§21). The expression *soli magisterio* is taken up again in *Dei verbum*, in the second paragraph of number 10, but the context indicates a notable difference. *Dei verbum* speaks within the framework of the "holy people united with their shepherds" and then of the "union in spirit between the prelates and the faithful."[38] Joseph Ratzinger tells us that "this short section presents us also with an important achievement of a renewed theology of the laity, seen here in connection with the theology of the word and making clear not merely the secular function, but also the truly ecclesial and spiritual function of the layman."[39] Therefore in this section "the contrast between the 'listening' and the 'teaching' Church is thus reduced to its true measure."[40]

This important explanation of the classical distinction does not prevent us, however, from being able to maintain the *soli magisterio* in the second paragraph of *Dei verbum* §10 and to maintain, therefore, the affirmation that Scripture also "structures" the ecclesial body. In this way we are permitted to understand that the Church is not a body without form, but rather a body in which exist, by the will of God, those who, by a special mission, have "the task of authentically interpreting the word of God, whether written or handed on" (*DV* §10).

3.3. Conclusion

We will now try to offer an assessment of the road we have traveled. We began with a presupposition: understanding the phenomenon of scripture, or writing, helps us to understand the reality of Sacred Scripture. In our first part we discovered that scripture is simply a "supplement of the spoken word." There

38. Translator's note: I have followed the Spanish translation of the Council's words, *exercenda profitendaque singularis fiat Antistitum et fidelium conspiratio*. The English translation, "it becomes on the part of the bishops and faithful a single common effort," does not get at *conspiratio* as well as the Spanish translation.

39. Ratzinger, "Dogmatic Constitution on Divine Revelation," 3:196.

40. Ratzinger, "Dogmatic Constitution on Divine Revelation," 3:197.

we saw that it is not "original" like the word, but that it is from the beginning linked to the human necessity of representing the word. Scripture is the social body of the word. Then we saw also that definite functions in the social body correspond to scripture: it structures the social body, gives it cohesion, and at the same time, puts it in relationship with other cultures, with other social bodies.

In the second part, we tried to see how this whole previous reflection helped us to understand a very singular scripture: Sacred Scripture. We went through three phases: the Word and Scripture; Scripture and Tradition; Scripture and the Church.

In the first phase we understood the exact difference between a Word of revelation (*Verbum Dei*), which is in the origin (as the originating/original), and a Scripture, which represents the Word and is in the beginning, always obligated to refer to the Word of which it is the body.

In the second phase we dealt with a limited conception of the Tradition, which sees in it only "supplemental contents" to Scripture. Our purpose was to understand Tradition within a wider framework, in the historical and ecclesial linking that keeps Scripture and the Word continuously joined together. It is this state of being joined together that allows Scripture not to lose its vital contact with the Word. Precisely in order to understand better this decisive point, the third phase of our journey came about, which helped us to understand the Tradition as "Scripture within the Church." Here we approached above all the dogma of the ecclesiality of Scripture and of its interpretation. Scripture is the body of the Word as the Church is the Body of Christ. Precisely in this way—in this analogous usage of the term "body"—we can understand the place that the Church and Scripture occupy in common. The precise functions that are assigned to scripture, in general, in the social body, find a new position and a new recognition in Sacred Scripture. It also gives cohesion and intercultural force to the People of God, at the very same time that it becomes a structuring principle of the body itself. It thus becomes easier to understand the existence of a Magisterium capable of "authentically interpreting" Sacred Scripture.

4

The Ecclesial Reading of Scripture

Luís Sánchez-Navarro

In the previous chapters we have shown the mutual implication between Scripture and the Church; this fundamental fact conditions the interpretation of Scripture. In the first volume of his *Jesus of Nazareth*, Benedict XVI affirms:

> The connection with the subject we call "People of God" is vital for Scripture. On one hand, this book—Scripture—is the measure that comes from God, the power directing the people. On the other hand, though, Scripture lives precisely within this people, even as this people transcends itself in Scripture. Through their self-transcendence (a fruit, at the deepest level, of the incarnate Word) they become the people of *God*. The People of God— the Church—is the living subject of Scripture; it is in the Church that the words of the Bible are always in the present.[1]

It is not easy, however, to situate oneself before this collection of seventy-three books that form what has been called "the Bible." One of the first impressions that strike readers when they approach this work which is so singular is the distance. By distance we mean chronological distance: we are speaking about certain literary works composed some thousands of years ago. And we also refer to cultural distance: not only because of such an evident aspect as the languages in which they are written (which, despite their vast and permanent cultural influence, are a relic of the past), but also—and above all—because the mentality of modern readers, and even more so postmodern

---

1. Benedict XVI, *Jesus of Nazareth, I: From the Baptism in the Jordan to the Transfiguration*, trans. Adrian J. Walker (New York: Doubleday, 2007), xxi.

readers, finds itself to be at the opposite end of the spectrum from the mentality of an ancient Near Eastern inhabitant. Taking all this into account, one might be expected to approach the Bible with a mix of curiosity and distance.

How is it possible, therefore, to sustain with a minimum of coherence the words of Pope Benedict that head up these pages? How can one affirm that today, in the midst of the twenty-first century, a group of people exists for whom "the words of the Bible are always in the present"? The community in which this is verified, will it not also be a relic of the past, irremediably incapable of "synchronizing" with the time in which it lives?

4.1. Scripture in the Church

The Church is conscious that when she reads Sacred Scripture she does not read something that is foreign; the Apostolic Exhortation *Verbum Domini* has put this into relief once again. The Church was born of the word of God, and is in a certain way the same word of God; on the other hand, Scripture was born from and for the Church. This circularity between both realities situates them in a very unique relationship.[2] It obeys Scripture's own nature.

a) Scripture as locutio Dei

The Second Vatican Council defined Scripture in this way: "Sacred Scripture is the speaking of God [*locutio Dei*] inasmuch as, by the inspiration of the divine Spirit, it is consigned to writing" (*DV* §9).[3] A strange intersection of concepts: Scripture is a "speaking consigned to writing." As Albert Vanhoye has noted,

> The expression chosen by the Council to define Scripture is surprising, because, taken literally, it affirms that the written text is, in fact, an action of *speaking*, "*locutio*"; the rest of the phrase accentuates this effect of surprise, as the verb "*consignare*" is placed there in the present tense and not in the past, as one may have expected. . . . The result is that Sacred Scripture is not defined in its final form, as a text already separated from its author, but in the moment of its being put into writing, as a 'living act' . . . , a living act that we are in the process of recording. In the end, the conciliar definition leads to a reversal of the relationship between the written text and the oral message. The word "*locutio*" normally designates an oral message; it is applied by the Council to a written text, the text of the Bible.[4]

2. Cf. chapter 2 of this volume, "The Word of God and the Church in the New Testament."

3. Translator's note: This is my translation based on the Latin and the Spanish.

4. Albert Vanhoye, "The Reception in the Church of the Dogmatic Constitution 'Dei Verbum,'" 104–125 in *Opening Up the Scriptures, Joseph Ratzinger and the Foundations of Biblical*

Scripture is therefore a "speaking of God," in the sense that its origin is the divine communication. But it is also an ongoing speaking: the definition— *locutio Dei*—points to the present. *Locutio*, like *traditio*, is a verbal noun that indicates an action. Therefore, what is specific about Scripture is that in it God speaks; he speaks because he spoke in the moment of its production, and he speaks even now. The previous paragraph of *Dei verbum* manifests this double dimension of God's speaking, historical (in the past) and present, to this end employing the same verbal root from which the noun *locutio* comes: "And thus God, who spoke of old [*qui olim locutus est*], uninterruptedly converses [*colloquitur*] with the bride of His beloved Son" (*DV* §8). The biblical books can be, in a certain sense, compared to the great voices of the past, such as the classics of literature, for example; but they are much more than that. In *Don Quixote* the voice of Cervantes resounds, a voice loaded with wisdom and thus permanent strength, but it irremediably belongs to the past. In the Bible, the voice that is discovered is alive.

The God who spoke continues to speak. And he does it through the Church, to which he directs his word.

b) The Church, addressee of Scripture

The Bible is not written for an isolated subject. The type of reader for whom the Bible is written is not a monad, even though the rationalist-illuminist mentality conceives him or her to be so: a pure consciousness, for which relationship does not represent a fundamental reality. This is the person, fundamentally, that the Protestant vision of free interpretation presupposes: someone who reads Scripture as a present word, yes, but from and for his or her own subjectivity, independent from what that same Scripture can suggest to others—including the community of faith. This vision leads to subjectivism; in identifying the voice of God with one's own subjectivity, true listening becomes difficult. Then the Bible does not reveal the presence of the Other, and otherness becomes impossible. On the other hand, the reader who lives in the Church recognizes

---

Interpretation, ed. José Granados, Carlos Granados, and Luis Sánchez-Navarro (Grand Rapids: Eerdmans, 2008), 106 (originally "La recepción en la Iglesia de la Constitución dogmática *Dei Verbum*," 147–173 in *Escritura e interpretación: Los fundamentos de la interpretación bíblica*, ed. Carlos Granados and Luis Sánchez-Navarro, LP 42 [Madrid: Palabra, 2003], 149–150). "Scripture is consignment to writing, consignment inspired by the Holy Spirit in God's act of speaking. Therefore, Scripture contains the Word of God in the form of writing, but before this Word of God there has been a living act, whose consignment was inspired by the Holy Spirit." Roger Schutz and Max Thurian, *La Palabra viva del Concilio: Texto y comentarios de la Constitución sobre la Revelación* (Madrid: Studium, 1967), 99.

in the Bible the true voice of God; only in the objectivity of ecclesial life can one experience this relationship with Sacred Scripture. In order to be truly perceived, the Word of God has to be measured not only by the written text, but also by the community of faith. It is not only that God speaks to *me*, but that he speaks to *us*, in plural; and that he speaks to me to the extent that I form part of a body.

And it is the case that Scripture is not conceived for the sake of an individual, but for the sake of a community. This fundamental theological affirmation is verified with a historical-literary study of each one of the books that form Scripture, and of the canonical collection as such. Even in those writings whose explicit addressee is an individual personage (Theophilus, Timothy, Titus, Philemon, Gaius), this person is always addressed insofarto an ecclesial community, in which oftentimes he holds an ecclesial function. What is said to us regarding John's Book of Revelation, can be applied to the whole of Scripture: it is "what the Spirit says to the churches" (Rev 3:22).

c) A community that reads by listening

The Bible is therefore a completely unique book. In order to do justice to its very nature it is not enough to read what is said in it. One has to read it, yes, and understand it according to its own proper measure; to this end, an appropriate methodological arsenal is required. But this is not sufficient. The Bible is a book that must be read with ears wide open; this is a reoccurring theme in biblical teaching, which can be synthesized in the characteristic expression of Jesus: "He who has ears to hear, let him hear." And it is such that, as we have seen, Scripture's letter channels a living voice; in Scripture *Deus loquitur*. As Ambrose of Milan affirms, "We hear him when we read the divine oracles."[5] Scripture's singularity lies in the fact that its author is not only alive, but that he is also present to whoever reads with faith, in such a way that the word of the past becomes present: the reading leads to a dialogue, in which—as Benedict XVI teaches—"we come to understand ourselves and we discover an answer to our heart's deepest questions" (*VD* §23). He who approaches Scripture as a word of the past cannot hear all of its truth; its proper genius is lost—so to speak. Moreover: the believing reader (who is, from the point of view of the sacred author, the "typical reader") approaches Scripture precisely because it is a word of the present. This is clear when the believer encounters biblical

5. "Illum audimus, cum divina legimus oracula." Ambrose, *De officiis ministrorum*, book 1, chapter 20, paragraph 88 (PL 16:50); cited in *DV* §25. Translator's note: I have translated from the Latin, taking my cue from the Spanish here. The English translation says "the divine saying."

passages of difficult interpretation, whether they be of the Old or the New Testament; they are disconcerting to him precisely because he does not see how to actualize them—which is his basic intention in reading Scripture.[6]

Outside of the Church, the Bible is only a collection of books from the past, as illuminating and enriching as they may be; and therefore exegesis becomes, not a fountain of certainties, but a conglomeration of hypotheses; "whenever Sacred Scripture is separated from the living voice of the Church, it falls prey to disputes among experts."[7] And it is the case that only in the community formed by the Word is that Word found to be present here and now; the Church is the place of its interpretation: "There are dimensions of meaning in the word and in words that only come to light within the living community of this history-generating word."[8] In fact, one could describe the Church as a community of persons that proclaims Sacred Scripture while listening to God speaking in it; as Pope Benedict XVI teaches, "Entering into communion with the Word of God, we enter a communion of the Church that lives the Word of God."[9] This is the hermeneutic that allows us to open up the mysterious significance of the Book of books; it is the hermeneutic of faith, of which Pope Benedict XVI speaks (*VD* §34–36).[10] It is the hermeneutic that finds its natural habitat in the life of the Church.

6. Benedict XVI has dedicated his attention to the necessity of an adequate interpretation of these passages in the exhortation *Verbum Domini*: "The 'dark' passages of the Bible" (§42).

7. Benedict XVI, Homily at the Mass of Taking Possession of His Cathedral (May 7, 2005); English trans. "Presiding in Doctrine and Presiding in Love," *L'Osservatore Romano* 38, no. 19 (May 11, 2005): 3–4, at 3

8. Benedict XVI, Address to Representatives from the World of Culture at the Collège des Bernardins, Paris (September 12, 2008); English trans. "Basis of Genuine Culture: Seek God, Listen to Him," *L'Osservatore Romano* 41, no. 38 (September 17, 2008): 5–7, at 6.

9. Benedict XVI, Celebration of the Third Hour, Address at the Opening of the 12th Ordinary General Assembly of the Synod of Bishops (Synod Hall, October 6, 2008); English trans. "God's Word More Stable Than Any Human Reality," *L'Osservatore Romano* 41, no. 41 (October 8, 2008): 5. This vision is concordant with the ecclesiology—we could say "logocentricity"—of Ratzinger/Benedict, about which the following has been affirmed: "The sweeping 'Word-centeredness' of Benedict's ecclesiology is truly remarkable and unparalleled among theologians of his generation, Catholic or otherwise." Scott Hahn, *Covenant and Communion: The Biblical Theology of Pope Benedict XVI* (Grand Rapids: Brazos Press, 2009), 48–49. "What is unmistakable in Benedict's recovery of Christian origins is the essential unity of the Church and the Word" (53).

10. Cf., on the subject of the 1993 document of the Pontifical Biblical Commission: Peter S. Williamson, *Catholic Principles for Interpreting Scripture: A Study of the Pontifical Biblical Commission's "The Interpretation of the Bible in the Church,"* SubBi 22 (Rome: Pontifical Biblical Institute, 2001), 95–108: "A Hermeneutic of Faith."

d) The life of the Church, the key for reading

In the text that opens this chapter, Benedict XVI spoke about the Church as "the living subject" of Scripture; this points to the life of the Church as the fundamental element of the interpretation of Scripture. In a way analogous to how Jesus' life became the interpretive criterion of the Scriptures of Israel, the life of the Church is also such a criterion; it is the living body of Jesus in history.

"And they devoted themselves to the Apostles' teaching and fellowship, to the breaking of bread and the prayers" (Acts 2:42); with these words Luke describes for us the daily life of the Church in Jerusalem after the event of Pentecost. He does not speak to us in this brief summary about the reading of the Bible, but not because it was absent; rather because that reading completely permeated the indicated activities. "The teaching of the apostles" fundamentally consisted in the reading of the sacred books in the light of Jesus resurrected (cf. Acts 2:14–36; 3:12–26); the "communion" of goods (*koinōnia*) was the form in which the community lived the ideal proposed by Moses to Israel: "But there will be no poor [LXX: *endeēs*] among you" (Deut 15:4);[11] it is the ideal situation that had never been realized in the historical Israel[12] and that now the nascent Church was living as a sign of the fulfillment of God's promise. "The prayers" very probably designate the Psalms of Israel, understood in the new light of the paschal mystery.[13] But above all the breaking of the bread, the new liturgical rite originated in the Last Supper of the Lord, is what will determine the ecclesial form of reading Scripture. This rite probably already included the proclamation of sacred writings; but, above all, the whole of it was imbued with biblical categories that led to a new reading, according to the key of fulfillment, of the entire biblical corpus. With his self-oblation, Jesus had inaugurated the New

---

11. Cf. Acts 4:34–35: "There was not a needy person among them, for as many as were possessors of lands or houses sold them, and brought the proceeds of what was sold and laid it at the apostles' feet; and distribution was made to each as any had need." Nestle-Aland cites Deut 15:4 in the margin of Acts 4:34.

12. Deut 15:11: "For the poor will never cease out of the land; therefore I command you, You shall open wide your hand to your brother, to the needy and to the poor, in the land."

13. The presence of the Psalms in the nascent Church, as much in her first decisions (Acts 1:16—Ps 41:10; Acts 1:20—Ps 69:26, 109:8) as in her primitive preaching (Acts 2:25–36—Ps 16:8–11, 110:1). The prayer of the new community after the liberation of Peter and John is a true Christian *derash* of Ps 2:1–2 (Acts 4:25–30). Translator's note: *derash* is derived from the Hebrew verb for *inquire* or *seek*; in Jewish exegesis it is the comparative or metaphorical meaning of a biblical text.

Covenant prophesied by Jeremiah (Jer 31:31) and prefigured in the covenant of Sinai (Exod 24:8).[14]

The earthly life of Jesus was the living exegesis of Israel's Scripture, an exegesis respectful of the law and at the same time radically new;[15] and so also is the faith, as well as the life of the Church. In her are overcome the apparent contradictions that the biblical writings present at times, and that end up being tensions which keep that ecclesial life living and efficacious. In this way, the confession of faith expressed in the apostolic symbol contains an interpretive synthesis of the biblical testimony; the Creed, the doctrines, and the ecclesial dogmas do not exist without the interpretation of Scripture.[16] In a similar way, the ecclesial structures of authority, doctrine, and liturgy are not historical additions externally imposed on the Scriptures, but rather dimensions that are historically constitutive of the Word;[17] in the words of Ratzinger, "If one takes into account, however, that the Sacred Scriptures come from God through a subject which lives continually—the pilgrim people of God—then it becomes clear rationally as well that this subject has something to say about the understanding of the book."[18]

Finally, every interpretation that is separated from the life of the Church and from her historical experiences can never pass beyond the category of hypothesis.[19] In his apostolic exhortation, Pope Benedict reflected this tenet when speaking, in his conclusion to the great first part ("Verbum Dei"), about "the saints and the interpretation of Scripture" (VD §§48–49). The interpretation of the Bible "would remain incomplete were it not to include listening to *those who*

14. Cf. Luis Sánchez Navarro, *Testimonios del Reino: Evangelios sinópticos y Hechos de los Apóstoles* (Madrid: Palabra, 2010), 120–122.

15. "As a good Jew, Jesus lived even in his body the ideal of 'fulfilling the Torah.' In his culture, the fufillment of the Scriptures was a *practice* related to the art of memory. This was modelled by the tradition of Scripture. . . . Jesus lived it so well that he became for his disciples the book itself: 'I said: "Lo, I come"; in the roll of the book it is written of me' [Ps 40:7]." Olivier-Thomas Venard, "Del canon bíblico a la vida Cristiana," 213–236, in *Palabra de Dios, Sagrada Escritura, Iglesia*, ed. Vicente Balaguer and Juan Luis Caballero, SIT 29 (Pamplona: EUNSA, 2008), 216–217.

16. Hahn, *Covenant and Communion*, 58. The rule of faith "constitutes the real 'hermeneutic' of Scripture, the key derived from Scripture itself by which the sacred text can be interpreted according to its spirit." Benedict XVI, *Jesus of Nazareth, II: Holy Week, From the Entrance into Jerusalem to the Resurrection*, trans. Philip J. Whitmore (San Francisco: Ignatius Press, 2011), 99.

17. Hahn, *Covenant and Communion*, 61.

18. Joseph Ratzinger, Address on the 100th Anniversary of the Pontifical Biblical Commission (May 5, 2003); English trans. "Relationship between Magisterium and Exegetes," *L'Osservatore Romano* 36, no. 30 (July 23, 2003): 8–9, at 9.

19. Cf. Hahn, *Covenant and Communion*, 42.

have truly lived the word of God: namely, the saints. Indeed, *'viva lectio est vita bonorum'"* (*VD* §48).[20] Moreover, what is said about men and women who with greater transparency express the sanctity of the Church, can be applied with greater reason to the same holy Church. In order to perceive the *logos* of the Gospel and Scripture in their totality, the best path is to contemplate the life of the Church, the community forged by that *logos*. In her we discover the permanent tension between faithfulness to the gift received and actualization of that word in the diverse moments of history; a very fruitful tension. Biblical exegesis cannot prescind from this fact without being radically impoverished; an interpretation of Scripture that is not capable of accounting for the lived experience of the Church, and in particular of its most authoritative exponents (the saints), will have difficulty being considered scientifically correct.

But then we can ask ourselves: what is the concrete path, the suitable "method," for this ecclesial reading?

4.2. The path for reading Scripture "in the Church"

In order to read Scripture in the Church, we are offered diverse paths. Fundamentally they are of two orders: natural (methods of the human sciences) and supernatural (the truths of Revelation). But we should note that the point of departure is one only: human reason, illuminated and purified by faith, which *searches for understanding* by employing all available resources for it. And hence the concrete path is also unique: the one that reason, illuminated and strengthened by faith, points out.

a) Reading in history

This path therefore has a double dimension, human and supernatural, which is already expressed in *DV* §12. The human dimension, which obeys the "carnal" reality of Scripture, is represented by the historical methodology: the historical and philological methods are keys for understanding the word of God.[21]

---

20. Benedict XVI here quotes St. Gregory the Great, *Moralia in Job*, book 24, chapter 8, paragraph 16 PL 76:295).

21. Cf. Joseph G. Prior, *The Historical Critical Method in Catholic Exegesis*, TG.T 50 (Rome: Editrice Pontificia Universita Gregoriana, 1999). In these pages we prefer not to talk about the "historical-critical method," because by this name one normally understands a concrete methodology (source criticism, form criticism, redaction criticism), which is questionable in its determined procedures, and whose historical exercise has also very frequently been accompanied by rationalist philosophical presuppositions. The term, on the other hand, could be improved. For one thing it is redundant, because every scientific method is critical; so it would be

The first point is that the historical-critical method—specifically because of the intrinsic nature of theology and faith—is and remains an indispensable dimension of exegetical work. For it is of the very essence of biblical faith to be about real historical events.[22]

The supernatural dimension, for its part, is manifested in the criteria exhibited by the paragraph cited from the dogmatic constitution of Vatican II, derived from the fact of divine Revelation: the unity of all Scripture, the living Tradition of the Church, and the analogy of faith. However, in recent decades, the conciliar passage mentioned has generally been interpreted as if it implied two successive methodological stages, such that after a first purely historical—and therefore "scientific"—interpretation, a second stage would follow, the "theological" one. This explanation prevents the mutual encounter of both categories, which continue in an irreducible parallelism. Pope Benedict affirms as much in *Verbum Domini*:

> In this regard we should mention the serious risk nowadays of a dualistic approach to sacred Scripture. To distinguish two levels of approach to the Bible does not in any way mean to separate or oppose them, nor simply to juxtapose them. They exist only in reciprocity. Unfortunately, a sterile separation sometimes creates a barrier between exegesis and theology, and this "occurs even at the highest academic levels."[23]

The hermeneutic of faith requires us to speak, on the contrary, not about two phases of interpretation, but of two dimensions of only one interpretive moment, or—as Pope Benedict XVI teaches—of "two methodological levels" (*VD* §34). But let us note further: it would be erroneous in biblical exegesis to start with a merely human exegesis, because the supernatural dimension is original; just as a recent monograph affirms in its title: "From faith is born exegesis."[24] The place where both paths meet is history; but a history in which

enough to speak of the "historical method." But, moreover, under this name are included the proper methods of very diverse sciences (archaeology, paleography, history, philology, etc.); for this reason we believe that it is better to speak, in general, of "historical methods" or "historical methodology."

22. Benedict XVI, *Jesus of Nazareth, I*, xv.

23. *VD* §35, quoting *Propositio* 27 of the Twelfth Ordinary General Assembly of the Synod of Bishops. Then he details "the most troubling consequences" of this mode of proceeding. Cf. Ignacio Carbajosa, *De la fe nace la exégesis: La interpretación de la Escritura a la luz de la historia de la investigación sobre el Antiguo Testamento*, EstBib 43 (Estella: Verbo Divino, 2011), 15–20; English trans. *Faith, the Fount of Exegesis: The Interpretation of Scripture in Light of the History of Research on the Old Testament,* trans. Paul Stevenson (San Francisco: Ignatius Press, 2013).

24. Carbajosa, *De la fe nace la exégesis*.

the revelation of God has occurred, and which thus becomes a history transformed, a history with an irreducible element of newness.

> The opinion that faith as such knows absolutely nothing of historical facts and must leave all of this to historians is Gnosticism: this opinion disembodies the faith and reduces it to pure idea. The reality of events is necessary precisely because the faith is founded on the Bible.[25]

History is thus the place where the word of God resounds. And therefore one must listen with attention, employing scientific methods that are necessary so that this voice of "transformed history" can ring out with clarity, without distortions.[26] The rationale and the methods of historical and literary science need to be united by the living faith of the Church, to whom the word of God is permanently directed.[27] The only way to avoid biblical spiritualism just as much as biblical fundamentalism—two readings that detach themselves from the facts of history—is to give critical attention to that constellation of historical facts that characterize the biblical text, and that allow one to capture its message with precision.

Well, the Church again appears to be the place of this reading, since it is the community that has arisen from that history and lives from it. Ecclesial faith knows that historical investigation is not opposed to it; on the contrary, faith *requires* historical investigation. For faith is not a mythical narration, but rather it sinks its roots into reality:

> This necessity is the result of the Christian principle formulated in Jn 1:14, "*Verbum caro factum est.*" Historical fact is a constituent dimension of the Christian faith. The history of salvation is not mythology but rather true history, and is therefore to be studied alongside serious historical research methods.[28]

The Church is not afraid of history being studied scientifically. Quite the opposite: she looks for and even needs it, because in this study she discovers what constitutes her.

---

25. Ratzinger, "Relationship between Magisterium and Exegetes," 9.

26. "Unlike the historical-critical method, which originated in modern philosophy and epistemology, this hermeneutic [of faith] grows organically out of Benedict's reflection on the data gained from scientific historical study of the Scriptures themselves." Hahn, *Covenant and Communion*, 62.

27. Hahn, *Covenant and Communion*, 44.

28. Benedict XVI, Address during the 14th General Congregation of the Synod of Bishops (October 14, 2008); English trans. "Modern Exegesis Necessary for a Living Faith Today," *L'Osservatore Romano* 41, no. 43 (October 22, 2008): 13; cf. *VD* §32.

> Because in the biblical word God comes towards us and we towards him, we must learn to penetrate the secret of language, to understand it in its construction and in the manner of its expression. Thus it is through the search for God that the secular sciences take on their importance, sciences which show us the path towards language.[29]

The Church has only one condition: that the study be rigorously scientific; that its conclusions, therefore, depend not on the prejudice of the investigator, but rather on the facts of history.

b) Christ, subject of Scripture

Paying attention to history leads the Church to center her attention on Christ. It is well known that the aim of the New Testament is to show Jesus of Nazareth as the one to whom "the law and the prophets" pointed; it is a central aim in the Christian faith, which "is based not solely on events, but on the conformity of these events to the revelation contained in the Jewish Scriptures."[30] This aim is historically justified. If the resurrection of Jesus has a historical dimension—and has it in a double measure, because it has left its footprints in history, and because it has generated events that are undoubtedly historical—then Jesus the Messiah appears in an absolutely singular situation in the long history attested by the biblical writings.[31]

This is what the Church expresses when she confesses Jesus as the central subject of all of Scripture, the Old Testament and the New. She does not intend with this confession to empty of its own meaning the history attested by the books of the Hebrew Scripture; she does not try to superimpose, without further ado, the image of Jesus over so many other historical images of the Old Testament, blurring them or erasing them directly. She tries to recognize how, in him, these images—always real—acquire a new level of reality in which their

---

29. Benedict XVI, Address to Representatives from the World of Culture, 5.

30. Pontifical Biblical Commission, *The Jewish People and Their Sacred Scriptures in the Christian Bible* (Vatican City: Libreria Editrice Vaticana, 2001), §7. "The New Testament is nothing other than an interpretation of 'the Law, the Prophets, and the Writings' found from or contained in the story of Jesus. Now, this 'Law, Prophets, and Writings' had not yet, at the time of Jesus, grown together to form a definitive canon; rather, they were still open-ended and, as such, offered themselves spontaneously to Jesus' disciples as a testimony to him, as the Sacred Scriptures that revealed his mystery." Joseph Ratzinger, *Milestones: Memoirs 1927–1977,* trans. Erasmo Leiva-Merikakis (San Francisco: Ignatius Press, 1998), 53 (originally *Aus meinem Leben: Erinnerungen 1927–1977* [Munich: Deutsche Verlags-Anstalt, 1998]).

31. Recently even the importance of the resurrection of Jesus for the formation of the canon of Scripture has been affirmed: Venard, "Del canon bíblico a la vida cristiana," 226–227.

most notable, most original aspects come to light. The light that Jesus sheds on the Old Testament is certainly selective; but it selects those elements in which the saving plan of God is manifested in a relevant way. In this it coincides with the Jewish tradition, at least in part. David, in both traditions, will not be the sinner (adulterer and murderer), but rather the king under whose command the unified Israel became great, and who in his prayer exalted the mercy of God. Solomon, in both traditions, will not be the polygamous idolater of his last days, but rather the young king who incarnates the wisdom of Israel. What is new is that, according to the intention of the New Testament, Jesus assumes these figures (and others no less relevant: Isaac, Jacob, Moses, Joshua, etc.) and confers on them a new relevance, elevating them to a transcendent level.

This intention is not original to the writers of the New Testament, but rather—as they testify in chorus—it goes back to the earthly Jesus himself, just as the Gospels testify: "I have come not to abolish [the law and the prophets], but to fulfill them" (Matt 5:17); "And beginning with Moses and all the prophets, he interpreted to them in all the scriptures the things concerning himself" (Luke 24:27); "It is they [the Scriptures] that bear witness to me" (John 5:39); "for [Moses] wrote of me" (John 5:46). Essentially, the beginning of the fourth Gospel is nourished by this reality: Jesus, the Son of God, is the Logos Creator; he is thus the voice that resonated in the scriptures of Israel, and that in the culminating moment of history "became flesh." As the Letter to the Hebrews affirms in its solemn beginning, "In these last days [God] has spoken to us by a Son . . . through whom also he created the world" (Heb 1:2). Jesus of Nazareth, Messiah and Son of God, is the indisputable subject of the New Testament; but at the same time he appears as the *telos* of the entire Old Testament economy (cf. Rom 10:4), in such a way that he acquires an unforeseen protagonism—let us say, "in hope"—in the scriptures of the Old Covenant, which thus appear to us as an open-ended reality that is aimed at its fulfillment.[32] As then-Cardinal Ratzinger would affirm in 1997, "If the Old Testament does not speak of Christ, it is not a Bible for Christians."[33]

32. Ignacio Carbajosa has demonstrated the radical openness constitutive of the Old Testament, just as much in its collective whole as in its diverse *corpora*: Ignacio Carbajosa, "El Antiguo Testamento, realidad abierta," 21–50 in *Entrar en lo Antiguo: Acerca de la relación entre Antiguo y Nuevo Testamento*, ed. Ignacio Carbajosa and Luis Sánchez Navarro, PreDi 16 (Madrid: Universidad Eclesiástica San Dámaso, 2007).

33. Joseph Ratzinger, *Many Religions, One Covenant: Israel, the Church, and the World*, trans. Graham Harrison (San Francisco: Ignatius Press, 1999), 18.

c) One single Book

This leads us to address another characteristic of the ecclesial reading of the Bible: the Church is precisely that community which reads *the* Bible, in other words, which sees the seventy-three books that compose it as one single Book. The transition of *ta biblia* ("the books") to *hē biblia* ("the Bible"), a phenomenon of a lexical nature, reveals a whole understanding of that reality: plurality is resolved into unity. With this, one does not pretend to erase the differences and discontinuities existing among the diverse biblical writings, whose mere enumeration would take us many pages. Every edition of the Bible includes, recognizes, and conserves all those differences; equally, the liturgical proclamation always carefully recognizes which book is being read in the assembly: the proclamation of the prophet is not the same as that of the psalm, the Apostle, or the Evangelist. But at the same time, the Church recognizes how these writings form a "macrotext" that gives a new meaning to each one of them, because they are understood, not as isolated works, but as parts of a whole.[34] This was something, furthermore, that was not far from the minds of its human authors.[35]

Dei verbum §12 says that "serious attention must be given to the content and unity of the whole of Scripture" as an indispensable prerequisite of ecclesial interpretation; it is to this aim that canonical exegesis responds (*VD* §34), a method that, having arisen in the field of scientific exegesis, proposes "reading the individual texts of the Bible in the context of the whole."[36] This does not presume to do violence to them, forcing them to fit together into a framework that is foreign to them. Completely the contrary: a calm study of the biblical books manifests their mutual implication, such that it becomes impossible to study any one of them critically without making reference to the others that have preceded it or those that drink from the same springs. The canonical approach, therefore, appears as a path that allows one to combine the historical and theological exigencies. It is "an essential dimension of exegesis. It does not contradict historical-critical interpretation, but carries it forward in an organic way toward becoming theology in the proper sense."[37]

34. Cf. Carlos Jódar Estrella, "La relación Antiguo-Nuevo Testamento y la configuración de la Biblia como texto," 69–84 in *Entrar en lo Antiguo*, ed. Carbajosa and Sánchez Navarro, 82–83.

35. For example: both at the beginning of Matthew ("the book of the genealogy," *biblos geneseōs*: Matt 1:1) and at the beginning of John ("in the beginning," *en archē*: John 1:1), the authors powerfully refer back to Genesis, thus presenting their respective narratives in continuity with the history that begins in the first book of the Torah.

36. Benedict XVI, *Jesus of Nazareth, I*, xix; cf. xviii.

37. Benedict XVI, *Jesus of Nazareth, I*, xix. Regarding the canonical method, see Augustín Giménez González and Luis Sánchez Navarro, eds., *Canon, Biblia, Iglesia: El canon de la Escritura y la exégesis bíblica*, PreDi 30 (Madrid: Universidad Eclesiástica San Dámaso, 2010).

d) The Church and the Book

As we well know, the Christian faith is not a "religion of the Book," but it is founded upon the living Word of God made flesh.[38] As Pope Benedict affirms in *Verbum Domini*:

> Finally, the word of God, attested and divinely inspired, is sacred Scripture, the Old and New Testaments. All this helps us to see that, while in the Church we greatly venerate the sacred Scriptures, the Christian faith is not a "religion of the book": Christianity is the "religion of the word of God," not of "a written and mute word, but of the incarnate and living Word."[39]

But these words show, at the same time, how the pilgrim Church cannot prescind from that Book: if Scripture is an object of singular veneration in the Church, it is because it represents an indispensable element in her life and is therefore inseparable from sacred Tradition. "Consequently the Scripture is to be proclaimed, heard, read, received and experienced as the word of God, in the stream of the apostolic Tradition from which it is inseparable" (*VD* §7, citing *DV* §10). Moreover, "Scripture is above all and by nature 'tradition.'"[40] Regarding the importance of Scripture for ecclesial life, the apostolic exhortation of Benedict XVI bears witness when he invites us to rediscover the richness of the Word of God attested by Scripture and its capacity for vitalizing all the dimensions and activities of the Church.[41]

Christianity is not, certainly, a "religion of the Book": revelation is not produced by means of written words, but by means of historical events that are experienced, testified to, and transmitted, which lead to a personal encounter with Christ.[42] But it is certainly a "religion with a Book": the presence of the apostolic testimony consigned to Scripture is so deep and essential that the Church could not be understood in herself without this great Book of books.[43]

---

38. Cf. CCC §108.

39. *VD* §7. The citation is from St. Bernard of Clairvaux, *Homilia super "missus est,"* homily 4, paragraph 11 (PL 183:86B).

40. Ratzinger, "Relationship between Magisterium and Exegetes," 8.

41. See principally the second part, "Verbum in Ecclesia" (*VD* §§50–89).

42. Cf. Benedict XVI, *Deus caritas est* (December 25, 2005) (Vatican City: Libreria Editrice Vaticana, 2006), §1.

43. "It is true that at the origin the orally transmitted word occupies a fundamental place. But the oral itinerant teaching does not exclude primitive Christianity from being able to be considered a 'textual community.' The communal life revolved around the books. So much so that it is difficult to imagine the followers of Jesus as forgers of traditions about their founder without an accompaniment of writings that explained and supported this phenomenon." Juan Chapa, "La materialidad de la Palabra: manuscritos que hablan," *Estudios Bíblicos* 69 (2011): 9–37, at 11.

4.3. Conclusion: a living book

The ecclesial reading of Scripture has an originality irreducible to any other approach to Scripture. It is a vital phenomenon: the Church grows with her reading, and at the same time makes this Word grow in her understanding of it and in its efficacy; as Gregory the Great said, *divina eloquia cum legente crescunt* ("divine words grow with the reader").[44] And the word of God "is living and active" (Heb 4:12); the Church makes her own the word that, by incarnating itself in the life of Christians, perennially shows to the world its beauty, and it is therefore always current and capable of transforming the hearts of men.

For the Church, Scripture is thus a *living book*, whose word does not represent simply an ancient object of archaeological investigation, but rather contains a reality that is present and therefore permanently in the now, capable of illuminating the path for men of all ages and cultures with the light that comes from God. And therefore, as Benedict XVI affirms, Scripture has a mysterious inhabitant: "The Church knows well that Christ lives in the Sacred Scriptures."[45] In effect, that collection of writings is the most distant thing from a dead letter; it contains a secret of divine life that makes it unified and present, rendering it contemporaneous— "synchronous"—with men of all ages. According to the always current words of the Second Vatican Council, in the ecclesial reading of Sacred Scripture,

> God, who spoke of old, uninterruptedly converses with the bride of His beloved Son; and the Holy Spirit, through whom the living voice of the Gospel resounds in the Church, and through her, in the world, leads unto all truth those who believe and makes the word of Christ dwell abundantly in them (see Col. 3:16). (*DV* §8).

44. Gregory the Great, *Homilies on Ezekiel*, book 1, homily 7, paragraph 8 (PL 76:843D) (cited in *VD* §30); trans Theodosia Tomkinson, *Homilies on the Book of the Prophet Ezekiel*, 2nd ed. (Etna, CA: Center for Traditionalist Orthodox Studies, 2008), 118. Cf. Pier Cesare Bori, *L'interpretazione infinita: L'ermeneutica cristiana antica e le sue trasformazioni* (Bologna: Il Mulino, 1987).

45. Benedict XVI, Address to the Participants in the International Congress Organized to Commemorate the 40th Anniversary of *Dei Verbum* (September 16, 2005); English trans. "Make 'Lectio Divina' a Cornerstone of Your Life," *L'Osservatore Romano* 38, no. 38 (September 21, 2005): 7.

PART II

Christ, Exegete of the Fulfillment

5

How Should We Read the Old Testament?
With Christ, Exegete of the Fulfillment

Carlos Granados

How should we read the Old Testament? Jean-Louis Ska translates this question into the following: Should we still read the Old Testament? Is it not perhaps an obsolete text, compromised by a series of anthropological and religious conceptions that are already outdated; a text that obliges us to imagine a violent God and human beings without hope for a life beyond this world?[1] Our aim in these pages is to give a preliminary response to this question. We will not try to offer a solution to particular problems, but instead we will reflect on the keys to reading the Old Testament which allow us to situate these problems in their proper context. How can a Christian reader be adequately positioned when encountering the texts of the Old Testament, in order to understand them in their ultimate intended meaning?

5.1. A new principle: the Old Testament as "testimony of Christ"

"Christians therefore read the Old Testament in the light of Christ crucified and risen" (CCC §129). Christians read the Old Testament as a testimony of Christ. But is this reading possible? Is it true when Jesus said in the New Testament that Moses wrote of him (John 5:46) and that Abraham saw his day (John 8:56)? But what scope and significance do these expressions have?

---

1. Cf. Jean-Louis Ska, "Come leggere l'Antico Testamento?," 23–48 in *Metodologia del Antico Testamento*, ed. Horacio Simian-Yofre (Bologna: EDB, 1994).

Reading the Old Testament as a testimony of Christ is possible and is, in fact, a radical exigency for Christian believers. For the first Christians it was not possible to say that Jesus was the Word, the Son of God, without pursuing a *new reading of the Old Testament.* This key for reading was not for them, nor can it be for us, simply one more among other possible readings, but rather it is the definitive and unifying one. Gerhard von Rad (an exegete who is by no means suspected of fundamentalism) can affirm that "one should truly speak about the testimony of Christ (*Christuszeugnis*) in the Old Testament."[2]

Walter Brueggemann has presented, however, serious objections to a Christological reading of the Old Testament. (We will look at this position in more detail later on [in Chapter 10].) For Brueggemann this reading is not credible or responsible, because it causes the Old Testament to lose its independence as an autonomous voice, subordinates the interpretation to a prior dogmatic prejudice, and impedes dialogue with our Jewish brethren.[3] What should we say to these objections?

a) Reading the Old Testament as an "open book"

Joseph Ratzinger, in his autobiographical book *Milestones,* speaks to us of the moment in which he understood more fully "why the New Testament is not a different book of a different religion that, for some reason or other, had appropriated the Holy Scriptures of the Jews.... *The Scripture we today call Old Testament is in itself open* to both ways [to the Christian interpretation and to the Jewish]."[4] This experience enlightens us about the first tenet of Brueggemann to which we need to respond: the "letter" of the Old Testament is not "autonomous" in the sense of "autoreferential," but rather it is in itself "open" to some sort of fulfillment. How should we read the Old Testament? As a book that is open and expectant.[5]

In the prophets this openness is clearly perceived; they speak about a future that is not simply fulfilled with the return to the land after the exile, but

2. Gerhard von Rad, "Typologische Auslegung des Alten Testaments," 272–288 in *Gesammelte Studien zum Alten Testament,* ed. Gerhard von Rad (Munich: Kaiser, 1973), 288.

3. Walter Brueggemann, *Theology of the Old Testament: Testimony, Dispute, Advocacy* (Minneapolis, MN: Fortress, 2005), 105–107.

4. Joseph Ratzinger, *Milestones: Memoirs 1927–1977,* trans. Erasmo Leiva-Merikakis (San Francisco: Ignatius Press, 1998), 53–54, emphasis added (originally *Aus meinem Leben: Erinnerungen 1927–1977* [Munich: Deutsche Verlags-Anstalt, 1998]).

5. Cf. Ignacio Carbajosa, "El Antiguo Testamento, realidad abierta," 21–50 in *Entrar en lo Antiguo: Acerca de la relación entre Antiguo y Nuevo Testamento,* ed. Ignacio Carbajosa and Luis Sánchez Navarro, PreDi 16 (Madrid: Universidad Eclesiástica San Dámaso, 2007).

rather they hope for a new creation (cf. Isa 65:17) and an unheard-of new thing that still needs to be realized (cf. Jer 31:22). The last book of the Hebrew Bible (which is 2 Chronicles according to the canonical collection of the Pharisees) also ends with an opening: "Whoever is among you of all his people, may the LORD his God be with him. *Let him go up*" (2 Chr 36:23). This ending demonstrates that the Bible, in the Hebrew canon, has a structure that is open to the future, because what appears to be a concluding invitation ("let him go up") is one that opens up a path to ultimate fulfillment.

The Old Testament is not a closed text to which we Christians added the New Testament. It is a text that in itself is open to fulfillment. The Christian reading of the Old Testament is not, therefore, the only one possible. It is necessary to affirm this in order to understand better that the "action of Christ" is radically free, not bound or demanded by a prior stringent logic. This affirmation is also necessary so that in our reading of the Old Testament we know how to recognize the processes through which, little by little, determinate connections are realized. Reading the Old Testament in the school of the New is not equivalent to reading all of the New Testament in the Old.

The verification that the "letter" of the Old Testament is, in fact, open allows us also to say that a Christological reading of it 1) does not annul its "autonomy," but rather is a new mode of giving meaning to that "autonomy"; 2) begins with a presupposition (as every reading does) fully corresponding to the structure and the trajectories of the book; 3) is the condition of possibility for a dialogue with our Jewish brethren that can be truly constructive and not lost in confusion.

b) The necessity of "conversion"

We will therefore speak about reading the Old Testament in light of the New. But we must be attentive with this formulation. The terms Old and New Testament do not refer, in the first place, to a collection of books, but rather they make reference above all to two Economies, two Dispensations, two Covenants. In fact, until the second century AD, this terminology of the "Testaments" was not employed to refer to a collection of books.[6] The expression "Testament" referring to a collection of books finds its foundation in an *event*, an occurrence, in the "action of Christ" that marks a passage, a change in time. The newness of the Christian reading of the Old Testament does not come from

---

6. Henri de Lubac, *Exégèse médiévale: Les quatre sens de l'Écriture*, 4 vols. (Paris: Aubier, 1959–1964), 1:309: the writing of Melito of Sardis (d. 175) apparently contains the first mention of the phrase "Old Testament" referring to a collection of books.

the fact that some pages have been added to the text, but from the fact that the Passover (=the passing/passage) of Jesus has taken place.[7]

The "passage" from the Old to the New Testament does not come about, therefore, simply when one finishes reading the last of the prophets (Malachi) and begins with the first evangelist (Matthew); it is not going past the page of a book; nor is it only the changing of culture, of the age, or of language (from Hebrew in the Old, to Greek in the New); it is not even to be elevated to a higher level of spiritualization. The "passage" is the "action of Christ," and passing with him from the Old to the New requires a "conversion" of the subject.

What conversion? What does it involve? Speaking in the words of Origen, it is the "conversion (*metanoia*) from the letter to the spirit";[8] it is a "transformation" of the subject who is reading, which implies a new mode of reading. The force that we want to give here to the term "conversion" can be perceived if we realize that the same term, *conversio*, is, at the same time, employed by the Fathers to refer to 1) the change in mentality that Jesus asks of the Christian (Mark 1:15); 2) the passage from the Old to the New Testament (as we have just seen); 3) Eucharistic "transubstantiation" (the *conversio* from bread to the Body of Christ). The qualitative change that occurs in the "passage" from the Old to the New Testament is of this order of magnitude.

Conversion from the letter to the spirit. Regarding this phrase, in order to avoid any misunderstandings, we do not want to say that the books of the Old Testament are "letter" and those of the New Testament are "spirit." We have already said that the Old and the New Testaments are not above all a collection of books. It is not about passing from a written text to another much later (which would be simply to pass from one "letter" to another). It is about the "passage" in which a "letter" that is more ancient (that of the books of the Old Testament), and is in itself open, as we will see shortly, is filled with meaning upon being inhabited by the "spirit" that from the beginning was destined for it. The books of the New Testament are the written testimony of that "passage." But one can also read the New Testament in a way that reduces the books to "letter" without perceiving the "spirit" that inhabits them. Again we repeat that a "conversion" in the reading subject is necessary. How does a Christian read the Old Testament? As a subject "converted" by the action of Christ,

---

7. Translator's note: The Spanish word used here, which is *Pascua*, ultimately derives from the Hebrew word *pesaḥ* (Passover), and it can refer to Israel's Passover or to the Christian celebration of Easter.

8. Origen, *On Matthew*, book 10, chapter 14, paragraph 18: *tēn apo tou grammatos epi to pneuma metanoian.*

who recognizes in the "letter" of the Old the "spirit" that comes from the New Covenant.

c) Reading the Old Testament as "fulfillment–rupture–transcendence"

The Christian reads the Old Testament with the key of "fulfillment." Christ has brought to fulfillment all that was written. "Salvation" signifies being able to read the New Testament as the fulfillment of the Old, understanding that all is brought about as "was necessary," "according to the Scriptures." Let us briefly examine what is implied by the notion of "fulfillment," which is so important for our reading of the Old Testament.

> [T]he concept of the fulfilment of the Scriptures is a complex one, since it has three dimensions: a basic aspect of *continuity* with the Old Testament revelation, an aspect of *discontinuity* and an aspect of *fulfilment and transcendence (VD* §40).[9]

In this text from *Verbum Domini*, Benedict XVI places at the center of his approach to the Old Testament the concept of "fulfillment." The Catechism does the same (CCC §139). According to the text of *Verbum Domini*, this category of "fulfillment" presupposes a tension: Jesus Christ is radically new, and Jesus Christ is the faithful "yes" of God to every exigency of the law, to every expectation of the promise, to every aspiration of humanity and of the Jewish people, since their respective beginnings. And all of this is in one single act. The character of this tension could be illustrated with the double biblical maxim: 1) "Therefore a man leaves his father and his mother and cleaves to his wife" (Gen 2:24); 2) "Honor your father and your mother" (Exod 20:12; Deut 5:16). One must "abandon" the Old Testament in order to be able thus "to honor it," that is to say, to lead it to its "fullness" (its glory). St. Augustine can affirm, therefore, that Jesus is, with respect to the Old Testament, *finis perficiens, non interficiens* ("an end that perfects, not that destroys");[10] and Leo the Great illustrates this tension with the example of the boy who when he changes and passes into adulthood fulfills his destiny (*dum mutatur, impletur*).[11]

Verbum Domini identifies the continuity with the "prophetic" side of Scripture, while it locates the elements of discontinuity in the "institutional" side of Scripture; it thus says:

9. The 2001 document of the Pontifical Biblical Commission, *The Jewish People and their Sacred Scriptures in the Christian Bible* (Rome: Libreria Editrice Vaticana, 2001), speaks about "continuity–discontinuity–rupture" (§§64–65).

10. Augustine, *Tractates on the Gospel of John*, tractate 55, paragraph 2.

11. Leo the Great, Sermon 58, chapter 1.

The Old Testament is itself replete with tensions between its institutional and its prophetic aspects (§40).

In this sense, the Sabbath and the dietary prescriptions are no longer binding for Christians (rupture), while the prophets with their foresight anticipated the arrival of the new (continuity).

One must certainly affirm, in the first place, a rupture. *Figuram res exterminat,* sings an Easter hymn ("the reality destroys the figure").[12] But we must clarify that this rupture does not imply a contradiction. "Transcending" that which is institutional in the Old Testament is not here simply equivalent to "transgressing it," but rather to recognizing the ultimate and definitive meaning to which were oriented all the rites of worship of the Old Testament. The rupture with certain forms (for example, the Sabbath rest) should not impede us from discovering their profound meaning, but on the contrary it should oblige us to do so. In this sense, Benedict XVI speaks about a "transcendence" of the Old Testament that is not a "transgression."[13]

We must understand what *Verbum Domini* affirms in this sense. Benedict XVI does not advocate for a purely "spiritual" or "interior" interpretation that would eliminate all the instances of [Israel's] ritual worship and abrogate its exterior (institutional) aspects. Rather, it is about a form of fulfillment in which a new thing that breaks in (that of Jesus) uncovers the authentic and profound meaning (the "intention") of the institutional realities, the sacrifices and rites of the Old Testament, and it is in this way capable of renewing the exterior forms. The sacramental economy is the mature fruit of this logic.

5.2. One mode of reading: "typology"

After what has just been said, the question that emerges for us is now more concrete. How can we read the history of the Old Testament after Christ? Is there not perhaps the risk of "losing history"? Is there not the danger of turning it into an excuse for talking about "ideas," "pure categories," of projecting onto it Christian "convictions" and finally turning history into a collection of *symbolic schemas dressed up as events*?

---

12. Adam of St. Victor, as cited in de Lubac, *Exégèse médiévale,* 1:316.

13. Benedict XVI, *Jesus of Nazareth, I: From the Baptism in the Jordan to the Transfiguration,* trans. Adrian J. Walker (New York: Doubleday, 2007), 120.

a) The response of the early Christian tradition

The solution that the early Christian tradition found for responding to this question was what is called "allegory." Today this word is much disparaged, because it has been confused with its worst degenerations and with its pagan precedents.

Allegory has had, in effect, bad press. It refers to "two modes of understanding" Sacred Scripture: historical and allegorical (or "literal" and "spiritual/ mystical").[14] Sadly, these "two modes" have been misinterpreted at times with people thinking, mistakenly, that the "spiritual" or "allegorical" reading was manifestly *a-historical*, belonging to the world of ideas, in the sphere of the subjectivity of the interpreter, who looked for the strangest applications of the Christian mystery in the ancient accounts. This interpretation does not do justice to the intention of our ancestors. What was their aim?

The best Christian tradition, with the "spiritual sense," looked precisely to *save history*. But in order to save it, the interpreters had to refer history to something greater than itself. And they referred it to the event of Christ. The worst thing about "historical criticism" is not that it reduces everything to history, but that it reduces history only to history. The best thing about the spiritual sense, to which the Fathers of the first Christian period referred, is that it opens history beyond itself, in order to save history in this way.

Henri de Lubac has shown, in a convincing way, the radical difference, in this sense, between "Greek allegory" and "Christian allegory." For a "Greek allegory" certainly existed.[15] This name they applied to their interpretations which updated the myths and ancient religious writings. The Greek thinkers and teachers thus tried to transform the Homeric stories of doubtful morality into pious songs with a moralizing end, by way of teachings that would serve the initiated. Their way of proceeding was called "allegory," and at times

---

14. De Lubac, *Exégèse médiévale*, 2:405: The whole medieval age, the heir of the Fathers, says it thus: "Sacra Scriptura duobus modis intelligitur, historice et allegorice."

15. The first antecedents of allegory can be located in the symbolic language of Pythagorean and Orphean practices. First the term *huponoia* ("supposition" and, later, "underlying meaning") was used. Towards the first century BC this term was replaced with *allēgoria* ("to say another thing"), which seems to go back to Crates of Mallus. The "allegory" developed above all around the Homeric writings, intending to provide interpretations that would rescue the moral or sapiential meaning of the past and allow Plato to be reconciled with Homer. See, for example, what Pseudo-Heraclitus says (first century AD?) in his *Allegories of Homer*: "All [of Homer's verses] would be impious if he did not speak allegorically (*ēllēgorēsen*)" (*Allegoriae* 1.2); see the edition of the *Allegorías de Homero* by Esteban Calderón Dorda, María Antonia Ozaeta Gálvez, and Antonino Liberal (Madrid: Gredos, 1989).

"theology" and also "physiology." It was in any case a naturalistic method: it sought to eliminate anything remaining that was historical or personal in order to elevate the meaning of a text to a-temporal, philosophical, elements, to those meanings that referred to the nature of things (the *phusis*; and so "physiology": *phusiologein*).

"Christian allegory" was very different. Even though they use a number of similar procedures, the two approaches to allegory have neither the same foundation nor the same end.[16] It happens, however, that the analogy of vocabulary and of method has brought many to think that an analogy of thinking and *forma mentis* also exists. There is nothing further from the truth.[17] "Pagan allegory" and "Christian allegory" are not to be confused with each other.

The decisive difference between the two can be described in their *sense of history*. In effect, the exegesis practiced by the first Christian generations is distinguished from that practiced in Hellenistic circles *according to how they value history*.[18] In a world fundamentally estranged from history, the Christian interpretation never renounced it. Therefore it is curious that today this exegesis is accused of the contrary: of being *a-historical*. Perhaps it is because what certainly did not exist in this Christian interpretation was that eagerness for "history for the sake of history," for simple *curiosity*. History was understood as a "teacher of life"; if one turned to it, it was above all to find there responses to present situations; they looked more for the meaning of history, and in particular the theological meaning of history. Therefore, the Fathers read history using a point of view, a reference that was beyond history. They looked not only to narrate but also to understand the historical fact.[19]

16. De Lubac, *Exégèse médiévale*, 2:396.

17. See Jean Pépin, *Mythe et allégorie: Les origines grecques et les contestations judéo-chrétiennes* (Paris: Études Augustiniennes, 1976). Of great interest for this whole question is also de Lubac, *Exégèse médiévale*, 2:373.

18. St. Augustine highlights how the faithfulness of the Bible to history is a characteristic of the biblical book: "History narrates what has been done, faithfully and with advantage; but the books of the haruspices, and all writings of the same kind, aim at teaching what ought to be done or observed, using the boldness of an adviser, not the fidelity of a narrator" (*De doctrina Christiana*, book 2, chapter 28, paragraph 44; trans. J. F. Shaw, NPNF 1/2:549).

19. "Our ancient exegetes did not have any idea, thanks be to God, of that 'absolutized History' which is one of the principal idols invented by our age. On the other hand, they did have a sense of biblical history, or even universal history, because they held on to its principle of discernment in the Mystery of Christ, the absolutely ultimate final cause." De Lubac, *Exégèse médiévale*, 2:490; English trans. E. M. Macierowski, *Medieval Exegesis: The Four Senses of Scripture, Volume 2* (Grand Rapids: Eerdmans, 1998), 71–72.

The error of many has been to understand the "allegorical sense" as a "second literal sense," when in reality it concerns an interpretive exercise of making reference to the real, and it concerns the openness of the text to its meaning, which comes through the words and realities that have been revealed in the history of salvation. In the "allegory" of the Fathers, therefore, not only was the word decisive, but also the "historical fact," the reality of which the text speaks.[20] With this presupposition, Bede can give the definition of allegory: *allegoria est, cum verbis sive rebus mysticis praesentia Christi et Ecclesiae sacramenta signantur* ("There is allegory when the presence of Christ and the sacraments of the church are signified through mystical words or signs").[21]

b) The response of Verbum Domini: "typology"[22]

Obviously, what has just been said does not mean that we have to eliminate the last two hundred years of exegesis and return to the ancient allegorical methods of the Fathers. Even if someone wanted to do so, it would be impossible. And besides, the period of historical criticism has brought us many good things; it has liberated us (and this alone is a great deal) from the naivety of thinking that a biblical text was produced by one single hand, finished and canonized from time immemorial, and thus disconnected from a redaction history, from literary genres defined by the surrounding culture, from a social and political system, etc. The problem now is: *how can we read the history that the text narrates keeping in mind the history through which the text has been transmitted to us?*

> The Church, as early as apostolic times, and then constantly in her Tradition, has illuminated the unity of the divine plan in the two Testaments through typology (CCC §128).

Benedict XVI has reaffirmed in *Verbum Domini* the current and undeniable validity of "typology" in biblical interpretation:

> From apostolic times and in her living Tradition, the Church has stressed the unity of God's plan in the two Testaments through the use of typology; this procedure is in no way arbitrary, but is intrinsic to the events related in the sacred text and thus involves the whole of Scripture. Typology "discerns in God's works of the Old Covenant prefigurations of what he accomplished in the fullness of time in the person of his incarnate Son" (CCC §128).

20. De Lubac, *Exégèse médiévale*, 2:493.

21. De Lubac, *Exégèse médiévale*, 2:500; trans. Eric Knibbs, *On the Liturgy: Amalar of Metz*, vol. 1 (Cambridge, MA: Harvard University Press, 2014), 203.

22. Translator's note: The author's discussion of typology here is closely followed later in chapter 12, section 2; see the note on "Original Publications" at the end of this volume.

Christians, then, read the Old Testament in the light of Christ crucified and risen. (VD §41)

In our opinion, it is necessary in this day and age to speak of "typology." Perhaps one should prefer this term to "allegory," which is more worn out and despised. The term "typology" has, moreover, diverse advantages, because it binds together the following:

- a *logos*, and here we refer to the field of reason and science,

with

- a *type*, that is to say, a model, in the "ethical" and "aesthetic" sense of the word, which allows us to understand the moral and prefigurative reach of biblical interpretation.

Let us read what Danielou says in this regard:

> Hence arises a new kind of symbolism, which is characteristic of the Bible. . . . It is called *typology*, from the wording of two passages in the New Testament: one where it is said of Adam that he "was the type (τύπος) of him who was to come" [Rom 5:14]; and another where baptism is called the "type" (ἀντίτυπος) of the Flood [1 Pet 3:18] . . . .

> So understood, in the strictest sense, typology is an intrinsic element of Christian doctrine . . . it was the basis of all sound scriptural interpretation in Patristic times. . . . But this use of figure, this strictly historical kind of symbolism, is something altogether different from the use of allegory by such as Philo, and by some of the Fathers.[23]

We ask ourselves: Is a "typological" interpretation of the biblical text still credible today?

Our response is this: it is not only credible but necessary, though we must always keep in mind that this "typology" never loses *the history through which the text has been transmitted to us*, which has so interested the exegetes of recent centuries. It is precisely each epoch of this history that has left written in the biblical book a "type," a segment of the story (reinterpreted or corrected by a tradition) through which is revealed to us how, little by little, the diverse figures continue to be developed, as they advance, not without drama or dead ends, toward their fulfillment.

In a very general way we could say that "typology" is a relationship between two elements of which the first (type) prefigures and announces the second

---

23. Jean Danielou, *The Lord of History: Reflections on the Inner Meaning of History*, trans. Nigel Abercrombie (Chicago: Regnery, 1958), 140–141.

(antitype). How do we apply this to the interpretation of the Bible? *Verbum Domini* gives us some paths for understanding it correctly:[24]

1. Biblical typology *does not have an arbitrary character*; that is to say, it does not consist in a game of relationships and comparisons whose only criteria would be the subjectivity of the interpreter and his greater or lesser imagination for relating two events narrated in the Bible (for example, the "passage through the Red Sea" in Exodus 14 and "the passage through the Jordan" in Joshua 3). Its basic principle is that the sacred writer wrote more than what he was conscious of writing (a sentence that applies to every writer and, in a paradigmatic way, to the sacred writer). This fact that the writing transcends the consciousness of the author is the condition of possibility for a typological exegesis, because it means that the text is objectively open to more: it is *objectively* well-suited for prefiguring future events (which are also much later than the time in which the human author lived) and for being prefigured by much earlier moments of the story (perhaps not present in the memory of the human author). The intent of typology will be rash if it proceeds without some regulation, but it will produce a stale exegesis if it hopes that it will be fully guaranteed by "science."

2. Typology *is applied to the story*. A "type" or "figure" is before all else a stage or phase that the whole story goes through before its fulfillment. The Catechism speaks of figures as "intermediate stages [of the biblical story]" (CCC §130). A "type" is not "the ark of Noah" without "the voyage of Noah's ark on the chaotic waters" or "the construction of Noah's ark." This affirmation implies moreover that the figure is realized in the event. An immediate corollary is that typology affects all of Scripture: that is to say, it is not reduced only to certain verses cited in the New Testament.

3. Typology is *deeply rooted in history*. Each figure is unrepeatable and concrete in its singularity: it is identified with a particular time and name. Along with this unrepeatable character there is also an "insistence" that basically consists in the fact that figures repeat themes, symbols, semantic structures, typical scenarios, opposition of terms, key concepts, and other series of significant elements.

In this history, "typology indicates the dynamic movement toward the fulfilment of the divine plan when 'God [will] be everything to everyone' (1 Cor 15:28)" (CCC §130). This dynamism develops thanks to a tension between the "singularity" of each figure and the "repetitiveness" of certain elements in

---

24. For everything that follows, see also Carlos Granados, "Cumplimiento y exégesis figurativa en P. Beauchamp," *Estudios Bíblicos* 64 (2006): 19–29.

the figures (to which we have just referred). Precisely from this tension one can enunciate the fundamental postulate of typology: *the ultimate truth of the "figure" is given in its capacity to dialogue with other figures (which are similar though differentiated) which continue to reveal it, leading it toward its ultimate destination.*

A brief example will demonstrate what perspectives are opened up: the waters separated at creation, the sign of victory over chaos (Gen 1); the waters crossed and overcome again by the keel of Noah's boat (Gen 6–9); the waters separated in order to open up a passageway for a victorious people in the Red Sea (Exod 14); the waters separated in order to make way for a people that would enter into the land (Josh 3:14–17); the waters separated in order to see the death and the birth of a prophet (2 Kgs 2:8); the waters separated in order to make way for a people returning from exile (Isa 43:2); the waters from which the baptized Christ emerges in order to initiate the path of his public life (Luke 3:21–22); the waters separated in order to make way for the sons reborn into faith (Rom 6). In all of these cases we are faced with distinct "figures," diverse moments of the story. We perceive, however, a unity (a persistence) in the content of the figure (to go through and to separate the waters), which invites us to place them in relationship with each other, not only linking "creation," "the history of Israel," and "fulfillment in Christ," but also establishing many other similarities and differences that enrich the content of each figure (and which permits us, for example, to read Christian baptism in light of Noah, of the people of Israel, of Joshua, of Elisha, etc.).

4. Exegesis according to figures, as *Verbum Domini* finally points out, has a progressive character. What it signifies in the first place is that the figure is "deficient" (therefore it can progress). The episodes of Abraham's life, for example, demonstrate this clearly. "It is not exactly traditional to speak about the education of Abraham. Pious tales of the patriarch regard him as a precocious monotheist even before God calls him, a man who smashed his father's idols, a man who sprang forth fully obedient and knowledgeable about the ways of the Lord. But a careful reading of the biblical text shows otherwise: Abraham indeed goes to school, God Himself is his major teacher, and Abraham's adventures constitute his education, right up to his final exam, the binding of Isaac."[25] Typology helps us, precisely, to understand this pedagogical path of God with men by putting certain events into relation with others and making comprehensible the path that each one opens up.

25. Leon Kass, *The Beginning of Wisdom: Reading Genesis* (Chicago: University of Chicago Press, 2003), 251.

5. Is there some criteria that allows us to discern how a figure walks toward its fulfillment? We can here refer to a fundamental one: the "concentration" of the figures. As the figures get closer to the fulfillment, they become more concentrated. The Messianic line is united with the sacerdotal and the prophetic in order to point to a Messiah who is Prophet and Priest. The reader of the Old Testament contemplates this slow process of "concentration," which is not always linear and which one has to study in its slow development. The figures are concentrated in order to point to the One. This concentration also implies an "excess": the figure accumulates and unites within itself so many elements that it is overflowing. The path toward fulfillment implies a logic of superabundance, a sort of increasing paroxysm according to figurative logic.

5.3. The application of freedom and the *telos*: anagogy and tropology

Littera gesta docet, quid credas allegoria
Moralis quid agas, quo tendas anagogia

This couplet is the work of a Scandinavian author of the thirteenth century, named Augustine of Dacia. His formulation made a lasting impression in the medieval period and fixed in the popular and Scholastic memory the four classical senses of Scripture: "letter" (*littera*: the historical or literal sense), "allegory" (*allegoria*: the meaning of faith), "tropology" (*moralis*: the moral sense), and "anagogy" (*anagogia*: the sense that speaks about the end, about teleology). The celebrated *adagio* distinguished, therefore, alongside "letter" and "allegory" a "moral" sense and a "teleological" sense. In reality, the "moral" and the "teleological" senses were nothing more than two applications of the "spiritual sense." This means that the pair "literal sense and spiritual sense" developed later, making it so that from the "spiritual sense" were born three other senses: the "allegorical," the "anagogical," and the "moral." *The tradition, in any case, thus demonstrates how to give central importance in the interpretation of the biblical text to two dimensions: a) the ethical, or moral, application; b) the application of the "end," or teleology.*

Reading the Old Testament in the school of the Christian tradition means understanding its "moral" sense and its "final" sense.

a) The "moral" sense

The moral sense ("tropological") allows us to understand that the revealed word does not belong to the past, but that it is living and effective here and now. De Lubac has shown us how in the tradition of early Christianity one finds the adverbs *moraliter* and *quotidie* combined in order to refer to this sense, in such a way that interpreting Scripture "in the moral sense" (*moraliter*) and interpreting it "in the daily sense" (*quotidie*) go together.[26] This same tradition helps us to understand the value of the moral sense by linking it with the idea of the "three advents" of Christ. There are in effect three advents of the Lord: the first, in the flesh; the last, in glory; and the daily coming (above all in the Eucharist and the Word). Therefore, it is said that the allegorical sense refers to the first coming of Jesus; the moral sense, to the second (the "daily" coming); and the anagogical sense, to the third, in glory. The "tropological sense" is, then, the one that allows us to taste Scripture in the choices of daily life, in this time in which the Lord comes "in secret."

An excess of centralization in the legislative texts has put at risk the "moral sense" of Scripture, which can easily be conceived as a fine tuning of the Decalogue for its present-day use. In reality, the "moral sense" is discovered above all in the narrative texts of the Bible: that is where the most ancient Christian tradition discovered the "figures" (*tupoi*) in which one could recognize the moral sense.

We know that from the first appearance of literature, this has served as an eminent form of moral instruction (cf. also 2 Tim 3:16).[27] We know that already the Greeks bound up ethical reflection with the tragedy as a literary genre in which they proposed the great ethical questions of the day. In Scripture, therefore, the linking of a "moral sense" to the biblical narration should by no means be strange to us. The modern recovery of the *narrative sense* of ethics does no more than to walk in this sense and give us new tools for understanding the importance that must be attributed to stories in the moral life.

Here it is not about the patriarchs and the prophets being morally irreproachable and thus becoming "types" of moral conduct.[28] It is therefore not about a "moralist" application of the narration.[29] The question is what the bibli-

---

26. De Lubac, *Exégèse médiévale*, 2:562.

27. For what follows, this is of particular interest: Juan José Pérez Soba, "*Lectio divina* y acción del cristiano," in "*Dichosos los que escuchan la palabra": Exégesis bíblica y lectio divina,* ed. Andrés García Serrano and Luis Sánchez Navarro (Madrid: Universidad Eclesiástica San Dámaso, 2012), 89–118.

28. See what St. Ambrose points out about Abraham: "Instruant te Patriarchae, non solum docents, sed etiam errantes" (*On Abraham*, book 1, chapter 6, paragraph 58 [PL:14:442A]) (taken from De Lubac, *Exégèse médiévale*, 2:460).

29. What is characteristic of the stories in Scripture is the fact that they are not "moralist"; frequently they do not approve of or condemn certain actions, leaving the judgment up to the

cal story decisively reveals for the moral life. Paul Beauchamp points out three attributes:[30]

In the first place, in the biblical story the true meaning of freedom is revealed. "The contingency of the story is precisely the place of our freedom."[31] In the story is presented a possible good, but not a necessary one, and therefore it is linked to a "choice." The first place of morality in the Bible is not the law but the story. Without narration, the law is "a law of slaves," because it will inevitably forget the historical gift that founds it and the promise that should be realized in history through its fulfillment. For this reason, before establishing his covenant, God always narrates the history of the gift (cf., for example, Exod 19:4: "You have seen what I did to the Egyptians, and how I bore you on eagles' wings and brought you to myself"). The narration requires a new form of freedom: that of the "grateful son." To read the *moral sense* of the letter of the Old Testament is, in the first place, to recognize the choices that are at play, their foundation, their meaning, and above all their openness to a later fulfillment.

In the second place, the story obliges us to recognize the meaning of the *path* that has to be attributed to the moral life, by situating us in a "temporality," in the stages that develop between the beginning and the end of the story. The most ineluctable characteristic of the story is that it has to begin and end. The "choice" is not made in a vacuum, but within this framework; and it is not realized once and for all, and for good, but it continues developing along a path. To read the *moral sense* of the letter of the Old Testament is always to bring to light the "path," the reality of a covenant that does not remain in the first "yes" but develops within a history marked by infidelity, sin, idolatry, etc.

In the third place, the story is where ethics and aesthetics are found. We have already spoken about the term *tupos*, which links both ideas. By means of figures, the story "represents" and "makes sensible" the truths of the body, helping us to escape from a morality based in ideas, concepts, and the pure sense of duty. Each biblical story is very concrete and particular; only in this way, with this concrete reality, can it serve as a "home" for a moral proposal.

---

reader. De Lubac, *Exégèse médiévale*, 2:458, demonstrates how this thinking was clearly present in St. Augustine: "neque approvabit hoc Scriptura, neque reprovabit" [. . .] "iudicanda nobis permittit, non laudanda praescribit" [. . .] "narrata ista sunt, non laudata." The reader is called to choose. St. Irenaeus will say also: "Scripturae non increpant, sed simpliciter sunt positae, nos non debere fieri accusatores [. . .], sed typum quaerere."

30. See Paul Beauchamp, "Cumplir las Escrituras: Un camino de teología bíblica," 170–184 in *Biblia y ciencia de la fe*, ed. Carlos Granados and Agustín Giménez, Ensayos 311 (Madrid: Encuentro, 2007), (originally published in *Revue biblique* 99 [1992]: 132–162).

31. Beauchamp, "Cumplir las Escrituras," 175.

The aim for universality should always begin with a concrete reality, from a place in which the good becomes possible. That place is the story. To read the *moral sense* of the letter of the Old Testament is also to be attentive to discovering every universal exigency to which the concreteness of the story gives voice.

All that has been said could be concluded, in the end, by adding that the "moral" reading follows naturally upon the fact (indicated earlier) that a [personal] "conversion" is necessary in order to read Scripture in a Christian sense.

b) The "theological" sense

What the ancient writers called "anagogy" is nothing more than discovering the "theological" sense of the "figures." The word "anagogy" comes from *an-agogē* (or *ana-agogē*), which implies an "ascending," as if to say that one needs to discover the sense that leads the interpretation of the Old Testament to what is above, to the *sursum* of the heart which elevates us to our ultimate destiny. *It is necessary, therefore, to read the Old Testament as a path to an end* ("telos").

Effectively, an interpretation based on "fulfillment" (to which we alluded earlier) is a "theological" interpretation, that is to say, oriented toward the end (*telos*). The "archaeological" preoccupation is typical of the historical-critical method: it intends to recover the original nucleus of the text, separating it from later additions (this is "literary criticism"); it also intends to individuate the stages that have led to the final redaction of the text (this is the "redaction history"); it investigates the basic literary forms and their original vital scope (this is "form criticism"). For its part, the "theological" interpretation gives more importance to the ultimate sense, to the question of *for what purpose* more than that of *because of what*. Historical-critical exegesis has interested itself a great deal with the pre-history of the texts; a laudable and useful interest while it remains within the reasonable limits of what it can know. But it has neglected the question of the end of the texts, the future reality that opens up the meaning of an ancient text and uncovers new and unheard of dimensions; [it has neglected] the form in which the texts continue to reveal that new reality and thus prepare for what is to come. This is the theological sense of the biblical texts.

5.4. Typology: is it a fundamentalist interpretation?

Despite all that has been said, a suspicion may still remain in the reader. Is a fundamentalist model of exegesis being thus proposed, a "typological" model that is opposed to the advances of biblical science? A passage from Henri de Lubac, which is still relevant today, can shed light for us in this respect:

When faced by the unanimity of centuries, a unanimity that abounds with witnesses from the very first generation of Christians right to the time of recent ecclesiastical documents, one has every good reason to be astonished at seeing some contemporary authors not only criticizing certain particular features of a complex theory (certain procedures, applications, and excrescences), but going so far as to reject the naming of a "spiritual sense," to denounce it as equivocal. But then what word in what language cannot lend itself to being equivocal? Furthermore, these same authors speak as if what were at stake here was a matter of mere novelty, a question of terminology arising from a personal choice, indeed, from suspect patterns of thought.[32]

The proposal of a typological exegesis is not therefore "a thinking that is suspect"; it is an interpretation anchored in a deep tradition. The proposal of a typological exegesis is not fundamentalist but rather fundamental, because it affects the foundation on which one can build a "science of faith."

We have wanted to show that "typology" is a fruitful way of reading the Bible, responding to the exigencies of the "historical fact" and of its meaning: a reading of the Bible that does not leave it in the pure past, but rather opens it up to the horizon of the *telos* ("anagogical" meaning) and to that of the choices that guide the reader's concrete life ("tropological" meaning).

32. De Lubac, *Exégèse médiévale*, 1:357; English trans. Mark Sebanc, *Medieval Exegesis: The Four Senses of Scripture* (Grand Rapids: Eerdmans, 2000), 1:262.

6

Old and New: Conflict or Fulfillment?

Luis Sánchez-Navarro

The Letter to the Hebrews, one of the most unique and dense writings of the New Testament, contains in its central part an affirmation that can seem surprising. After citing at length the prophecy of Jeremiah about the New Covenant (Jer 31:31–34; Heb 8:8–12), the author of this homily affirms: "In speaking of a new covenant he treats the first as obsolete. And what is becoming obsolete and growing old is ready to vanish away" (Heb 8:13). In the face of these unequivocal words, the reader asks himself: is it the case that we Christians have decreed the death of the Old Testament? The writings of the Old Covenant—are they only the forebears of the New Testament, eminent forebears undoubtedly, but already dead, or at least definitively superseded?

In order to give a response to this question, we must remember above all the rule belonging to Sacred Scripture.

6.1. Scripture, testimony of Revelation

The biblical books are indissolubly linked to the Revelation of God, since they testify to it truthfully. But they are not in themselves the Revelation: this consists in an encounter between God and human beings, an encounter that takes place in history and only becomes reflected in the inspired writings in a later phase (*DV* §2).

> In today's theological lingo, it is common to term the Bible "Revelation" without qualification. This usage would never have occurred to the ancients. Revelation is a dynamic event between God and man, which again and again

becomes reality only in their encounter. The biblical Word attests to Revelation, but does not contain it in the sense of absorbing it and turning it into a sort of thing that one could stick in one's pocket. The Bible attests to Revelation, but the concept of Revelation as such is broader.[1]

In this way, we can say that the Old Testament is the written and inspired testimony of the Old Covenant; and that the New Testament is that of the New Covenant—with the added observation that, in reality, "Testament" and "Covenant" are two different translations of the same Hebrew term (*bərît*) and the Greek term (*diathēkē*); and that, therefore, even though we would conventionally apply a term to the historical event and another to its literary expression, we find ourselves before a single reality (the event and its testimony). This gives us a clue for dealing with the relationship between the Old and the New Testament: it depends on the one that exists between the Old and the New Covenant.

6.2. Unity of Scripture and unity of Covenant

The fact that a "New Covenant" exists does not mean that the first one has been revoked; the biblical texts (both the Old and the New Testaments) that point in that direction must refer to certain constitutive elements of the Covenant, in particular to their ritual aspect; but not to the Covenant in itself, because—as Paul firmly affirms, referring precisely to Israel—"the gifts and the call of God are irrevocable" (Rom 11:29). In the New Testament, the adjective "new" (*kainos*), in its theological sense, does not refer generally to a reality that displaces another; on the contrary, it indicates a "renewal" of the old reality. Frequently *kainos* in the New Testament functions as a Derash technique (that is: the interpretation of Scripture by applying it to current times) in order to express the eschatological *plenitude* of a reality of revelation already existing.[2] It is not about a revoking, but rather a culminating of the revelation of God; in the programmatic words of Jesus, "Think not that I have come to abolish the law and the prophets; I have come not to abolish them but to fulfil them" (Matt 5:17).

1. Joseph Ratzinger, "Biblical Interpretation in Conflict," trans. Adrian Walker, 1–29 in *Opening Up the Scriptures: Joseph Ratzinger and the Foundations of Biblical Interpretation*, ed. José Granados, Carlos Granados, and Luis Sánchez-Navarro (Grand Rapids: Eerdmans, 2008), 26.
2. Domingo Muñoz León, *Derás: Los caminos y sentidos de la palabra divina en la Escritura, Parte I: Derás targúmico y Derás neotestamentario*, BHBib 12 (Madrid: Consejo Superior de Investigaciones Científicas, 1987), 236–239: "El cumplimiento expresado como Novedad (superación)."

The biblical writings testify to the one Covenant of God, that Covenant that the Letter to the Hebrews—with the Old Testament expression—calls the "eternal covenant" (Heb 13:20).[3] In fact, in Scripture we find diverse covenants of God: with Noah (Gen 9:9–17), with Abraham (Gen 15:18; 17:2), with Jacob/Israel (Gen 28:10–22), with the people of Israel on Sinai (Exod 19:2), with David (Ps 89:4; Sir 45:25). In the Letter to the Romans, Paul speaks of the "covenants" (plural) belonging to Israel (Rom 9:4). It is evident that the successive covenants do not presuppose the disappearance of the antecedent ones, but rather they realize and complete them. In this way the covenants allow the one Covenant to advance. That Covenant whose eschatological plenitude was already announced by the prophets: "Behold, the days are coming, says the LORD, when I will make a new covenant with the house of Israel and the house of Judah" (Jer 31:31); "I will make with them a covenant of peace" (Ezek 34:25). Or, in an expression typical of Isaiah: "Behold, the former things have come to pass, and new things [*kaina*] I now declare, before they spring forth I tell you of them" (Isa 42:9). In the letters to the Romans and the Galatians,

> Paul, with his distinction between the covenant with Abraham and the covenant with Moses, has rightly interpreted the biblical text. This distinction, however, also supersedes the strict opposites of the Old and the New Covenant and implies that all history is a unity in tension: the one Covenant is realized in the plurality of covenants.[4]

6.3. The Old and New Testaments: a mutual implication

The New Covenant certainly is nothing more than a realization of that eternal Covenant: it constitutes the definitive manifestation of God that clearly exceeds the previous ones, as we can conclude from the solemn beginning of the Letter to the Hebrews: "In many and various ways God spoke of old to our fathers by the prophets; but in these last days he has spoken to us by a Son" (Heb 1:1–2). This manifestation awaits its eschatological consummation, but it does not allow for a further fulfillment: this Son, superior not only to the prophets but also to the angels (Heb 1:4), "he appointed the heir of all things" (Heb 1:4). However, the New Covenant does not erase the preceding covenants in order to begin with a *tabula rasa*, but rather it assumes them. It does not annul them:

3. See in particular: Gen 9 (covenant with Noah); Gen 17 (with Abraham); Exod 31:16 (Sabbath). In the Prophets it appears as an eschatological promise: cf. Isa 55:3; 61:8; Jer 39:40; Ezek 16:60; 37:26.

4. Joseph Ratzinger, *Many Religions, One Covenant: Israel, the Church, and the World*, trans. Graham Harrison (San Francisco: Ignatius Press, 1999), 57.

on the contrary, it gives them their maximum perfection. The figure subsists in the prefigured reality, just as the promise subsists in its fulfillment. Neither the reality nor the promise would be intelligible or possible if they prescinded from that previous genesis.

For its part, the Old Testament is not closed in on itself either; on the contrary, it is a plan of the future. This can seem paradoxical, but the unitary reading of the writings of the Old Testament manifests their projection toward the future; the *promise* is a fundamental element in them. We have mentioned some particularly significant prophetic passages; but the promises are present in many other passages, the first of which (Gen 3:15: "I will put enmity between you and the woman, and between your seed and her seed; he shall bruise your head, and you shall bruise his heel") was already called by Christian antiquity the *protoevangelion*. We should also mention the blessings of Jacob (Gen 49), or the prophecy of Nathan about the house of David (2 Sam 7). Despite centering on the events of the past, on the history of Israel, the Old Testament contains a solid orientation toward the future. The Hebrew Bible, in each one of its parts (Law, Prophets, Writings), is presented to the reader as a reality open to a later fulfillment.[5] Moreover, the Old Covenant appears as an itinerary for the journey which every Christian is called to take. "The passage through what is Jewish, that is, the Old Testament, is still today an essential necessity of the Christian consciousness."[6] The light of the resurrection, in the end, allows us to discover in the writings of the Old Testament a luminous testimony of Jesus Christ.[7]

From all this it is shown that the Old Testament and the New are not opposed realities, but rather they are mutually implicated; the conciliar teaching treats their relationship in this way.[8] Saint Augustine expressed it with an excellent couplet: *Novum in Vetere latet, et in Novo Vetus patet* ("The New is latent in the Old, and in the New the Old is made clear"). The Bishop of Hippo

---

5. See the previous chapter, and also Ignacio Carbajosa, "El Antiguo Testamento, realidad abierta," 21–50 in *Entrar en lo Antiguo: Acerca de la relación entre Antiguo y Nuevo Testamento*, ed. Ignacio Carbajosa and Luis Sánchez Navarro, PreDi 16 (Madrid: Universidad Eclesiástica San Dámaso, 2007), 28–38.

6. Paul Beauchamp, *Testamento bíblico* (Magnano: Edizioni Qiqajon, 2007), 118 (originally *Testament biblique: Recueil d'articles parus dans "Études"* (Paris: Bayard, 2001).

7. Brevard S. Childs, "Da el Antiguo Testamento testimonio de Jesucristo?" 170–183 in *Biblia y ciencia de la fe*, ed. Carlos Granados and Agustín Giménez, Ensayos 311 (Madrid: Encuentro, 2007) (originally "Does the OT Witness to Jesus Christ?" 57–64 in *Evangelium, Schriftauslegung, Kirche: Festschrift für Peter Stuhlmacher zum 65*, ed. Jostein Ådna et al. [Göttingen: Vandenhoeck und Ruprecht, 1997]).

8. See chapter 8 below.

postulated therefore the interpenetration of both Testaments: one is not conceivable without the other, to the point of mutually requiring each other for their interpretation. The unity of Scripture is a truth that is constitutive of the Christian faith; it will lead to the affirmation of the Second Vatican Council that we must interpret biblical writings by attending "to the content and unity of the whole of Scripture" (*DV* §12).

6.4. Continuity in the discontinuity

This does not mean that this unity lacks tensions; there are in it a multitude of "discontinuities," demanded by the unheard-of new thing that the Incarnation of the Son of God implies and by the fullness of revelation that he brings, incomparable to that mediated by the greatest of all the prophets. But this pertains to the same logic of fulfillment. "Fulfillment presupposes at the same time total continuity and radical rupture, fidelity and complete change at the same time. Just as the butterfly that flutters in the air brings to fulfillment the caterpillar that was crawling along."[9] The Pontifical Biblical Commission has explained it as a complex relationship:[10]

1. *Continuity*: the new events conform to what has been announced; the fundamental biblical themes are seen to be continued in Christ and the Church. All in a universal perspective: Jesus Christ, the descendant of Abraham (cf. Gal 3:16), offers salvation to the entire world.

2. *Discontinuity*: the passage from the Old Testament to the New Testament entails ruptures, even while presupposing continuity in what is essential. This is manifested above all in the institutional aspect (priesthood, temple, cultic worship, sacrifices, purity, imperfect laws, restrictive interpretations, etc.). The change of emphasis, all the same, has already begun in the Old Testament and thus constitutes a legitimate reading of it.

3. *Progress*: the New Testament bears witness that Jesus brings to fulfillment the Scriptures in his person and mission, particularly in his paschal mystery. This progress affects all the great themes:
   • *God*: one (monotheism) and triune (Father, Son, and Holy Spirit)
   • *Human beings*: Christ is the perfect image of God; human beings are called to become an image of Christ, "a new creation." Christ has become the universal mediator of salvation.

---

9. Roland Meynet, *Morto e risorto secondo le Scritture* (Bologna: EDB, 2002), 22.

10. Pontifical Biblical Commission, *The Jewish People and Their Sacred Scriptures in the Christian Bible* (Vatican City: Libreria Editrice Vaticana, 2001), §§64–65.

- *The people*: the Church is composed of Israelites who have accepted the New Covenant in Christ and of other believers who have been united to them; she exists thanks to her adherence to Jesus, the Messiah of Israel, and her links with the apostles, all Israelites. Therefore, far from substituting for Israel, the Church remains in solidarity with it. In referring to the land of Israel, the New Testament advances much further in the process of symbolization that was already initiated in the Old Testament and intertestamental Judaism.

In a similar way, Benedict XVI in *Verbum Domini* (§40) speaks about continuity, rupture, and fulfillment/transcendence; and he explains: "The mystery of Christ stands in continuity of intent with the sacrificial cult of the Old Testament, but it came to pass in a very different way, corresponding to a number of prophetic statements and thus reaching a perfection never previously obtained." The "rupture," which affects determinate aspects, is not total, but rather it is the appropriate modality of the fulfillment: "The paschal mystery of Christ is in complete conformity—albeit in a way that could not have been anticipated—with the prophecies and the foreshadowings of the Scriptures" (*VD* §40).

To sum up: the Christ–Church event (=New Testament), by means of a complex relationship with the Old Testament (continuity/discontinuity/ progress), causes a full but not previously perceptible meaning to emerge from the Old Testament, which leaves aside secondary aspects and is manifested in all the themes revealed there.

6.5. The gospel of the Kingdom: a logic of fullness

All that we have spoken about so far explains to us the origin of the ministry of Jesus. From the beginning he shows his firm consciousness of a mission: to bring definitive fulfillment to the salvific plan of God. This he expresses by means of the category of "gospel," the object of his first preaching: "Repent, and believe in the gospel" (Mark 1:15). The "Good News" in which his proclamation consists must be understood on the basis of the Old Testament passages that speak of the mission of the Servant of YHWH: to bring good news ("evangelize") to the poor (cf. Isa 61:1). In Isaiah 52:7 this same verb has as its content the announcement of the kingdom of God: "How beautiful upon the mountains are the feet of him who brings good tidings, who publishes [evangelizes] peace, who brings good tidings of good, who publishes [evangelizes] salvation, who says to Zion, 'Your God reigns.'" Jesus, by announcing the "gospel of the

Kingdom" (Matt 4:23), is presented as he who incarnates this mysterious Old Testament figure.

And what is this "Kingdom" that Jesus proclaims like? Does it amount to the reconstitution of the historical kingdom of Israel, just like that which was realized in its greatest splendor with David and Solomon? It does not seem that this is the case; and this can be gathered precisely from the undercurrent of the Old Testament. For that Kingdom which is promised for the time of fulfillment is a reality into which not only the Jews must enter, but also all the nations: "Say among the nations: 'The LORD reigns!' Yea, the world is established, it shall never be moved; he will judge the peoples with equity" (Ps 96:10). The gospel of the Kingdom appears, therefore, in virtue of the Old Testament undercurrent, as the eschatological fulfillment of the prophetic Scripture that, by being this fulfillment, will mark the beginning of the mission among the Gentiles. It is thus about bringing to fullness the plan of God. His work of salvation will have the same universal reach as his work of creation had.

This is manifested in all the New Testament traditions. Next we will go over the three principal traditions (Synoptic, Johannine, and Pauline).

6.6. The Synoptic Gospels: the fulfillment in Jesus

The three primary gospels present Jesus to us as the one whose mission is synthesized in this expression: "fulfilling the Scriptures."[11] Already from the first steps of his ministry (baptism, temptations in the desert, first preaching), Jesus shows himself as depending radically on the Scriptures, which are the testimony of the divine will. The inaugural preaching of Jesus in the Gospel of Luke is not without the declaration of fulfillment "today" of the prophecy of Isaiah 61:1–3 (Luke 4:18–21). The whole Sermon on the Mount in the Gospel of Matthew is shown to be dominated by the fundamental principle of fulfilling "the Law and the prophets" (Matt 5:17), in such a way that the teaching of Jesus ends up being incomprehensible without the Old Testament. In no way does Jesus consider the Old Testament outmoded or surpassed; on the contrary, it is his principal font of inspiration. One can appreciate this, for example, in the controversy about divorce (Matt 19:3–9 || Mark 10:3–12): Jesus' teaching interprets the texts of Genesis 1–2. "When he began to preach and teach, he drew

---

11. Luis Sánchez Navarro, "Jesús y las Escrituras: el testimonio de los Sinópticos," 71–101 in *Vetus in Novo: El recurso a la Escritura en el Nuevo Testamento*, ed. Filippo Belli, Ignacio Carbajosa, Carlos Jódar Estrella, and Luis Sánchez Navarro, Ensayos 290 (Madrid: Encuentro, 2006).

abundantly from the treasure of Scripture, enriching this treasure with new inspirations and unexpected initiatives."[12]

Referring to his future passion, Jesus does not present it as a failure of his mission; on the contrary, he will insist on its necessity, as the Scriptures testify: "And taking the twelve, he said to them, 'Behold, we are going up to Jerusalem, and everything that is written of the Son of man by the prophets will be accomplished'" (Luke 18:31). The transformation of his existence and of his earthly mission becomes comprehensible in this light, which is not a word of failure but of life. "Jesus understood the increasing opposition he had to face on the way to Calvary in the light of the Old Testament, which revealed to him the destiny reserved for the prophets. He also knew from the Old Testament that in the end God's love always triumphs."[13] When in the Garden of Olives he is delivered into the hands of his persecutors, Jesus solemnly expresses the meaning of this handing over: "Day after day I was with you in the temple teaching, and you did not seize me. But let the scriptures be fulfilled" (Mark 14:49). Regarding the two disciples going on the road to Emmaus, finally, the resurrected Christ will reproach them: "'O foolish men, and slow of heart to believe all that the prophets have spoken! Was it not necessary that the Christ should suffer these things and enter into his glory?' And beginning with Moses and all the prophets, he interpreted to them in all the scriptures the things concerning himself" (Luke 24:25–27). The prophetic Scriptures have acquired in Jesus an unexpected fulfillment that has radically renewed them: the new wine has renewed the wineskins (cf. Mark 2:22).

In this way, and through bringing the Scriptures to their eschatological fulfillment, the risen Jesus will be able to entrust to his disciples the universal mission: "Go therefore and make disciples of all nations" (Matt 28:19); "Go into all the world and preach the gospel to the whole creation" (Mark 16:15); "You shall be my witnesses in Jerusalem and in all Judea and Samaria, and to the end of the earth" (Acts 1:8). The Church, in the hope of her definitive consummation, already lives the time of fulfillment: the time of proclaiming the gospel to all peoples, so that all men see the salvation of God (cf. Ps 98:3).

---

12. John Paul II, Address to Members of the Pontifical Biblical Commission (April 11, 1997); English trans. "Old Testament Essential to Know Jesus," *L'Osservatore Romano* 30, no. 17 (April 23, 1997), p. 2, §3.

13. John Paul II, Address to Members of the Pontifical Biblical Commission, §3.

6.7. John: "It is they that bear witness to me"

In the Gospel of John as well, Scripture appears in close relationship with the mystery of Christ. Already in the prologue the evangelist affirms: "For the law was given through Moses; grace and truth came through Jesus Christ" (John 1:17). Jesus, the Logos of the Father, is therefore the definitive revealer; but he was preceded by the gift of the Law that, handed on by Moses, already presupposes in itself a sublime gift from God.

Upon seeing him for the first time, John the Baptist will exclaim: "Behold, the Lamb of God, who takes away the sin of the world" (John 1:29). With these mysterious words he signals him as the Servant of YHWH (Isa 53:7) who with his sacrifice (similar to that of Isaac: Gen 22) will save the entire world from its sins; the universal horizon of these words leaves no place for doubts: in Jesus the eschatological fulfillment of the promise arrives. The two disciples of the Baptist, given such an indication, will be able to follow Jesus; their experience will bring one of them, Andrew, to say a little later to his brother Peter: "We have found the Messiah" (1:41)—that is to say, the Anointed One promised by the Scriptures. The following day another neo-disciple, Philip, in his conviction will say to Nathanael: "We have found him of whom Moses in the law and also the prophets wrote, Jesus of Nazareth, the son of Joseph" (1:45). We thus see that a decisive factor leading the first disciples to follow Jesus was their perception that he was the one announced by the Law and the Prophets.

This conviction penetrates the whole gospel narrative. To the subtle observation of the Samaritan woman—"I know that Messiah is coming (he is called Christ); when he comes he will show us all things" (4:25)—Jesus responds: "I who speak to you am he" (1:46). A little later, in the polemics with the Jews, Jesus will say: "You search the scriptures because you think that in them you have eternal life; and it is they that bear witness to me; yet you refuse to come to me that you may have life" (5:39–40). Jesus thus situates himself audaciously, from the point of view of Israel's Scriptures, as the object of their testimony. And he insists: "If you believed Moses, you would believe me, for he wrote of me" (5:46). The Law of Moses had Jesus as its ultimate object. Later, with even greater audacity, he will affirm in the temple: "Your father Abraham rejoiced that he was to see my day; he saw it and was glad" (8:56). Such a claim provokes an intent to stone him, but Jesus is able to escape (8:58). The consciousness of Jesus is very clear: Scripture acquires its meaning in him, the one to whom it points and about whom it gives testimony.

This will be definitively established in the passion of Jesus. The "farewell discourse" (John 13–21) begins with this solemn declaration: "Having loved his own who were in the world, he loved them to the end" (13:1). This "end," in Greek *telos* (end, objective), is reached in the moment of his death on the cross, as the use of two verbs derived from this same word shows: "After this Jesus, knowing that all was now finished (*teleō*), said (to fulfil the scripture [*teleioō*]), 'I thirst.' . . . When Jesus had received the vinegar, he said, 'It is finished (*teleō*)'; and he bowed his head and gave up his spirit" (19:28–30). Jesus loved his own until the end, which is to say, until the perfect fulfillment of the Father's saving plan, to which the Scriptures testify. This reaches its first concrete instantiation in the episode that follows, the piercing of Jesus' side with the lance: "For these things took place that the scripture might be fulfilled, 'Not a bone of him shall be broken.' And again another scripture says, 'They shall look on him whom they have pierced'" (19:36–37). The mysterious flowing forth of water and blood from Christ's side is understood by the astonished eyewitness as a fulfillment of Scripture that allows us to discover in Jesus the true Paschal Lamb, who with his sacrifice attracts all men to himself. But this understanding of Scripture in light of Jesus will be possible only through the resurrection: "When therefore he was raised from the dead . . . they believed the scripture and the word which Jesus had spoken" (2:22). The Beloved Disciple, the one who contemplated the pierced side, will be the first to believe upon entering the empty tomb: "Then the other disciple, who reached the tomb first, also went in, and he saw and believed; for as yet they did not know the scripture, that he must rise from the dead" (20:8–9). To believe in Jesus means to understand Scripture. The mutual implication could not be shown more strongly.

6.8. Paul: the fulfillment of time

The apostle Paul is a particularly interesting witness to the theme that occupies our thoughts. He is a Jew by birth, formation, and piety, which is particularly shown by his fervent faithfulness to the traditions of the fathers (Gal 1:13–14; Phil 3:5); his knowledge and living out of Scripture cause him to affirm, in his autobiographical confession, that he was "as to righteousness under the law, blameless" (Phil 3:6). However, his encounter with Jesus brings him to completely reevaluate his previous experience. The one whom Paul earlier had considered to be a blasphemer worthy of being persecuted, is now the "first-born of all creation" (Col 1:15); in the Letter to the Galatians Paul identifies Jesus' birth from "a woman" as "the fullness of time" (Gal 4:4), meaning the moment that marks the fulfillment of the promises of God. Paul's acceptance of Jesus Christ has brought him to a new reading of the Tanakh, "Law, Prophets, and Writings," up until then so familiar to him.

He thus discovers the "mystery" that was latent in the writings of the Old Covenant. This mystery is Christ (Eph 3:4–5), whom he had been incapable of perceiving earlier; just as, in his time, happens with his Jewish contemporaries, his brethren. He will explain it to the Christians of Corinth by employing the image of Moses' face covered with a veil in order to not blind others with its brightness (cf. Exod 34:29–35):

> But their minds were hardened; for to this day, when they read the old covenant, that same veil remains unlifted, because only through Christ is it taken away. Yes, to this day whenever Moses is read a veil lies over their minds; but when a man turns to the Lord the veil is removed. (2 Cor 3:14–16; cf. Exod 34:34)

This passage, which is very relevant because it is the only time in all of the New Testament that the expression "old covenant" (i.e., Old Testament) appears, reflects the great discovery of Paul. Before, he read Scripture, but he could not see Christ because a veil impeded him. Now that he has received the gift of faith, it is possible for him to discover Christ in a multitude of passages in that same Scripture. Jesus was already in that ancient letter, but Paul was not capable of perceiving him. Paul was missing the light of the Spirit: "The Lord is the Spirit" (2 Cor 3:17). Now he can see the reality, so much so that he will come to affirm that the final objective (*telos*) to which all of the Law points is Christ (Rom 10:4).

And it is the case that the Christian event, even though it has presupposed a radical surpassing of the Law, has not occurred independently of it: "But now the righteousness of God has been manifested apart from the law, although the law and the prophets bear witness to it" (Rom 3:21). Paul cannot speak of Christ without consulting the Scriptures.

> The God of Jesus Christ, such as Paul experiences and communicates, is the God of Abraham, Isaac, and Jacob, who has not backtracked on his faithfulness or in his mode of relationship with humanity. For Paul, utilizing Scripture is indispensable not so much as an external proof or guarantee of his affirmation, and even less as a way of arriving at the faith, but rather as a foundation of the very veracity of his discourse.[14]

In some cases, and in spite of recognizing the holiness of the Law, he will debate against it, arguing that historically it was not capable of efficaciously helping human beings to overcome sin (see especially Rom 7:7–13). But at the same time he recognizes in the prophetic Scriptures an exceptional witness in

---

14. Filippo Belli, "'Testimoniada por la ley y los profetas.' Rom 3:21: Pablo y las Escrituras," *Revista Agustiniana* 43 (2002): 413–426, at 425.

favor of the gospel of Jesus the Messiah: "Paul, a servant of Jesus Christ, called to be an apostle, set apart for the gospel of God which he promised beforehand through his prophets in the holy scriptures" (Rom 1:1–2).

6.9. Recapitulation: Jesus "according to Scriptures"

Jesus was incomprehensible without Scripture; now Scripture is incomprehensible without Jesus. The Old and New Testaments are inseparable, because they represent the two "sides of the coin" (preparation and fulfillment) of one single reality: the saving plan of God for all human beings. Conformity with the Old Testament is constitutive of the Christian faith, which "is not based solely on events, but on the conformity of these events to the revelation contained in the Jewish Scriptures."[15] Paul affirms as much in a traditional formulation: "For I delivered to you as of first importance what I also received, that Christ died for our sins *in accordance with the scriptures,* that he was buried, that he was raised on the third day *in accordance with the scriptures*" (1 Cor 15:3–4). All the attempts that—beginning with Marcion (second century) and arriving at national socialism (twentieth century)—have tried to tear the New Testament out of its biblical matrix have ended by disintegrating this same New Testament and the Christian faith in its totality.

6.10. Conclusion: the New—the full manifestation of the Old

In the first verse of the New Testament we read: "The book of the genealogy of Jesus Christ, the son of David, the son of Abraham" (Matt 1:1). The credentials of the undisputed protagonist of these twenty-seven writings cannot be more eloquent: he is the "son of the promise" made to David and before him to Abraham. This claim of the New Testament, from its very beginning, reveals to us to what extent the relationship with the Old Testament is necessary for being able to read and understand the writings that testify to the New Covenant realized in the blood of Jesus (cf. Luke 22:20). That passage of the Letter to the Hebrews with which we opened our reflection, and which seemed to put in crisis the very validity of the Old Covenant, does nothing but confirm everything we are saying. For are not the prophetic oracles perhaps what allow us to recognize in the person and the work of Jesus the definitive fulfillment of the Covenant on the part of the faithful God? There is, certainly, a conflict; but it is not resolved in the annulment of one of its terms, but in an unexpected fulfillment.

---

15. Pontifical Biblical Commission, *The Jewish People and Their Sacred Scriptures in the Christian Bible,* §7.

7

The Old-New Relationship, Hermeneutical Key to Scripture

Luis Sánchez-Navarro

There are two words in this title that we have to clarify: "key" and "hermeneutical." We are talking about a noun and an adjective that, united, express the meaning of the "Old Testament–New Testament relationship" on which these pages turn. "Key" means an instrument that allows one to open or close something.[1] According to our postulate, therefore, if we neglect the Old Testament–New Testament relationship, Sacred Scripture remains opaque. For its part, "hermeneutical" refers to interpretation; the verb *hermēneuō* and its derivatives signify "to explain," "to interpret," "to translate." This indicates to us the sense in which Scripture remains closed to us if we do not pay attention to the relationship mentioned above.

According to our thesis, therefore, the Old Testament–New Testament relationship is necessary in order to "open up" the Scriptures, not from a linguistic, literary, or historical point of view, but from an interpretive one. For the first, a philological competency in Semitic and Hellenistic Greek languages is required; for the second, an adequate knowledge of the literary genres of Middle Eastern antiquity is needed. In order to study the Scriptures from the point of view of history, we need to apply historical methods, to the extent that it is possible and keeping in mind the limits of the sources at our disposal. But in order to *interpret* Scripture it is necessary, keeping in mind the methodologies

---

1. Cf. Rev 3:7: "The words of the holy one, the true one, who has the key of David, who opens and no one shall shut, who shuts and no one opens."

just mentioned (which are indispensable), to pay attention to the relationship between the two great parts that compose it, the Old and the New Testaments.[2]

But is this a supposition that is more ideological than real, or does it obey internal motivations of that Scripture itself?

7.1. The New and the Old: what the Bible says

The stories of the resurrection of Jesus in Luke give us a primary answer, which refers to the interpretation of the Old from the New. And the Book of Jeremiah does the same thing regarding the inverse relationship.

a) The New: key to the Old

The dialogue of the two disciples with Jesus (who is still unrecognizable to their eyes) on the road to Emmaus is well known. After they describe with precision the lived events of the two past days and show evidence of the disillusionment that envelops them (Luke 24:13–24), their companion on the road directs a surprising reproach at them: "O foolish men, and slow of heart to believe all that the prophets have spoken! Was it not necessary that the Christ should suffer these things and enter into his glory?" (Luke 24:25–26). Then the evangelist sums up Jesus' subsequent discourse—which he does not reproduce—with these words: "And beginning with Moses and all the prophets, he interpreted to them in all the scriptures the things concerning himself" (24:27). The Greek verb employed in this last verse is *diermēneuō*, "to explain, interpret"; it is the only time that it appears in the Gospels. Luke uses it again in Acts 9:36 with the meaning "to translate";[3] outside of the Lukan work, the term appears only in 1 Corinthians, referring to the interpretation of tongues (*hermēneia glōssōn*: 1 Cor 12:10; 14:26).[4] The well-known charism of the Church in Corinthians enlightens us with respect to the words of the Resurrected Jesus on the road to Emmaus: just as speaking in tongues ends up being unintelligible if there

2. "No less serious attention must be given to the content and unity of the whole of Scripture if the meaning of the sacred texts is to be correctly worked out. The living tradition of the whole Church must be taken into account along with the harmony which exists between elements of the faith" [translator's note: the Latin is *analogia fidei*, "the analogy of faith"] (*DV* §12c). Cf. Benedict XVI, *VD* §34.

3. It is thus synonymous with *methermēneuō*, the verb that is most used in the New Testament with this meaning: Matt 1:23; Mark 5:41, 15:22, 34; John 1:38, 41; Acts 4:36, 13:8. In John 1:42 and 9:7 we find with this same meaning the verb *hermēneuō*.

4. *Diermēneuō*: 1 Cor 12:30; 14:5, 13, 27; *diermēneutēs*: 1 Cor 14:28. In the Old Testament this verb appears only in 2 Mac 1:36.

is not an interpreter, a translator, in a similar way, what refers to Jesus in all the Scriptures, if it is not interpreted in light of the passion of that same Jesus, ends up being like a coded language whose key is unknown.[5] Luke audaciously proposes the historical person of Jesus as the interpretive criterion of Israel's Scriptures.[6]

A few verses later, after the sudden disappearance of the Lord, we hear the two disciples saying, "Did not our hearts burn within us while he talked to us on the road, while he opened to us the scriptures?" (Luke 24:32) This time we have a different verb, *dianoigō*, "to open completely." It functions as a synonym of the verb that we had encountered before; in fact it is often translated as "to explain."[7] But the metaphor is different: earlier it was about explaining or translating something unintelligible, but here it is about "opening." The final apparition of the Resurrected Jesus in Luke contains, with the same verb *dianoigō*, a slightly different expression that allows us to specify the verb in verse 32: "Then he opened their minds to understand the scriptures" (Luke 24:45).[8] Opening the Scriptures (24:32) is equivalent to opening the mind in order to understand the Scriptures (24:45). And this opening is made a reality through the *interpretation* of what, in these Scriptures, refers to Jesus (24:27).

The story of Emmaus therefore contains two concepts that we used in the title of this chapter; it thus allows us to show how the mystery of Jesus is the key that opens the Scriptures, by interpreting them, to a new meaning.[9] If we keep in mind that the New Testament is the written testimony of the event of Jesus Christ, a believing testimony that attests to the fulfillment in Jesus of

5. The question of the Ethiopian eunuch to the deacon Philip is illustrative in this respect: "About whom, pray, does the prophet say this, about himself or about someone else?" (Acts 8:34)

6. It is a teaching similar to the one that, using the image of the veil, Paul explains regarding the reading of the Old Testament in 2 Cor 3:12–18.

7. It is translated thus in the *Biblia de Jerusalén* (Bilbao: Desclée de Brouwer, 1998) and the *Sagrada Biblia* of the BAC (Madrid: 2010). Manuel Iglesias, *Nuevo Testamento* (Madrid: Encuentro, 2003) translates, with greater precision: "when he was opening for us [the meaning of] the Scriptures." In Acts 17:3 we find an identical use of this verb: "opening them [the Scriptures] and showing that Christ had to suffer and to rise from among the dead and that, 'This Christ is Jesus, whom I proclaim to you.'"

8. Cf. Acts 16:14: "One who heard us was a woman named Lydia, from the city of Thyatira, a seller of purple goods, who was a worshiper of God. The Lord opened her heart [*diēnoixen tēn kardian*] to give heed to what was said by Paul."

9. Cf. Luis Sánchez Navarro, "Jesús y las Escrituras: el testimonio de los Sinópticos," 71–101 in *Vetus in Novo: El recurso a la Escritura en el Nuevo Testamento*, ed. Filippo Belli, Ignacio Carbajosa, Carlos Jódar Estrella, and Luis Sánchez Navarro, Ensayos 290 (Madrid: Encuentro, 2006), 96.

the ancient promises, we can extend the reach of this evangelical episode in order to affirm that the New Testament is a key that opens the Old, "which only now, it claims, can be understood as a unity and as a meaningful totality."[10] This allows us to verify the title put forth, at least in part: the relationship with the New Testament appears to be a hermeneutical key for the Old Testament, which lacks significant unity without the New Testament.[11]

Can we affirm also the inverse: that the relationship with the Old Testament is a key of interpretation for the New Testament?

b) The Old, key of the New

If the New is the interpretive key of the Old, to which it gives fulfillment, then the Old for its part offers the key for interpreting the New. For the premise is necessary for the fulfillment. In the Christian Bible the New is the "final cause" of the Old,[12] which in turn is necessarily presupposed by the New Testament, which simply could not exist without it.[13]

Above all we need to focus on the name: "New Testament," that is, "New Covenant." Its significance remains closed if we prescind from the Old: every new thing presupposes an anterior state, without which it lacks meaning. But, also, the expression "New Covenant" proceeds from the Scriptures of Israel (Jer 31:31); this prophecy of Jeremiah, of notable importance within this prophetic book,[14] already points to a new realization of the Covenant with YHWH, a realization that will be different from the first: God will write the law, no

---

10. Joseph Ratzinger, "Biblical Interpretation in Conflict," trans. Adrian Walker, 1–29 in *Opening Up the Scriptures: Joseph Ratzinger and the Foundations of Biblical Interpretation*, ed. José Granados, Carlos Granados, and Luis Sánchez-Navarro (Grand Rapids: Eerdmans, 2008), 12.

11. With this we do not affirm that the Hebrew Scriptures lack unity; but they have *another* significant unity that is distinct from the Christian Old Testament, as the very order of the books in both canons makes manifest. Regarding the differences between the Old Testament and the Hebrew Bible, see Carlos Jódar Estrella, "Lectura cristiana del Antiguo Testamento," 25–29 in *Diccionario de Teología*, ed. César Izquierdo, Jutta Burggraf, and Félix María Arocena Solano (Pamplona: EUNSA, 2006).

12. "The deeds that occurred in the Old Testament have their basis in a future deed in light of which it first becomes possible to understand them correctly." Ratzinger, "Biblical Interpretation in Conflict," 24.

13. "A New Testament separated from the Old, however, cannot hold together even on its own terms, because, according to its own claim, it exists only thanks to this unity." Ratzinger, "Biblical Interpretation in Conflict," 25.

14. It is "one of the most profound and moving passages in the entire Bible." John Bright, *Jeremiah*, AB 21 (Garden City, NY: Doubleday, 1965), 287.

longer on stone, but on human hearts (Jer 31:33).[15] The Incarnation of the Son
of God and his saving work imply a radical new thing; but in turn they do not
become a reality from nothing, but rather they are preceded by a history which
they fulfill. That history, to which the books of the Old Testament bear witness, therefore becomes necessary for the interpretation of the Incarnation and
Christ's salvific work. It is significant that the only time that we find in the Bible
the expression "Old Covenant" (*palaia diathēkē*: 2 Cor 3:14) it is in the context
not of abolition but of full manifestation: the mystery of Christ does not presuppose the extinction of that ancient Covenant, but rather the correct understanding of it.[16] The New does not destroy the Old, but rather it fully brings it
to reality.[17]

An example, closely related to Jeremiah 31, can serve to concretize the
question for us. Jesus would not have been able to speak of a New Covenant
in his blood without the precedent of the Covenant established by God with
his people, sealed with the blood of young bulls and witnessed to in the books
of the Jewish people's Scriptures;[18] "The words of Jesus over the cup proclaim
that the prophecy in the Book of Jeremiah is fulfilled in his Passion. The disciples participate in this fulfilment by their partaking of the 'supper of the Lord'

15. "[N]ot like the covenant which I made with their fathers when I took them by the hand
to bring them out of the land of Egypt, my covenant which they broke, though I was their husband, says the LORD" (Jer 31:32). Ezekiel interprets it as the gift of a heart of flesh in place of
the heart of stone (Ezek 36:26).

16. This unique mention makes reference, moreover, to the *Scripture* of the Old Covenant,
as the insistence on "reading" shows: "But their minds were hardened, for to this day, when
they read the old covenant, that same veil remains unlifted, because only through Christ is it
taken away. Yes, to this day whenever Moses is read a veil lies over their minds; but when a man
turns to the Lord the veil is removed" (2 Cor 3: 14–16; cf. Exod 34:34).

17. The Letter to the Hebrews prefers to speak of "the first covenant" (*prōtē diathēkē*: Heb
9:15). The importance that this writing gives to the New Covenant is shown in the passage from
Jer 31:31–34 in the very center of the letter (Heb 8:8–12: which is the longest Old Testament
quotation in the New Testament); cf. Albert Vanhoye, *Carta a los hebreos*, Comprender la
Palabra 34 (Madrid: Biblioteca de Autores Cristianos, 2014), 84–88. One must note that, even
though in the Old Testament this expression does not appear, the "old Covenant" is necessarily
implied in the "new Covenant" that Jeremiah compares to "the covenant that I made with your
fathers" (Jer 31:32).

18. The Covenant of Sinai is realized through the declaration of Moses: "Behold the blood
of the covenant which the LORD has made with you in accordance with all these words" (Exod
24:8).

(1 Cor 11:20)."[19] By employing a cultic terminology, Jesus situated the new rite in the wake of the Old Testament sacrifices, in such a way that it becomes incomprehensible without them. The Old Testament thus becomes the key to the New; and also vice versa, because the sacrifice of the Eucharist shows with complete clarity what the Old Testament sacrifices signified in a veiled way. On the other hand, the Eucharist causes the sacrifices to disappear: in the Church the sacrifices of animals or any other type of similar ritual offerings are not celebrated. But those sacrifices have not totally been extinguished, because they subsist in the sacrifice that has brought them to fullness, in such a way that the promise subsists in its fulfillment. According to the fundamental principle enunciated by Jesus at the beginning of his public life, they have not been abolished, but brought to their fullness (cf. Matt 5:17).

All of these facts reveal, in the end, the profundity of the relationship between the Old Testament and the New Testament; both collections of writings—testimonies of the respective stages of revelation—become mutual keys of interpretation. The "fulfillment" that characterizes this relationship is not a simple reality with no complexity; it is described by the Exhortation *Verbum Domini* with the inseparable triplet of continuity, rupture, and transcendence (§40).[20] This is a theme that merits a deeper investigation; next we will present some particularly fruitful approaches.

7.2. Two recent proposals for understanding

Among the authors who have recently dealt with the Old Testament–New Testament relationship and the overcoming of their division when one interprets Scripture, two stand out: Brevard S. Childs and Paul Beauchamp. Even though they proceed from different backgrounds (the first North American, and the second European; the first Presbyterian, and the second Catholic), the two of them have in common not only their specialty (the Old Testament) but also their interest in biblical theology.

19. Pontifical Biblical Commission, *The Jewish People and Their Sacred Scriptures in the Christian Bible* (Vatican City: Libreria Editrice Vaticana, 2001), §40. Two different redactions of the words of Jesus over the chalice exist: "This is my blood of the covenant" (Matt, Mark) and "This cup . . . is the new covenant in my blood" (Luke, 1 Cor).

20. See also the Pontifical Biblical Commission, *The Jewish People*, §§64–65 (continuity, discontinuity, and progress). On the hermeneutic of "fulfillment" in the New Testament, see Belli et al., *Vetus in Novo*, 53–63; Stefano Romanello and Roberto Vignolo, eds., *Rivisitare il compimento: Le Scritture di Israele e la loro normatività secondo il Nuovo Testamento*, Biblica 3 (Milan: Glossa, 2006), xxiii–xxxi.

a) Brevard S. Childs: the canon of the Old Testament and New Testament, differentiated testimony of Christ

Brevard Childs (d. 2007) developed the "canonical method," which intends to show the meaning of each biblical book, understood not in an isolated way, but insofar as it forms part of a canon; with the adjective "canonical" he expresses synthetically the diverse factors implied in the formation of the biblical literature, and in particular "the reception and acknowledgement of certain religious traditions as authoritative writings within a faith community."[21] He brings this to the field that we are treating, since necessarily one has to deal with the relationship between the two great groups of writings that compose the Christian canon, the Old and New Testament. The relationship between them is fundamental: "The Old is understood by its relation to the New, but the New is incomprehensible apart from the Old."[22] And they are related in Christ, about whom each gives a distinct testimony.[23]

Childs insists on the uniqueness of the Old and the New Testaments, which cannot be assimilated, but rather must be interpreted with full respect for their own characteristics. But that does not imply that an abyss intervenes between the Old and the New;[24] on the contrary, as we have said, they are related according to the object of their testimony.

> The two testaments have been linked as Old and New, but this designation does not mean that the integrity of each individual testament has been destroyed. The Old Testament bears its true witness as the Old which remains distinct from the New. It is promise, not fulfillment. Yet its voice

21. Brevard S. Childs, *Biblical Theology of the Old and New Testaments: Theological Reflection on the Christian Bible* (Minneapolis, MN: Fortress, 1993), 70.

22. Childs, *Biblical Theology*, 77.

23. In this way our author affirms that Christology is at the foundation of the Christian canon: "The authority assigned to the apostolic witnesses derived from their unique testimony to the life, death, and resurrection of Jesus Christ. Similarly, the Old Testament functioned as Christian scripture because it bore witness to Christ. The scriptures of the Old and the New Testament were authoritative in so far as they pointed to God's redemptive intervention for the world in Jesus Christ." Childs, *Biblical Theology*, 64.

24. As happened *de facto* in Christian exegesis starting with the Enlightenment. "It became a truism that the New Testament had been influenced by the Old, but that the Old Testament could in any way be interpreted by the New—recall Augustine's famous formulation—was an idea dismissed as hopelessly anachronistic." Brevard S. Childs, "On Reclaiming the Bible for Christian Theology," 1–17 in *Reclaiming the Bible for the Church*, ed. Carl E. Braaten and Robert W. Jenson (Edinburgh: T&T Clark, 1996), 13.

continues to sound and it has not been stilled by the fulfilment of the promise.[25]

In turn, the New contains a radical new thing, thanks to which it offers its specific testimony: "It tells its own story of the new redemptive intervention of God in Jesus Christ."[26]

Moreover the relationship between the two is not exhausted in the object of their testimony, despite the fact that this represents their fundamental connection. "Yet the complexity of the problem arises because the New Testament bears its totally new witness in terms of the old, and thereby transforms the Old Testament";[27] the New thus freely interprets the Old "as a transparency of the New."[28]

In summary, we can say that, for Brevard Childs, the Old and New Testaments represent two voices that give a differentiated but concordant testimony of Christ. Their interpretation, in the end, is about the reality attested by the Scriptures;[29] this means that the relationship between the two Testaments represents a fundamental aspect of their interpretation.

b) Paul Beauchamp: Christ, fulfillment of the Scriptures

This French Jesuit (d. 2001) developed a project of biblical theology centered on the fulfillment of the Scriptures,[30] a fulfillment which is a complex fact, but which is realized in a single act: the "act of Christ." The complexity of the fulfillment of the Scriptures is derived from the variety of meanings of "fulfillment": realizing a prediction, fulfilling a promise, or causing a process to arrive at its end. "From this perspective, the Old Testament is given so that it can be explored as the prediction to be realized, the promise to be maintained, the process to be finalized."[31]

---

25. Childs, *Biblical Theology*, 77. "The Old Testament is to be understood in its own right because it has its own Jewish voice, which was never altered by the coming of Jesus Christ. Indeed, it was this very Jewish voice that bore witness to the gospel." Childs, "On Reclaiming the Bible," 13.

26. Childs, *Biblical Theology*, 78.

27. Childs, *Biblical Theology*, 78.

28. Childs, *Biblical Theology*, 78.

29. "In this sense, true biblical interpretation involves a *Sachkritik*, but one in which the *Sache* is defined in terms of the reality of Jesus Christ." Childs, "On Reclaiming the Bible," 15.

30. Paul Beauchamp, *L'un et l'autre Testament: I. Essai de lecture; II. Accomplir les Écritures* (Paris: Éditions du Seuil, 1976; 1990). Cf. Paul Beauchamp, "Cumplir las Escrituras: Un camino de teología bíblica," 170–184 in *Biblia y ciencia de la fe*, ed. Carlos Granados and Agustín Giménez, Ensayos 311 (Madrid: Encuentro, 2007) (originally published in *Revue biblique* 99 [1992]: 132–162).

31. Paul Beauchamp, "Lecture christique de l'Ancien Testament," *Biblica* 81 (2000): 105–115, at 106.

For this task Beauchamp focuses on the notion of "figure," thus developing a figurative (or typological) exegesis; his hypothesis is that typology, liberated from the restrictions suffered in a theological tradition influenced by Platonism, is not just one among multiple meanings of Scripture, but rather is the key that allows us to grasp their unity.[32] Thus the notion of figure

> allows . . . us to elaborate on a biblical theology of fulfillment. The Old Testament, in this perspective, is not only useful for understanding the New, nor is the Old just the preparation for the New, but rather the Old should be seen as a path that is continually necessary to travel, as a constant condition of access to the mystery of Christ, in whose action all the figures find their fulfillment.[33]

The first Testament anticipates the form of the final event whose presence will proclaim the New.[34]

The dynamic of fulfillment therefore accounts for the intimate relationship between Old and New, which Beauchamp—thus emphasizing their profound connection—calls "the one and the other Testament." This fulfillment is realized, as we have indicated, in the act of Christ, an act of obedience through which he is united with the Father[35] in such a way that the Old Testament–New Testament relationship has an essential Christological dimension.[36] "The articulation of the Old and the New Testaments is not preliminary to the knowledge of the event of Jesus, but rather it is internal to this knowledge. . . . Jesus is in the conjunction of the two Testaments, because he himself is this 'way' [the step from Old to New]."[37] The Old and the New Testaments thus end up being two voices that coincide in their testimony about Jesus.[38]

32. Angelo Bertuletti, "Introduzione: Un modello di teologia biblica," ix–xxxiv in Paul Beauchamp, *L'uno e l'altro Testamento. 2: Compiere le Scritture* (Milan: Glossa, 2001), xvii.

33. Carlos Granados, "Cumplimiento y exégesis figurativa en P. Beauchamp," *Estudios Bíblicos* 64 (2006): 19–29, at 19.

34. Bertuletti, "Un modello di teologia biblica," xxv.

35. Beauchamp, "Lecture christique de l'Ancien Testament," 110.

36. Cf. Massimo Grilli, *Quale rapporto tra i due Testamenti?: Riflessione critica sui modelli ermeneutici classici concernenti l'unità delle Scritture*, Epifania della Parola 10 (Bologna: EDB, 2007), 191–192.

37. Bertuletti, "Un modello di teologia biblica," x.

38. "If two independent witnesses, separated by time, see the same thing, according to what the assumed position allows them, then their testimony will have much more value and force. Precisely for this reason the task that summons the Old Testament to witness to Jesus Christ is a constitutive part of Christian theology. About this, the continuity of the tradition persuades us. This tradition is rooted in the New Testament." Beauchamp, "Is a Biblical Theology Possible?," 65–78 in *Opening Up the Scriptures*, ed. J. Granados et al., 73.

We can sum everything up by saying that for Paul Beauchamp, the one and the other Testament, whose difference is necessary to preserve the tension between them as a fountain of meaning, present a relationship so profound that the New fulfills the Old, which remains as a path that must be constantly travelled in order to approach Christ; in its turn the Old anticipates—in *figure*—the salvation to which the New testifies.

7.3. Some observations for the interpretation of this fact

After reviewing some basic data of Scripture and summarily expounding on the doctrine of two important recent scholars with regard to the Old Testament–New Testament relationship, we will offer a reflection that flows from what we have shown.

a) "The Book": Old and New Testament

From the literary point of view, neither the Old nor the New Testament by itself forms a book. It is the union of both that gives rise to the Book, the Bible,[39] in such a way that the New, by itself, is incomplete. In fact, the first verses of the New Testament canon, the genealogy of Jesus according to Matthew (Matt 1:1–17), are but a concise rereading of the Old Testament. Literarily the genealogy functions as a reminder, in terms of a key of fulfillment, of all that the reader has read up until that moment: in Jesus, who is the culmination of that long chain, the promises made by God to Abraham and David are fulfilled. Nor does the Old Testament have coherence on its own; its principal prophecies remain without an answer if we do not then read the New.[40] Only the Bible, made up of the Old and the New Testaments, forms *a book*. Related to this fact is the connection that we discover between Genesis 1–3 and Revelation 21–22, of which the canonical compilers were very conscious. To the creation of the heavens and the earth (Gen 1:1) correspond the new heavens and the new earth

39. The word "Bible" is significant in this respect. Originally it was a neuter plural: *ta biblia*. But in the modern languages it is singular (La Bibbia, la Bible, die Bibel, la Biblia, the Bible). The plurality—which, in virtue of the etymology, is never suppressed—has been at the same time conceived as a unity, in the singular form. This is only possible from a unitary, and therefore theological, consideration of *ta biblia*.

40. We mentioned earlier the prophecy of the New Covenant; to this we ought to add, among others, Deut 18:15–18 (the Lord will raise up a prophet like Moses) and Mal 4:5 (the eschatological sending of Elijah); cf. John 1:21. Cf. also Ignacio Carbajosa, "El Antiguo Testamento, realidad abierta," 21–50 in *Entrar en lo Antiguo: Acerca de la relación entre Antiguo y Nuevo Testamento*, ed. Ignacio Carbajosa and Luis Sánchez Navarro, PreDi 16 (Madrid: Universidad Eclesiástica San Dámaso, 2007).

(Rev 21:1–8). The road to the tree of life, closed because of sin (Gen 3:24), is now open through the work of Jesus Christ (Rev 22:2). Revelation, the true compendium of the New Testament, shows how the mystery of Christ constitutes a new creation that has definitively opened for human beings the doors of Paradise (cf. Luke 23:43), full access to the tree of life. Only then can we close the Book.

b) A hermeneutic of testimony

But the relationship between Old Testament and New Testament is not exhausted in the literary fact; moreover, it is not something of a primarily literary character. It makes reference to a fact that exceeds the written word: the real referent is the foundation that confers unity on the Bible.[41] Sacred Scripture represents the *written and inspired testimony* of that reality, of the revelation.[42] The testimonial condition is intrinsic to it: the biblical word seeks to testify to the truth to which it refers; and it does so in the double dimension of this truth, historical and salvific.[43] On the one hand the reality of the revelatory event is affirmed,[44] and simultaneously its transcendent meaning, which constitutes the ultimate objective of the sacred author, is manifested (cf. John 20:31). The experience that is at the origin of the testimony is situated in history, and at the same time is projected toward transcendence.[45] The revelatory event is pregnant with meaning; the testimony is therefore the appropriate medium for

41. It has been written that Beauchamp's biblical reading "is supported by a theory of the text entirely governed by the primacy of reference. His high regard for the Book, understood as the irreplaceable condition of access to the reality that it configures, depends on such a reading." Bertuletti, "Un modello di teologia biblica," x.

42. Cf. Benedict XVI, *VD* §18: "Indeed, the word of God is given to us in sacred Scripture as an inspired testimony to revelation."

43. See chapter 1 of this volume.

44. "One cannot testify *in favor of* a meaning, without testifying *that* something has happened which signifies this meaning." Paul Ricœur, "L'ermeneutica della testimonianza," 73–108 in *Testimonianza parola e rivelazione*, ed. Francesco Franco (Rome: Dehoniane, 1997), 88. "The testimony-confession could not be separated from the testimony-narration, without the result of transforming it into a gnosis." Ricœur, "L'ermeneutica," 94. [Translator's note: I have translated from the author's Spanish rendition.] We do not understand the historicity of the Gospels in terms of the precision belonging to modern historical science, but rather as the true reference to real events (which later the tradition and the evangelists were able to model in diverse ways; cf. *DV* §19).

45. "The Christian testimony has its font in a specific experience, situated in history and anchored by history, but in tension with regards to the absolute You." Edmond Barbotin, *Le Témoignage* (Brussels: Culture et Verité, 1995), 50. Translator's note: I have translated from the author's Spanish rendition.

accessing it. All of this reveals to us the necessity of having in mind the testimonial character of the sacred books in order to understand the relationship between the Old Testament and the New Testament.[46]

At the same time the biblical testimony is differentiated. The Old Testament gives witness to the relationship of God with humanity, which is concretized in his revelation to the people of Israel and his covenant with them; all the biblical books are articulated around this fundamental fact. And the New Testament attests to the final revelation of God in Jesus Christ: the primordial event (Christ) as well as what is born of it (the Church). Between the people of Israel and the Church there is a clear distinction, which, however, does not destroy the continuity between both realities.[47] This continuity of the subject of reference lays the foundation for the profound relationship existing between the two blocks of the Christian canon.[48] Moreover, this fact has a close connection with the inspired character of the biblical writings.[49] Scripture thus becomes, beyond all discontinuity, a unified reality: in its subject (the people of Israel–the Church), in its origin (the inspiration of God), and in its finality (the testimony of the revelation, which culminates in Christ). The consideration of the testimonial character of Scripture allows us to address the relationship between its two great parts, the Old and New Testament, making clear how they pertain to the same process; that is to say, the unity that underlies their diversity.

46. In fact we have seen that both Brevard Childs and Paul Beauchamp assign to this category a relevant role in their respective systems.

47. The concluding vision of the Book of Revelation serves as an illustration: the new Jerusalem, constructed on the twelve apostles of the Lamb (Rev 21:14), has twelve gates that are the twelve tribes of Israel (Rev 21:12). "Representing the twelve tribes of Israel, they are the foundation stones of the new Jerusalem [cf. Matt 19:28; Luke 22:30; Rev 21:12–14]" (CCC §765).

48. "Scripture is one by reason of the historical subject that traverses it, the one people of God. To read Scripture as a unity therefore means to read it from the Church as its existential locus and to regard the faith of the Church as its true hermeneutical key." Ratzinger, "Biblical Interpretation in Conflict," 6.

49. Cf. Bruce M. Metzger, *Il Canone del Nuovo Testamento* (Brescia: Paideia, 1997), 223. Joseph Ratzinger, *God and the World: A Conversation with Peter Seewald* (San Francisco: Ignatius Press, 2002), 153: "And inspiration means that the people who wrote the text—and in many cases, this was a process of collective development—speak as members of the people of God and speak out of the history of God's people. The fact that, through many stages of mediation, they bring the history of God's people and of God's guidance to verbal expression means that they, too, are anchored in God the subject."

7.4. Conclusion

The title of this chapter was perhaps audacious: to identify the hermeneutical key of the Christian Scriptures in the Old Testament–New Testament relationship. With this objective we began with some biblical facts in order to, in a second phase, focus on two relevant authors (Brevard Childs and Paul Beauchamp) who throw light on this question; then we expounded on some hermeneutical clarifications. It is a very broad theme that we have barely been able to sketch out; however, we believe that our brief tour here confirms the proposed thesis. The relationship between the Old Testament and the New Testament, a rich and complex relationship, is revealed as the condition of possibility for interpreting Scripture from the point of view that Scripture itself shows to be the appropriate field of interpretation: its unity. The Old Testament is only "opened" by the New, which for its part manifests every potentiality of the Old; as the great Augustine said, *in Novo Vetus patet*.[50] At the same time, if it is not understood in light of the Old, the New Testament ends up being a fulfillment which has not been preceded by the promise, and it thus represents an enigma. Both collections of books, the Old and New Testaments, form a single book, the Bible; their unity is supported in the reality about which they give distinct testimonies, in such a way that we can conclude by seeing in this multiform relationship the key to understanding the Bible. This relationship is thus a necessary reference for exegetical work.[51]

---

50. Augustine, *Questions on the Heptateuch*, book 2, chapter 73 (PL 34:623).

51. "The first presupposition of all exegesis is that it takes the Bible as *one* book. If it does so, then it has already chosen for itself a position that is rooted in much more than the literary aspects of the text. It has recognized this literature as the product of a coherent history, and this history as the proper locus of understanding." Ratzinger, "Biblical Interpretation in Conflict," 29.

8

Christians and the Old Testament:
The Teaching of Vatican II (*DV* §§15–16)

Luis Sánchez-Navarro

The Dogmatic Constitution *Dei verbum*, on divine Revelation, is counted among the principal contributions of the Second Vatican Council; as is generally recognized, it is one of the most innovative documents produced by the Council. One of the innovations lies in the fourth chapter, dedicated to the Old Testament. It is the first time that a conciliar document treats this question intentionally.[1] In this section the Council addresses the Old Testament in itself (*DV* §14) and in its relationship with the New Testament (*DV* §§15–16); in these pages I will discuss the second aspect.

Fifty years after the conclusion of the Council, in a moment in which biblical science asks itself about its foundation and about the road that will allow it to recover the unity of Scripture without renouncing the scientific character of exegesis, it is particularly appropriate to return to this aspect. It has not attracted the attention of scholars in any special way, but it does not lack importance for understanding the Christian Scriptures and the Christian faith.

8.1. The Old Testament in *Dei verbum*

The reference to the Old Testament in this conciliar document is not confined to chapter IV, which is expressly dedicated to it; it appears for the first time in §7

---

1. Stanislas Lyonnet, "La elaboración de los capítulos IV y VI de la 'Dei Verbum,'" 117–149 in *Vaticano II: Balance y perspectivas: Veinticinco años después (1962–1987)*, ed. René Latourelle, VeIm 109 (Salamanca: Sígueme,1989), 117.

IN THE SCHOOL OF THE WORD

(ch. II, on the transmission of Revelation) and we find it again in §11 (ch. III, on the inspiration and interpretation of Scripture) and §22 (ch. VI, on Scripture in the life of the Church). It is worthy of mention that *Vetus Testamentum* does not refer to the literary corpus, but rather to a salvific historical event characterized by an "economy" or divine plan (cf. §15). It is the Old Covenant. Its written testimony is designated as "the books of the Old Testament" (*libri Veteris Testamenti*, §§14–16). Apart from that, it is significant that the first two times that this is mentioned, it is closely united to the New: "Sacred Scripture of the two Testaments" (*Sacra utriusque Testamenti Scriptura*, §7); "the books of both the Old and New Testaments" (*libri . . . tam Veteris quam Novi Testamenti*, §11).[2]

All of this is related to the Council's teaching about Revelation, which is not understood as an aesthetic reality, a literary *corpus* that remains a perennial written expression of the divine will; but rather it is understood as a dynamic and dialogical reality, as a historical reality that implies the response of human beings to the God who reveals himself (cf. §§2–6). The books are its written and inspired testimony.[3] By treating of one single history, those books present a profound unity; they form one Sacred Scripture (§7), one single Book.

8.2. The relationship between *DV* §14 and *DV* §§15–16

After covering divine Revelation (ch. I) and its transmission (ch. II), as well as inspiration and interpretation of divine Scripture (ch. III), *Dei verbum* dedicates a chapter to the Old Testament. In §14[4] it treats of the Old Testament in itself, emphasizing creation and the covenant with the people of Israel and

---

2. Only in its final redaction does it seem to refer to a literary corpus: "That is why the Church from the very beginning accepted as her own that very ancient Greek translation of the Old Testament [*graecam illam antiquissimam Veteris Testamenti versionem*] which is called the Septuagint" (*DV* §22).

3. Cf. §17: "Now the writings of the New Testament stand as a perpetual and divine *witness* to these realities." And §18: "It is common knowledge that among all the Scriptures, even those of the New Testament, the Gospels have a special preeminence, and rightly so, for they are the principal witness for the life and teaching of the incarnate Word, our savior." "The Council considers the two orders of salvation in their totality and is not simply limited to the books that are the testimony of them." Béda Rigaux, "Dogmatische Konstitution über die göttliche Offenbarung," 558–570 in *Lexicon für Theologie und Kirche*, vol. 2, *Das Zweite Vatikanische Konzil: Dokumente und Kommentare*, ed. Josef Höfer and Karl Rahner (Freiburg: Herder, 1967), 558.

4. Cf. Ignacio Carbajosa, "La recuperación del Antiguo Testamento para la vida de la Iglesia: Estudio de *Dei Verbum* 14," 80–101 in *Un escriba en la corte del Rey*, Ensayos 475 (Madrid: Encuentro, 2012).

the self-revelation of God realized by these means; the economy of salvation perdures in the books of the Old Testament as a true word of God.

This "economy of the Old Testament" reappears at the beginning of §15, which demonstrates the finality of it in relation to the New Testament. Section 16, for its part, closes the chapter by underlining the unity of the books in both groupings. The Council thus offers an integrated doctrine about the meaning of the Old Testament, taken both on its own and in relation to the mystery of Christ, for Christians. In the following pages we offer an analysis of these two numbers of the constitution.

8.3. Diachronic analysis of *DV* §§15–16

It is well known that *Dei verbum* experienced a particularly complex process of redaction, which lasted a number of years.[5] For our work, we take as the point of reference the final redaction of the dogmatic constitution in light of the three previous redactions.[6] We will sometimes refer to the previous version of 1962, rejected by the first session of the Council (Schema I, *De fontibus*).[7] All of this will permit us to go deeper into the significance of the text and better perceive its finality and its newness.

a) DV §15: importance of the Old Testament for Christians

In the previous paragraph of the constitution the Council spoke about the "economy of salvation" of the Old Testament: this already contained, therefore, a saving power, as the historical Israel was able to experience in the fundamental moments of its existence. This salvific significance confers a perennial validity on the sacred books that testify to this economy. Now, however, the Council goes further and emphasizes the ultimate end of those writings: that is to say, from that economy, from that history of salvation. "In it we find an

---

5. Cf. Albert Vanhoye, "The Reception in the Church of the Dogmatic Constitution 'Dei Verbum,'" 104–125 in *Opening Up the Scriptures: Joseph Ratzinger and the Foundations of Biblical Interpretation*, ed José Granados, Carlos Granados, and Luis Sánchez-Navarro (Grand Rapids: Eerdmans, 2008), 104–105.

6. Cf. Francisco Gil Hellín, *Concilii Vaticani II Synopsis: Constitutio Dogmatica de Divina Revelatione Dei Verbum*, (Vatican City: Libreria Editrice Vaticana, 1993), 114–121. The official version of the document is found in AAS 68 (1966): 817–836. For a description of the history of this conciliar text, see José Perarnau, *Constitución dogmática sobre la Revelación divina: Edición, traducción, introducción, notas, comentario e índices*, Boletín Oficial del Obispado (Castellón de la Plana: Palacio Episcopal, 1966), 19–22.

7. The Latin text is found in Gil Hellín, *Synopsis*, 181–190.

abundance of symbols, images, words, and events that acquire a significance of prefigurations."[8]

As we know, the definitive redaction of the constitution dropped the titles that the previous redactions put before each paragraph, so that now the only titles in the official version are those of the chapters. But the one we attribute to this paragraph corresponds to the one that redactions II and III proposed: "The importance of the Old Testament for the Christian faithful" (*De momento Veteris Testamenti pro Christifidelibus*); it is notable to compare it with the one that figured in the first redaction: "The nature of the Old Testament and its books" (*Indoles Foederis Veteris Testamenti eiusque librorum*). Worth noting, first of all, is the substitution of *indoles* by the more significant *momentum*, which from the first instance underscores the importance of the Old Testament for Christians (who were not mentioned before, but are now). In the second place, the original title also spoke of "its books," while the latter omits this reference. As we have already indicated, this is coherent with the conciliar doctrine about revelation being a dialogical reality. What is truly important is the saving event; the written testimony of that event—despite its very elevated value[9]—is secondary; it is included in that event, emerges from it, and is oriented to it.

The principal reason for the Old Testament economy (DV §15a)

Veteris Testamenti oeconomia ad hoc potissimum disposita erat, ut Christi universorum redemptoris Regnique Messianici adventum praepararet, prophetice nuntiaret (cf. Lc. 24, 44; Io. 5, 39; I Pt. 1, 10) et variis typis significaret (cf. I Cor. 10, 11).	The plan of the old covenant was directed above all to preparing for the coming of Christ, the redeemer of all, and of the messianic kingdom, to announce this coming by prophecy (see Luke 24:44; John 5:39; 1 Peter 1:10), and to indicate its meaning through various types (see 1 Cor. 10:12).

In redaction III, regarding the Latin name of the Old Testament they opted, over and against the preceding redactions, for *testamentum* in place of *foedus*, a Latin term more in accord with the original meaning of the Hebrew *bərît* and the Greek *diathēkē* (pact, covenant) although less hallowed by the

---

8. Rigaux, "Dogmatische Konstitution," 560.

9. "The books of both the Old and New Testaments . . . because written under the inspiration of the Holy Spirit . . . have God as their author and have been handed on as such to the Church herself" (*DV* §11).

tradition; in fact, *Dei verbum* much prefers *testamentum* (used fourteen times) to *foedus* (used three times).[10] But the redactional emphasis of this paragraph falls on the adverb *potissimum* ("above all"), which modifies the principal verb and differentiates it from the preceding paragraph.[11] What has been said in it about the perennial value of the Old Testament retains all of its value; but the ultimate meaning, the "final cause" of the whole Old Testament economy, points beyond the Old Testament, toward the coming (*adventus*) of Christ and of his Kingdom. The Old Testament is *praeparatio evangelica* (*ut praepararet*).

Only in redaction III do we find the *potissimum*; the two previous redactions use *praesertim*, certainly synonymous, but lacking the expressive power of the superlative.[12] Let us note, however, that all of these redactions differ from *De fontibus*, where the Christological importance of the Old Testament was not presented as principal but rather as unique and exclusive.[13] *Dei verbum* presents a careful equilibrium between the substantive value of the Old Testament and its ordering to the New Testament. This allows us to understand that the Christological significance of the Old Testament is made possible thanks to the historical and salvific density of the events to which it testifies.

The Christological finality of the Old Testament is reinforced, as the Subcommittee indicates,[14] by the citations of the New Testament; these are more abundant than in redaction I, where only 1 Peter 1:10 and 1 Corinthians 10:11 are mentioned (the last text underlining the typological value of the Old Testament).[15] Both Luke 24:44 and John 5:39 constitute, within their respective gospels, principal testimonies about the relationship between Christ and

---

10. In the *Vulgate* there is a notable difference in this regard between the Old Testament and the New Testament. The Old Testament prefers *foedus* (used 226 times) over *testamentum* (71 times), while in the New Testament, *testamentum* appears 33 times and *foedus* only once (in Rom 1:31, without reference to the Covenant). It is probable that this fact influences the practice of the Constitution.

11. Translator's note: I have followed the Latin in translating *potissimum* as "above all"; the Gonzalez English translation uses "principal purpose."

12. As the Subcommittee indicates, "In place of *praesertim* is put *potissimum*, in order to express the Christological end of the Old Covenant." Gil Hellín, *Synopsis*, 114.

13. *De fontibus* 16b: "Consequently, the raison d'être and the importance of the whole Old Testament (*totius Veteris Testamenti ratio atque momentum*] resides in tending towards the New and being made clear in the New."

14. Gil Hellín, *Synopsis*, 114.

15. 1 Pet 1:10: "The prophets that prophesied of the grace that was to be yours searched and inquired about this salvation." 1 Cor 10:11: "Now these things happened to them as a warning [typologically: *tupikōs*], but they were written down for our instruction, upon whom the end of the ages has come."

Scripture.[16] These citations show that the Christological significance of the Old Testament was clearly perceived by the ancient Church.[17]

Importance of Old Testament Revelation (DV §15b)

| *Veteris autem Testamenti libri, pro condicione humani generis ante tempora instauratae a Christo salutis, Dei et hominis cognitionem ac modos quibus Deus iustus et misericors cum hominibus agit, omnibus manifestant.* | Now the books of the Old Testament, in accordance with the state of mankind before the time of salvation established by Christ, reveal to all men the knowledge of God and of man and the ways in which God, just and merciful, deals with men. |

The Christological finality does not diminish, as we have already indicated, the validity of the Old Testament teaching. The writings of the Old Testament manifest an authentic knowledge of the true God, "just and merciful"; the present tense of the verb (*manifestant*) indicates the present reality that the conciliar text attributes to these writings.[18] It is not a full knowledge, which will only arrive in Jesus Christ; all the same, the successive redactions attest to a process of validating the Old Testament testimony. Redaction I said that "the books of the Old Testament supply, *although not yet perfectly* [*etsi nondum perfecte*], the knowledge of God and man to believers." But now from redaction II on, we read in its place a reference to the "state of mankind before the time of salvation established by Christ"; with this, which implies an imperfection but does not make it explicit, they avoid directly qualifying the knowledge of God supplied by the Old Testament as imperfect, and they anticipate the "divine pedagogy" that is spoken about in this same paragraph. The imperfection of the Old Testament is pedagogical; it responds to the condition of its addressees who need salvation.

The comparison with redaction I indicates another revealing change: there it was said that the books of the Old Testament provide knowledge of God and of human beings "to believers"; but from redaction II until the final document it is affirmed that those books manifest this knowledge "to all" (*omnibus*). This is related to another change from redaction I: there they cited, in addition to the knowledge of God and of man, the ethical teaching of the Old Testament.[19]

---

16. Luke 24:44: "Then he said to them, 'These are my words which I spoke to you, while I was still with you, that everything written about me in the law of Moses and the prophets and the psalms must be fulfilled.'" John 5:39: "You search the scriptures, because you think that in them you have eternal life; and it is they that bear witness to me."

17. Rigaux, "Dogmatische Konstitution," 560.

18. Rigaux, "Dogmatische Konstitution," 561.

19. "[A]nd they teach the ways in which . . . any man whatsoever should behave rightly concerning God and his neighbors."

But now from the second redaction on, they drop this reference and extend for all men the validity of the knowledge of God and of man provided by the Old Testament.[20]

We find ourselves, therefore, with the written testimony of a knowledge which has not yet arrived at its full development but has been adapted to the human condition before the coming of Christ; yet despite this, it is valid and saving for all men. The Old Testament does not limit its radius of action to the people of the Covenant, but rather its teaching has universal reach. *Verbum autem Dei nostri manet in aeternum* (Isa 40:8).

The divine pedagogy witnessed to in the Old Testament (DV §15c)

Qui libri, quamvis etiam imperfecta et temporaria contineant, veram tamen paedagogiam divinam demonstrant.	These books, though they also contain some things which are incomplete and temporary, nevertheless show us true divine pedagogy.

Both this sentence and the following one were introduced into redaction II, but they have undergone a significant evolution. Redaction II said, "though they contain many imperfect and provisional [*provisoria*] things [*plura*]," while in redaction III we read, "though they contain some things [*quaedam*] which are imperfect and temporal [*temporalia*]." The definitive text reads: "though they *also* [*etiam*] contain some things which are incomplete and temporary [*imperfecta et temporaria*, without a substantive]." With this [last redaction] those elements of imperfection are toned down. And, without a doubt, the emphasis of this sentence goes back to the principal sentence: the affirmation of the divine pedagogy which connects to the "admirable condescendence" of God evoked in §13.[21] Redaction II said that these books "conserve [*servant*] the importance of a true divine pedagogy even for Christians [*etiam pro Christifidelibus*]"; the omission of this last phrase from redaction III intentionally gives universal value to this affirmation, as the Subcommittee explicitly affirms.[22]

The reference to the divine pedagogy witnessed to by the Old Testament was introduced in redaction II. But redaction III reinforced this reference: instead of "conserve the importance of," we read "show us true divine pedagogy." The

20. The Subcommittee explains: "The correction sufficiently implies that the ethical teaching of the Old Testament *does not have universal value* for every human epoch [non habet vim universalem *pro omni hominum aetate*]." Gil Hellín, *Synopsis*, 114.

21. Cf. Lyonnet, "La elaboración de los capítulos IV y VI de la 'Dei Verbum,'" 119.

22. "So that the text can have universal validity here, the words *etiam pro Christifidelibus* are omitted." Gil Hellín, *Synopsis*, 115.

subcommittee indicates as much: "this new correction insists sufficiently that God wants to use these books today as instruments for instructing men."[23] In all this we discover an allusion to the function of the Law as a pedagogue, which is affirmed by Paul.[24] But the proximate origin of this expression is found in the encyclical *Mit brennender Sorge* of Pius XI (1937);[25] there this assertion was for the purpose of stressing the value of the Old Testament writings in the face of a totalitarian ideology that justified its anti-Semitism with the theological devaluation of Hebrew Scripture.[26] This polemic now having been overcome, the expression [in the Council] recognizes in the Old Testament a very elevated value. For, if its writings testify to the divine pedagogy, this fact makes them a path that the Christian believer must traverse constantly in order to arrive at Christ. "The Church expressly uses the pages of the Old Testament to *introduce her children more and more profoundly into the mystery of salvation* and prepare them *to receive Christ* the Savior in their own life."[27]

Perennial teachings of the Old Testament (DV §15d)

Unde iidem libri, qui vivum sensum Dei exprimunt, in quibus sublimes de Deo doctrinae ac salutaris de vita hominis sapientia mirabilesque precum thesauri reconduntur, in quibus tandem latet mysterium salutis nostrae, a Christifidelibus devote accipiendi sunt.	These same books, then, give expression to a lively sense of God, contain a store of sublime teachings about God, sound wisdom about human life, and a wonderful treasury of prayers, and in them the mystery of our salvation is present in a hidden way. Christians should receive them with reverence.

23. Gil Hellín, *Synopsis*, 116.

24. Gal 3:24–25: "So that the law was our custodian [pedagogue] until Christ came, that we might be justified by faith. But now that faith has come, we are no longer under a custodian." It is, in addition to 1 Cor 4:15, the only time that we find the Greek term *paidagōgos* in the Bible.

25. Gil Hellín, *Synopsis*, 116.

26. "It is precisely in the twilight of this background that one perceives the striking perspective of the divine tutorship [pedagogy] of salvation [*die Heilspädagogik des Ewigen*], as it warns, admonishes, strikes, raises, and beautifies its elect. Nothing but ignorance and pride could blind one to the treasures hoarded in the Old Testament." Pius XI, *Mit brennender Sorge* (March 14, 1937), 145–167 in AAS 29 (1937), §15. The magisterial reference was also found in *De fontibus*; but there it served to underline the *indoles incompleta* of the Old Testament, while now it supports the affirmation about the divine pedagogy testified to in those writings. Its use is therefore now more in conformity with its original intention.

27. Augustin Bea, *La doctrina del Concilio sobre la Revelación: La palabra de Dios y la humanidad*, BRFT 16 (Madrid: Razón y Fe, 1968), 234.

The examination of the diverse phases of this last sentence of *DV* §15 attests to a process of the Old Testament writings increasing in value simultaneously with the redactional evolution.[28] In redaction I the sentence is totally absent. Redaction II recognized the necessity for Christians to read them attentively "especially because they luminously express a lively sense [*vividum sensum*] of the most holy and clement God." In redaction III it is said, no longer that one ought to read them attentively, but that one ought to receive them with devotion [*devote*][29]—not only because they express a lively sense of God but also "because they contain a store of sublime teachings about God, sound wisdom about human life, and a wonderful treasury of prayers."[30] This sentence went into the definitive redaction in its entirety, with one difference: the causal *quia* ("because") is replaced by *in quibus* (in which). One thus has the impression that the valuable things of the Old Testament are not, so to speak, the ultimate motive for accepting these books: this is based on the tradition of the Church, which has recognized them as inspired by God.[31]

The Old Testament contains, therefore, a series of inalienable teachings for the Christian. Above all about God himself: "In the New Testament this doctrine is not treated on its own, but rather it is presupposed and applied; and it is completely indispensable even for understanding God's mode of working with man in the New Covenant, and in particular for understanding the person and the mission of Christ."[32] In the second place, regarding man: the Old Testament anthropology—think about the first chapters of Genesis, for example—in its dogmatic and ethical aspects, constitutes an irreplaceable knowledge that will find its greatest splendor in the New Testament.[33] Finally, regarding the rela-

---

28. "Until arriving at the current form, the text grew in an organic manner." Perarnau, *Constitución sobre la Revelación*, 121.

29. The Commission explains that "in place of *legendi sunt* they put *devote accipiendi sunt*, because the reading of the books is better spoken about in chapter 6." Gil Hellín, *Synopsis*, 116.

30. Béda Rigaux mentions among these teachings the concept of the Messiah and his eschatological lordship, individual retribution after death, personal responsibility, and love of neighbor ("Dogmatische Konstitution," 561).

31. "For holy mother Church, relying on the belief of the Apostles (see John 20:31; 2 Tim. 3:16; 2 Peter 1:19–20, 3:15–16), holds that the books of both the Old and New Testaments in their entirety, with all their parts, are sacred and canonical because written under the inspiration of the Holy Spirit, they have God as their author and have been handed on as such to the Church herself" (*DV* §11).

32. Bea, *La doctrina del Concilio sobre la Revelación*, 230.

33. A significant example is the doctrine about matrimony: Jesus' innovation about the illicitness of divorce emerges from his interpretation of Genesis. Cf. Luis Sánchez Navarro, "Mt. 19:3–9: Una nueva perspectiva," *Estudios Bíblicos* 58 (2000): 211–238.

tionship between man and God: "the wonderful treasury of prayers," whose paradigmatic expression is found in the Psalms, forms a necessary part of the liturgy and the piety of the Church, and thus has substantially contributed to configuring genuine Christian spirituality.[34]

The final redaction of the document added another subordinate clause to this already long sentence, which underlines the historical-salvific significance of the Old Testament emphasized at the beginning of this paragraph: "and in them the mystery of our salvation is present in a hidden way [*latet*]";[35] the "mystery" will be spoken about again in §17.[36] The writings of the Old Testament, therefore, not only contain valuable teachings about God and man, but also they enclose the hidden mystery of our salvation; from this it follows that they are in every way essential for the Christian. With this affirmation, finally, is anticipated the citation of Augustine that we find in the following paragraph.

b) DV §16: unity of the two Testaments

The title that introduced this paragraph in redaction I was "The mutual relationship between the New and Old Testament"; the Subcommittee decided to change it starting with redaction II, because they considered that the paragraph spoke of the unity of both more than the relationship between them.[37]

Deus igitur librorum utriusque Testamenti inspirator et auctor, ita sapienter disposuit, ut Novum in Vetere lateret et in Novo Vetus pateret.	God, the inspirer and author of [the books of] both Testaments, wisely arranged that the New Testament be hidden in the Old and the Old be made manifest in the New.

This sentence is found without modification from the first redaction on, with a minor exception: starting from redaction II it says "inspirer and author of the books of both Testaments" where before we read simply "inspirer and author of both Testaments"; as the Subcommittee indicates, the word "books" is introduced because the inspiration affects the books in themselves.[38] The

---

34. "The Psalter has become the book of prayers *par excellence*, by which and with which the community is directed to God" (Bea, *La doctrina del Concilio sobre la Revelación*, 233).

35. This addition responds to the initiative of five conciliar Fathers, accepted by the Commission as an allusion to Messianism (Gil Hellín, *Synopsis*, 117).

36. "This mystery had not been manifested to other generations as it was now revealed to His holy Apostles and prophets" (*DV* §17).

37. Gil Hellín, *Synopsis*, 118.

38. Gil Hellín, *Synopsis*, 118. Translator's note: the English translation of *Dei verbum* does not include "the books."

clear allusion to the sentence of Augustine, *Novum in Vetere latet et in Novo Vetus patet,* was absent from *De fontibus* and expresses very appropriately the interpenetration of the Old and New Testaments;[39] this formula, which not only recognizes the contribution of the New Testament to the Old but also the positive value of the Old, which hides the New within it,[40] "is valid both for the field of exegesis and for the profound realities which are treated here."[41] The conciliar text shows (*ita . . . ut*) that this fact responds to the will and the wisdom of God, presented as the inspirer and author of both Testaments (along with what is evoked in §11 of the constitution, regarding the inspiration of Scripture). To devalue or negate this unity is something directly contrary to the revelatory and salvific plan of God. "The Old Testament is, now and always, a Christian book: not by a tolerant acceptance, but by something intrinsic and constitutive that, in the end, is manifested."[42]

Nam, etsi Christus in sanguine suo Novum Foedus condidit (cf. Lc. 22:20; I Cor. 11:25), libri tamen Veteris Testamenti integri in praeconio evangelico assumpti, in Novo Testamento significationem suam completam acquirunt et ostendunt (cf. Mt. 5:17; Lc. 24:27; Rom. 16:25–26; 2 Cor. 3:14–16), illudque vicissum illuminant et explicant.	For, though Christ established the new covenant in His blood (see Luke 22:20; 1 Cor. 11:25), still the books of the Old Testament with all their parts, caught up into the proclamation of the Gospel, (3) acquire and show forth their full meaning in the New Testament (see Matt. 5:17; Luke 24:27; Rom. 16:25–26; 2 Cor. 14:16) and in turn shed light on it and explain it.

The Council avoids a possible misunderstanding that could arise from the conception of the New Testament according to the idea of substitution. Christ indeed founded a New Covenant, just as the first two biblical texts cited express. But both Luke and Paul go back with this expression to Jeremiah 31:31, the prophecy of the New Covenant: the origin of the New is in the Old. A logic of substitution does not fit here, but rather a logic of fulfillment: this is how the

39. Augustine, *Questions on the Heptateuch,* book 2, chapter 73 (PL 34:623).

40. Cf. Lyonnet, "La elaboración de los capítulos IV y VI de la 'Dei Verbum,'" 121.

41. Rigaux, "Dogmatische Konstitution," 562. "Already the apostolic teaching cites and elaborates on the Old Testament, in order to clarify and deepen its message. The Fathers of the Church carry on this enterprise. They give proof that this recourse is justified, and elaborate on the basis of spiritual understanding a hermeneutic that allows Christians to grow in a religious life marked by the Word of God" (562).

42. Luis Alonso Schökel, "El Antiguo Testamento (DV 14–16)," 495–575 in *Comentarios a la constitución Dei Verbum sobre la divina revelación,* ed. L. Alonso Schökel, BAC 284 (Madrid: Biblioteca de Autores Cristianos, 1969), 496.

adjective *kainos* functions in the books of the New Testament.[43] The Council boldly signals, in the first place, that the New confers the full meaning on the books of the Old and demonstrates that meaning, but additionally, that the Old for its part illuminates and explains the New. Again they are presented as two intimately linked realities; the unity between the two Covenants causes their written testimonies to form *one* book. This is emphasized by the four New Testament citations provided, some of the most significant affirmations of fulfillment in the Gospels and the letters of Paul: Matthew 5:17, Luke 24:27, Romans 16:25–26, and 2 Corinthians 3:14–16.[44] Also on this point the document experienced an evolution.[45]

Upon comparing the final text with the previous redactions, we again perceive a progressive validation of the books of the Old Covenant. It passes from "the institutions of the Old Testament, fitting only for the time of preparation, were derogated by the New Law" (redaction I) to "the Old Testament gave way, by the death of Christ, to the New" (II), and from here to "Christ established the New Covenant in his blood" (III and *DV*; from this last redaction was rejected the proposal by a Father to add *prius veterans*, "declaring the first antiquated"[46]). The elimination of the references to the derogation and expira-

---

43. Cf. Domingo Muñoz León, *Derás: Los caminos y sentidos de la palabra divina en la Escritura, Parte I: Derás targúmico y Derás neotestamentario*, BHBib 12 (Madrid: Consejo Superior de Investigaciones Científicas, 1987), 236–239: "El cumplimiento expresado como Novedad (superación)."

44. Matt 5:17: "Think not that I have come to abolish the law and the prophets; I have come not to abolish them but to fulfil them." Luke 24:27: "And beginning with Moses and all the prophets, he interpreted to them in all the scriptures the things concerning himself." Rom 16:25–26: "Now to him who is able to strengthen you according to my gospel and the preaching of Jesus Christ, according to the revelation of the mystery which was kept secret for long ages but is now disclosed and through the prophetic writings is made known to all nations, according to the command of the eternal God, to bring about the obedience of faith . . ." 2 Cor 3:14–16: "But their minds were hardened; for to this day, when they read the old covenant, that same veil remains unlifted, because only through Christ is it taken away. Yes, to this day whenever Moses is read a veil lies over their minds; *but when a man turns to the Lord the veil is removed* [cf. Exod 34:34]."

45. In redaction I, no text is cited; redaction II goes back to Matt 5:17 *passim* and Rom 8:2–3. But redaction III omits these two texts "because they do not demonstrate this doctrine," and includes 2 Cor 3:14. The definitive redaction adds, at the petition of three conciliar Fathers, the references to Matthew, Luke, and Romans 16. The change of opinion regarding Matt 5:17 draws attention. Cf. Gil Hellín, *Synopsis*, 120–121. To these references we must add, finally, the ones that we see at the beginning of §15.

46. He wanted to allude to Heb 8:13: "In speaking of a new covenant, he treats the first as obsolete [*veteravit prius*]. And what is becoming obsolete and growing old is ready to vanish away."

tion of the Old Testament again shows us a growing appreciation of its religious content; to this is added the conclusive affirmation of the importance of the Old Testament for understanding the New Testament, introduced in redaction III (*illustrant*) and amplified in the final redaction for stylistic and doctrinal reasons: *illuminant et explicant*.[47] The conciliar Fathers had a special interest in clarifying all these teachings. "The books of the Old Testament not only receive meaning, but also they provide it; they reflect the light received from Christ in order to illuminate the books of the New."[48]

8.4. The challenge of the unity between the Old and New Testament

The process of redaction of the constitution *Dei verbum* gave rise, as we have been able to demonstrate, to a reevaluation of the Old Testament in its dimensions concerning history, doctrine (teaching about God and man), and prayer. But this fact does not mean that the Council advocates for an "Old Testamentism," a return to the Old that prescinds from the New. The Old Testament is valued in the context of the interest of manifesting its unity with the New Testament. In other words, in an ecclesial context.

The insistence on distinguishing "the writings" from the realities that form the Old and the New Testament shows the true nature of these [Scriptures] in the economy of revelation. They are the written and inspired testimony of God's revelation; they are not in themselves that revelation to which they give witness.[49] In this way, at the same time that their importance is underlined, it is clarified that revelation—the dialogue between God and human beings—transcends the writings; as this document will say later, "For in the sacred books,

47. "Three Fathers propose that, in place of *illustrant*, one should put *illuminant et explicant*. On the one hand, in order to put two other verbs in the place of *acquirunt et ostendunt*, but also to insist that Christ understands himself according to the Scriptures of the Old Testament." Gil Hellín, *Synopsis*, 121.

48. Alonso Schökel, "El Antiguo Testamento," 527. Cf. Lyonnet, "La elaboración de los capítulos IV y VI de la 'Dei Verbum,'" 121–124.

49. "In today's theological lingo, it is common to term the Bible 'Revelation' without qualification. This usage would never have occurred to the ancients. Revelation is a dynamic event between God and man, which again and again becomes reality only in their encounter. The biblical Word attests to Revelation, but does not contain it in the sense of absorbing it and turning it into a sort of thing that one could stick in one's pocket. The Bible attests to Revelation, but the concept of Revelation as such is broader." Joseph Ratzinger, "Biblical Interpretation in Conflict," trans. Adrian Walker, 1–29 in *Opening Up the Scriptures: Joseph Ratzinger and the Foundations of Biblical Interpretation*, ed. José Granados, Carlos Granados, and Luis Sánchez-Navarro (Grand Rapids: Eerdmans, 2008), 26.

the Father who is in heaven meets His children with great love and speaks with them" (§21).

The Council also firmly maintains the internal unity between the two Testaments. Not only is the Old ordained to the New; but also the New requires the Old in order to be illuminated and explained.[50] The Council uses bold expressions, although they are in line with the New Testament affirmations (as the biblical references are able to prove). Even though it is not a symmetrical relationship, one can speak about the Old and New Testaments as mutual hermeneutical keys. The understanding of one depends on the other. This has consequences for the order of interpretation:

> It is certain that our Constitution does not speak *directly* about this aspect, but rather about the mode in which the books *themselves* of the Old and New Testaments mutually illuminate each other; but from here one deduces an evident *conclusion*: whoever truly wants to comprehend the sacred books should allow himself to be guided by these very books, and therefore, by their mode of interpreting the Old Testament in light of the New and vice versa.[51]

With its interest in the Old Testament, the Council has put before our eyes a reality that, although traditional in the Church, has suffered contradictions in the history of theology, even recently. In the ancient Church, the paradigmatic case is that of Marcion.[52] In recent theology we must remember how the exclusive use of the historical-critical method, which relegates the text to the past, makes its prophetic dimension impossible, practically speaking.

> For, on this assumption, the continuity between the two Testaments that is asserted in the New Testament writings is precisely one of those elements of mystification that the historian has unmasked as a strategy of the later

---

50. "The Old Testament makes us better understand the meaning of the New by reminding us of its origin and its preparation, and its cultural and religious atmosphere, the fact of which is the fulfillment of the history of salvation, begun in the Old Covenant and continued without interruption or discontinuity in the New." Roger Schutz and Max Thurian, *La Palabra viva del Concilio: Texto y comentarios de la Constitución sobre la Revelación* (Madrid: Studium, 1967), 128.

51. Bea, *La doctrina del Concilio sobre la Revelación*, 238.

52. "The Old Testament, according to Marcion, came from a god unworthy of the name because he was vindictive and bloodthirsty, while the New Testament revealed a God of reconciliation and generosity. The Church firmly rejected this error, reminding all that God's tenderness was already revealed in the Old Testament." John Paul II, Address to Members of the Pontifical Biblical Commission (April 11, 1997); English trans. "Old Testament Essential to Know Jesus," *L'Osservatore Romano* 30, no. 17 (April 23, 1997), p. 2, §2a.

community to construct a legitimacy for itself. At the same time, however, it becomes clear as if in a sudden flash just how far this retrieval of the putative origin really is from what the New Testament actually says. After all, a constitutive feature of the New Testament is the awareness of its unity with the entire witness of the Old Testament, which only now, it claims, can be understood as a unity and as a meaningful totality.[53]

This fact has not impeded the recent development in theology of some interesting projects of biblical theology based precisely on the differentiated unity between the two Testaments;[54] but it certainly involves a path that still needs to be traversed.[55] The following words of Enrique Farfán serve as a demonstration of the fruitfulness of this approach and as closure to these pages; in them is shown, on the subject of Isaiah 41:17, the prophetic background of the culminating moment of the New Testament revelation: the death of Jesus, which John presents as the definitive fulfillment of the Scriptures.

> This dryness of the elected people (which the Lord promises to transform) perhaps also figures into the extreme aridity of the favored Son who is abandoned (cf. Mark 15:34): ἡ πέτρα δὲ ἦν ὁ Χριστός [and the rock was Christ] (1 Cor 10:4). To the Servant (Acts 8:35), [who is] the shoot from the land that is dry from our crimes (Isa 53:2, 6), corresponds the feeling of complete thirst that takes away the sin of the world. "In order to fulfil the Scripture" (Ps 69:22 only?), Christ thirsts (John 19:28). And God, by an unknown Moses, converts him into a spring (John 19:34).[56]

8.5. Conclusion

We conclude our reflections with the confirmation of this challenge, which remains open; it is necessary to go deeper, exegetically and theologically, into the unity of the New Covenant with the Old. We have shown that the Second Vatican Council, while progressively highlighting the value of the Old Testament books as written testimony of a salvific economy, also emphasized the Christological reality as the uniting factor of all of Scripture. It is probably one

---

53. Ratzinger, "Biblical Interpretation in Conflict," 12.

54. In the Catholic camp the effort of Paul Beauchamp is worth mentioning; and in the Protestant circle, Brevard S. Childs. See the previous chapter.

55. A comprehensive bibliography regarding this question can be found in *Vetus in Novo: El recurso a la Escritura en el Nuevo Testamento*, ed. Filippo Belli, Ignacio Carbajosa, Carlos Jódar Estrella, and Luis Sánchez Navarro, Ensayos 290 (Madrid: Encuentro, 2006), 225–259.

56. Enrique Farfán Navarro, *El desierto transformado: Una imagen deuteroisaiana de regeneración*, AnBib 130 (Rome: Pontifical Biblical Institute, 1992), 82.

of the conciliar teachings that most needs attention and development, because the Council presents the unity between the two Testaments as a fruitful path for the renewal of biblical studies according to the Spirit in which they were written (cf. *DV* §12). Numbers 15 and 16 of the constitution *Dei verbum*, in their letter and spirit—that spirit that is clarified in light of the history of its redaction—offer us the necessary elements of that renewal.

9

A Model for the Relationship between
the Old and New Testaments: 1 Corinthians 9:9

Carlos Granados

9.1. An unfortunate interpretation?

Paul proposes in 1 Corinthians 9:9 (and cf. 1 Timothy 5:17) an interpretation of the precept from Deuteronomy 25:4 that has led to criticism or reservations from more than one exegete. First, I give the text here:

> 1 Cor 9:9–11: For it is written in the law of Moses, "You shall not muzzle an ox when it is treading out the grain." Is it for oxen that God is concerned? Does he not speak entirely for our sake? It was written for our sake, because the plowman should plow in hope and the thresher thresh in hope of a share in the crop. If we have sown spiritual good among you, is it too much if we reap your material benefits?

Hans Conzelmann affirmed that "the quotation—Deut 25:4—is, contrary to Paul's exegesis, essentially a rule for the protection of animals."[1] In an even more severe way, Frank Crüsemann wrote with an ironic tone that "far from what Paul presupposed in his rhetorical question of 1 Cor 9:9s, God is quite concerned about the oxen," in order then to completely reject Paul's "symbolic or figurative interpretation," for "there should not remain any doubt that [in Deut 25:4] it is primarily and above all about a regulation referring to the

---

1. See Hans Conzelmann, *1 Corinthians: A Commentary on the First Epistle to the Corinthians* (Philadelphia: Fortress, 1975), 154–155.

proper way to act with domestic beasts."[2] What should we say about these and other similar opinions? What value should we give to the Pauline interpretation of the text?

Taking as a sample Paul's use of Deuteronomy 25:4 in 1 Corinthians 9, we will attempt to shed some light in these pages on the problem of the literal sense of the biblical text. The specific questions that will constitute our point of departure could be formulated in the following way: Is Paul proposing in 1 Corinthians 9:9-11 an allegorical and ultimately arbitrary usage (*ad usum*) of Scripture?[3] Can we really say that he is departing from the "literal sense" of the Old Testament text?

9.2. The laws referring to animals in the Old Testament

In order to confront the interpretative question just proposed, we begin with the Old Testament, trying first to understand the specific sense of the law of Deuteronomy 25:4.

The content of the law of Deuteronomy 25:4, in other words, that of a precept that imposes particular consideration toward the animal, continues to cause a certain perplexity, at least regarding its ethical value. It is thus necessary in the first place to try to understand its meaning. We should begin by noting that the same literary theme is present in other texts within the legal Old Testament *corpus*.[4] Here are some examples of laws that contain similar motives:

- The precept of leaving the female bird that is sitting on her eggs alive (Deut 22:6-7).
- The famous norm "You shall not boil a kid in its mother's milk" (probably referring to not eating a kid that still drinks its mother's milk; Exod 23:19; 34:26; Deut 14:21).[5]

2. See Frank Crüsemann, *Die Tora: Theologie und Sozialgeschichte des alttestamentlichen Gesetzes* (Gütersloh: Gütersloher Verlagshaus, 2005), 304, 308–309.

3. William Arndt, "The Meaning of 1 Cor 9:9, 10," *Concordia Theological Monthly* 3 (1932): 329–335, maintains that the Pauline argument assumes an allegorical and mystical understanding of Deuteronomy which, even without entirely violating the literal sense, does not depend on it either.

4. Julian Morgenstern, "The Book of the Covenant, IV," *Hebrew Union College Annual* 33 (1962): 59–105, at 100, even postulated the existence of a small autonomous compendium of laws referring to the care of animals.

5. See Gianni Barbiero, *L'asino del nemico: Rinuncia alla vendetta e amore del nemico nella legislazione dell'Antico Testamento (Est 23,4-5; Dt 22, 1-4; Lv 19, 17-18)*, AnBib 128 (Rome: Pontifical Biblical Institute, 1991), 165: "The prohibition to cook a kid in its mother's milk ex-

- The obligation to conduct a lost animal back to its owner and help the ass suffocated by the weight of its cargo (Exod 23:4–5; Deut 22:1–4).
- The Sabbath precept, which obliges one to give repose to the son, daughter, manservant, maidservant, ox, ass, and all the beasts of the household (cf. Exod 20:10; 23:13; Deut 5:14).

As we have said, in light of these examples there are immediate questions that arise which we can formulate in these terms: is the animal perhaps the subject of legal rights in Israel? In what sense is the world of ethics put into play when it is about the relationship between man and animal? Do we then provide some criteria of a general type that will help us to find a response?

1) The meaning of these laws referring to the care of animals can be seen as a way of representing (through a concrete expression that acquires the character of a symbol) the respect and the love toward the gift of life that has been entrusted to man by the Creator.[6]

2) The question of violence is also implicated in these laws about the protection of animals. Cruelty in the treatment of animals is condemnable not because the beast is the subject of an ethical right, but because through it man shows a senseless behavior, a reprehensible internal disorder. The relative similarity between man and animals makes the violence loosed upon them more shocking than using force on a plant; in fact, this becomes even more cruel when it produces the spilling of blood or when the animal is defenseless or injured.

3) Given the close relationship of this theme with the world of wisdom writings, which is where it is developed in a more consistent manner (cf., e.g., Prov 12:10),[7] we could understand its meaning from the attitude of the wise man described in Proverbs 27:23–27. This proverb says that the obligation of tending to domestic beasts with care has the purpose of assuring the provision of wool and milk in order to clothe and feed everyone in the household. In

presses that same respect for life in its birth and in its manifestations that inspired Dt 22, 6s." See further the work of Othmar Keel, in particular: *Das Böcklein in der Milch seiner Mutter und Verwandtes: Im Lichte eines altorientalischen Bildmotivs*, OBO 33 (Freiburg: Vandenhoeck und Ruprecht, 1980).

6. Thus the precepts referring to animals in Deut 22:1–4, 6 *passim*, will extend the consideration about the theme of human life in Deut 19–21, now expressing through a symbolic reference the respect towards this life that the creator causes (cf. Barbiero, *L'asino*, 149).

7. See, above all, the already cited work of Keel, *Das Böcklein*, 51; and also Luis Alonso Schökel and José Vílchez, *Sapienciales*, vol. 1, *Proverbios* (Madrid: Cristiandad, 1984), 291. Keel's book offers abundant documentation regarding the presence of this theme in the Eastern context.

this sense, the laws obliging one to respect animals could refer to the ethical responsibility of man toward those who depend on the survival of said beasts for their maintenance (the "household" and the "maidservants" in Prov 27:27), as well as even those who will be able to profit later (future generations).

4) As a corollary to the two previous observations, we can add that frequently these legal dispositions favor the protection of animals in order to inculcate respect for the human life that is subjugated (under the yoke) or threatened. The human–animal relationship is frequently represented in Scripture as a symbolic translation of justice which man is called to fulfill in his interpersonal relationships.[8] Therefore, in certain laws that regulate one's behavior with animals, one could see underlying them that statement of Matthew 12:12: "Of how much more value is a man than a sheep!"[9] We will see this shortly with regard to the subject of Deuteronomy 25:4.

This care for animals acquires, therefore, in certain cases, the value of a symbolic gesture whose ultimate beneficiary is not the animals but one's neighbor. This perspective is made evident, for example, in the law referring to the help that one should give to his enemy's ass, formulated in Exodus 23:4–5 in this way:

> If you meet your enemy's ox or his ass going astray, you shall bring it back to him (עֹזֵב לוֹ). If you see the ass of one who hates you lying under its burden, you shall refrain from leaving him with it, you shall help him to lift it up (עָזֹב עִמּוֹ).[10]

The subtle play of the pronouns in the emphatic position reveals who is the true receiver of the action. It is not directly the animal, but its owner, your enemy. That is to say, the meaning of the prescribed action is not "to aid the fallen beast" but "to help your enemy harness it again." The rabbinic tradition has clearly seen the parabolic meaning of this precept and the intention

---

8. Paul Beauchamp, "Création et fondation de la Loi en Gen 1, 1–2,4a: Le don de la nourriture végétale en Gn 1,29s," 105–144 in *Pages exégétiques*, ed. Yves Simoens, LeDiv 202 (Paris: Cerf, 2005), sees this perspective as realized in the theme of the "dominion over animals" (Gen 1:26–28) which is linked to the vegetarian regimen (Gen 1:29–30). Only after the flood is eating animal flesh permitted (cf. Gen 9:2–3) as an expression that the utopian regime of harmony and peace originally established cannot be recovered, once the reality of violence has been introduced into the world of interpersonal relationships (cf. Gen 9:6).

9. See in this respect, Luis Sánchez Navarro, "*Cuánto más vale un hombre* (Mt 12, 12): La dignidad humana en Mateo," 561–572 in *Una ley de libertad para la vida del mundo*, ed. Juan José Pérez-Soba, Juan Larrú, and Jaime Ballesteros, CMat 4 (Madrid: Universidad Eclesiástica San Dámaso, 2007).

10. See Barbiero, *L'asino*, 82–88.

to prescribe, through a symbolic type of gesture, the love toward him who is presented as an enemy.[11] "If Exodus 23:4s and Deuteronomy 22:1–4 ask one to restore to the enemy his lost ass and to help him to lift up his fallen ass, it is in order to overcome, with this demonstration of solidarity, the hate that reigned between the two persons"; in other words, it is about a demonstrative gesture.[12]

9.3. The meaning of the law of Deuteronomy 25:4

In light of these principles of a general type, what should we say about the law of Deuteronomy 25:4?

Crüsemann, as we indicated earlier, has vigorously reacted to any interpretation of a symbolic kind, affirming that Deuteronomy 25:4 "is a law about the treatment of domestic animals. . . . The ox, which is subjugated to man as a beast of burden and of work, receives here similar rights to those of a human being (cf. Deut 23:25)."[13] This affirmation of Crüsemann is understood also as a reaction to that tendency to forget or devalue the ecological component of Scripture. It seems to us, however, that Crüsemann makes a mistake in giving a directly ethical valence to the relationship of man with animals. In effect, it becomes enormously problematic to say that this animal, which the Israelite can kill and consume, and which YHWH regularly asks to be a sacrificial offering, is the subject of rights similar to those of a human being.

The posture of Walter C. Kaiser seems much more appropriate to us. This author, considering the broader context of this law (that is to say, Deut 24–25) and, in particular, some commandments like that of restoring a poor man's cloak (24:10–13), giving to the worker in need his wages on the same day (24:14–15), or leaving the gleanings and sheaves for the orphan, the stranger, and the widow (24:19–22), expresses the conviction that the legislator is not preoccupied in Deuteronomy 25:4 only with the oxen, but rather above all

11. In this sense, the midrash on the Psalms (99.4, §3), for example, says: "Or when a man going along the way sees his enemy's ass fallen down under its burden, he goes forward, lends a hand, and helps his enemy in loading and unloading. Then both men go into an inn, and the latter says: 'So-and-so is my friend after all, and I thought that he was my enemy.' They fall to talking with one another, and peace results between them. What was it that caused the two men to make peace and become friends? It was that the first man kept what is written in the Torah . . . (Exod 23:5)." *The Midrash on Psalms*, trans. William G. Braude, YJS 13 (New Haven, CT: Yale University Press, 1959), 2.

12. See Barbiero, *L'asino*, 337.

13. See Crüsemann, *Die Tora*, 309, which is based on the study of Eduard Nielsen, "'You Shall Not Muzzle an Ox While It Is Treading out the Corn,' Dt 25,4," 94–105 in *Law, History, and Tradition: Selected Essays by Eduard Nielsen* (Copenhagen: GEC Gads, 1983).

with the development of a form of humanity and compassion in the owner. "'It was the duties of *moral beings* to one another that God wished to impress' on mankind."[14]

The broader context, examined earlier, of other laws referring to animals in the Torah can effectively support this interpretation. The presumed perspective of this precept of Deuteronomy 25:4 is ethical, not because the animal is the subject of rights that are similar to human rights, but insofar as the mandate expresses, under the symbolic surface, a truth about the world regarding interpersonal relationships.

However, the recognition of this fact implies a powerful indeterminacy in the letter of Deuteronomy 25:4. If we admit that there is a symbolic surface whose application is not subsequently explained, it follows that the reader ought to specify its contents not only regarding the identification of the characters (the "ox" and the "owner") but also in reference to the very nature of the mandated action (to not muzzle). This indetermination has a positive value insofar as it confers on the text an interpretive potential that is much richer.

In this way, Deuteronomy 25:4 can be interpreted generically as a fitting gesture for expressing the respect owed to the Creator and the life that he causes in diverse manifestations. It would also express that ethical responsibility that concerns man in the care of the goods (in this case the ox) which serve him for the sake of giving his own [household] their necessary sustenance. But also in the background would be the theme of compassion, insofar as this precept intends to cause a series of internal dispositions that lead one to more humane behaviors toward one's neighbor. And from here it would follow that underlying the precept of Deuteronomy 25:4 is a type of argument that is *a fortiori* open to an extensive application within the immediate framework of chapters 24 and 25 (as Kaiser indicated): fulfilling the commandment of Deuteronomy 25:4 implies with all the more reason (when it is about a human person) that one ought to give payment to the worker in need on the same day (cf. Deut 24:14–15) or also to permit the stranger and the orphan to collect the fallen sheaves (cf. 24:19–22).

---

14. Walter C. Kaiser, "The Current Crisis in Exegesis and the Apostolic Use of Deuteronomy 25:4 in I Corinthians 9:8–10," *Journal of the Evangelical Theological Society* 21 (1978): 3–18, at 14; quoting Frédéric Louis Godet, *Commentary on the First Epistle of St. Paul to the Corinthians*, 2 vols., trans. A. Cusin (Grand Rapids: Zondervan, 1957), 2:11. We will return shortly to this article in order to evaluate the content of the thesis defended by Kaiser. See in a similar vein other authors like J. T. Noonan, "The Muzzled Ox," *Jewish Quarterly Review* 70 (1979–1980): 172–175.

9.4. The interpretation of Paul in 1 Corinthians 9:8–11

Now that we have analyzed the meaning of the Deuteronomic precept in its literary context, we can see how Paul interpreted it in 1 Corinthians.

In 1 Corinthians 9, the Apostle defends his right as a preacher to receive a material payment with many arguments: *first*, in verse 7, from human reasoning (*kata anthrōpon*, v. 8); *second*, in verses 8–11, from the authority of Scripture (*ho nomos*, v. 8); *third*, in verses 12–13, by examining the common practice in the Church and in other religions; *fourth*, in verse 14, by reminding us about the teaching of the Lord himself (*ho kurios dietaxen*, v. 14).

In particular we are interested in verses 8–11, which deal with the scriptural argument. It is fitting first of all to clarify what Paul does *not* affirm in these verses. In other words, the (implicit) response to the rhetorical question of 1 Corinthians 9:9 ("Is it for oxen that God is concerned?") does not turn the Apostle in any way into an "anti-ecological" person. To suppose this is to take the text out of its context and out of the thread of the argument, going against the most elementary hermeneutical norm. It is not infrequent, moreover, in a discourse, that in order to counter and give more force to the sentence itself, one blurs the subtle differences by employing hyperbolic language, as occurs in Matthew 9:13: "I have not come to call the just, but sinners."[15]

We will try to determine with greater precision what Paul is saying in 1 Corinthians 9:8–11.

His line of argumentation does not proceed, as that of some Gospel passages that assume the same literary motive of the animal (cf. Matt 6:26; 10:31; 12:12), from an argument *a fortiori* based on a maxim or on an anterior principle. Paul *does not* say: "The law of God applies to oxen; with how much greater reason does it apply to us, mankind," but rather he affirms in a direct way that the law refers literally "to us." Why? Because, as he explains in 1 Corinthians 9:10b, the law speaks about "the plowman" and prescribes that he has the right to collect his portion. For Paul, therefore, the law of Deuteronomy 25:4 does not refer only to brute animals but rather applies generally to the obligation of giving the worker his portion; in other words, it is interpreted, always according to Paul, in a sense similar to that of Deuteronomy 24:15: "You shall give him

---

15. See more examples: Jer 7:21; Hos 6:6; Matt 12:7; 1 Pet 1:12; and also Luke 14:12. In response to the ecological preoccupation of G. M. Lee, "Studies in Texts: 1 Cor 9:9–10," *Theology* 71 (1968): 122–123, Ethelbert William Bullinger, *Figures of Speech Used in the Bible* (Grand Rapids: Baker Books, 1968), 24, affirms that 1 Cor 9:9 employs the rhetorical figures of the ellipsis, in such a way that it is necessary to presuppose an "only" ("is God concerned [only] about oxen?").

his hire on the day that he earns it" (the text evoked in 1 Tim 5:17 immediately after the citation of Deut 25:4).

The Apostle would thus be directly understanding not an allegorical or figurative sense of Deuteronomy 25:4, but rather the sense to which the very letter in itself of the Deuteronomic command is open, that is, the "literal sense" of the precept. This affirmation requires some further clarifications that we will consider in the following paragraphs.

9.5. 1 Corinthians 9:8–11 and the "literal sense" of Deuteronomy 25:4

In a 1978 article, referring also to the interpretation of Deuteronomy 25:4 in 1 Corinthians 9:9, Kaiser follows a line of reasoning that is fairly similar to what we have proposed. In order to explain the Pauline exegesis of this Old Testament text, Kaiser begins with a distinction between *meaning* and *significance*. For *meaning* he understands the specific sense intended by the author of a text; in our case, it would be what the author of Deuteronomy 25:4 wanted to express with his words. For *significance* he alludes to every posterior "applicative sense" which puts the text in relation with other persons or situations; in our case it would be the application that Paul makes to the concrete circumstances of the evangelizer.

Kaiser demonstrates how, in 1 Corinthians 9:8–11, Paul has respected the meaning desired by the author of Deuteronomy 25:4, because effectively this law refers not only to oxen but above all to interpersonal relationships. To this *meaning* the Apostle would have added a *significance* that tries to apply the precept to the particular situation that occurs in the community.

This argument seems to "save" the Pauline interpretation, because the Apostle would not have jeopardized the "literal sense" intended by the legislator of Deuteronomy 25:4. We have to say, however, that this explanation does not turn out to be totally convincing for us.

Our interpretive proposal differs from Kaiser's because he more radically questions the very distinction between *meaning* and *significance*, that is, between a literal sense (which is already determined) and another applicative sense (which is open). Essentially underlying this proposal is the "linguistic reduction of the symbolic reach" itself (Paul Ricœur), which results in the distinction between the "proper sense" and the "figurative sense" of a text.[16] These distinctions only restrict *a priori* the horizon of meaning for the text. There

---

16. See Paul Ricœur, "Centinela de la inminencia," 179–198 in *Pensar la Biblia: Estudios exegéticos y hermenéuticos*, ed. André LaCocque and Paul Ricœur (Barcelona: Herder, 2001).

does not exist something like a literal sense already fixed and foreseen by the author once and for all in the moment of putting the text into writing; what exists is a "letter" open to a meaning.[17]

A fortiori, this affirmation is valid for Deuteronomy 25:4, for we have seen that this law, thanks to its symbolic layer, includes its own indetermination regarding not only the identification of the characters, but also the nature of what the mandated action supposes. This indetermination frees up an enormous interpretive potential. But (let us note well) it is a potential that is present in the very same letter, that is to say, the law itself of Deuteronomy 25:4, insofar as the symbolic law asks to be applied, and consequently, every application that adequately makes explicit one of its lines of meaning will be a literal sense.

In conclusion, therefore, what we want to argue in these pages is simply that the reading that Paul makes of Deuteronomy 25:4 in 1 Corinthians 9:9 is a literal sense of the text; in other words, it is the recognition (regarding a concrete case) of the openness and the movement inscribed in the very letter of the text.

17. See David J. A. Clines, *I, He, We, and They: A Literary Approach to Isaiah 53*, JSOTS 1 (Sheffield: University of Sheffield, 1976), 59–61: "Once it is recognized that the text does not exist as a carrier of information, but has a life of its own, it becomes impossible to talk of *the* meaning of a text, as if it had only *one* proper meaning. . . . We cannot even be sure that a literary text (or any work of art) 'originally'—whenever that was—meant one thing and one thing only to its author; even the author may have had multiple meanings in mind. . . . On the understanding advanced here, it is not a matter of being quite wrong or even quite right: there are only more and less appropriate interpretations, no doubt, according to how well the world of the poem comes to expression in the new situation."

10

Does the Old Testament Give Testimony of Christ? Canonical Exegesis and Postmodern Exegesis

Carlos Granados

> Brueggemann can perhaps be thought of as being *more* canonical than Childs, in that Childs so often and so obviously *starts out from* historical criticism and seeks to progress to the canonical reading, while Brueggemann for the most part, though condemning historical criticism if anything even more absolutely, in the handling of actual texts simply ignores it from the start.[1]

This affirmation of James Barr indicates to us very precisely the feeling of anyone who approaches for the first time Walter Brueggemann's *Theology of the Old Testament*.[2] His radical distancing from the historical-critical methods and his desire to pursue a "theology" of the Old Testament could seem to situate him in a position similar to that of Brevard Childs. However, there is an abyss between the two approaches. According to Brueggemann, the project of canonical reading is radically "reductionist" and is, for that very reason, quite different from the one that he proposes. To what is he referring? What is the critique that is directed at Childs from a "postmodern approach" like Brueggemann's? What foundation and what relevance does it have? In the following pages we intend to offer a response to these questions.

Brueggemann's *Theology of the Old Testament*, published in 1997, has had a

---

1. James Barr, *The Concept of Biblical Theology: An Old Testament Perspective* (London: SCM, 1999), 551.
2. Walter Brueggemann, *Theology of the Old Testament: Testimony, Dispute, Advocacy* (Minneapolis, MN: Fortress, 1997).

powerful impact in recent years. Its author, then a professor at Columbia Theological Seminary, stands out for his originality and audacity when it comes to offering novel and expressive perspectives which are presented as a veritable provocation for the reader. From his point of view the theology of the Old Testament should give a testimony of plurality, expressing a pluralism of affirmations of faith and of methods within the framework of a diversity of interpretive communities. Brueggemann affirms that it is a hermeneutical necessity to adopt the context of a postmodern and post-metaphysical society. For this reason, he proposes an approach to the text's claim to truth that is founded in the interaction of diverse affirmations within a series of processes, conflicts, and debates among a "plurality of voices," through which Israel arrives at the affirmations that it considers to be true.[3]

Within this framework, Brueggemann situates the approach of Childs in the "Centrist Enterprises"[4] (a significant title) and in his pages directs at Childs basically a double critique that will mark out the path of our exposition and will prepare us to offer a final evaluation: 1) his Christological exclusivism and 2) his ontological aim.

10.1. The Old Testament: does it give testimony of Christ?

Brueggemann's most radical criticism refers to the polemical affirmation made by Childs that the Old Testament witnesses to Jesus Christ.

This affirmation which is indispensable for Childs ends up being lethal in Brueggemann's eyes; therefore he affirms: "My own perspective, against that of Childs, suggests that such an overtly Christological reading of the Old Testament is not credible or responsible."[5] The risk that Brueggemann here perceives is that of a disappearance of the Old Testament, because it will fall "under the aegis of Christological claims."[6]

We will try to expound in the first part on Childs's true position on the matter (1.1) in order to go deeper into Brueggemann's criticism and counter-proposal (1.2) and to finish with an evaluation of the controversy from some personal reflections (1.3).

---

3. See Brueggemann, *Theology*, 5.
4. Brueggemann, *Theology*, 89.
5. Brueggemann, *Theology*, 93.
6. Brueggemann, *Theology*, 92, 730n13.

a) Christuszeugnis *according to Childs*

Childs expressed himself on this particular question in an article published in 1997, "Does the Old Testament Witness to Jesus Christ?"[7] Childs, confronting the accusation of Rolf Rendtorff that heavily criticized his claim of seeing in the Old Testament a "witness to Christ," adduces basically three arguments.[8] *First*, he argues from the very claim of the New Testament that in its relationship with the Old Testament it transcends the temporal sequence and affirms the original presence of Christ (Word of the Father). *In the second place*, in response to those who would accuse him of having a position that started with a "dogmatic prejudice," Childs reminds them that the presence of a dogmatic decision prior to the exegetical work is inevitable, and that the essential question refers more to the quality of the exegetical analysis and of the theological reflection in their relation to both the text and the object. *In the third place*, Childs in his own defense adduces the necessity of a single method of interpretation with diverse levels of reading, which takes seriously both the different dimensions that constitute the text and the distinct contexts in which it interacts.

This third point he then makes concrete by distinguishing a double interpretive process:[9]

1. "In the first instance, one seeks to hear the historic voice of Israel in its literal/plain sense"; a testimony that is open and expanding, fragmentary, at times contradictory, and always wrapped in obscurity.[10]

2. In the second instance, the interpreter assumes that there is a collection of canonical books with two distinct parts that have taken a unique and special form in the Christian community of faith. The interpreter now strives to reach a level of global theological construction that investigates "the full reality of the subject matter of Scripture, gained from a close hearing of each separate testament."[11] Here is where one can reach the possibility of reading the Old Testament as a "witness to Christ."[12]

---

7. The article appears in *Evangelium, Schriftauslegung, Kirche: Festschrift für Peter Stuhlmacher zum 65*, ed. Jostein Ådna et al. (Göttingen: Vandenhoeck und Ruprecht, 1997), 57–64.

8. See Childs, "Does the Old Testament Witness?," 59–62.

9. See Childs, "Does the Old Testament Witness?," 63.

10. Childs, "Does the Old Testament Witness?," 63.

11. See Childs, "Does the Old Testament Witness?," 62.

12. Cf. Brevard S. Childs, *Biblical Theology of the Old and New Testaments: Theological Reflections on the Christian Bible* (Minneapolis, MN: Fortress, 1993), 78, 85; the author explains that the testimony of the New and the Old is distinct and does not lose its specificity (78). In "The Canon in Recent Biblical Studies: Reflections on an Era," *Pro Ecclesia* 14 (2005): 26–45, he covers this theme clearly (45). See also the discussion of Childs's thought regarding this

b) Brueggemann's critique and proposal

Brueggemann radically criticizes this articulation in "two phases" (*first*, the interpretation of the Old Testament on its own terms; *second*, the reading of it in relation to the New Testament).[13] For him, this way of proceeding supposes the following: a) a separation of both of Childs's phases (because one cannot see how the two explications [one, hearing Israel's own voice, and the other, reading the Old Testament in light of the New] are related to each other); b) a disappearance of the singularity of the Old Testament (enveloped in New Testament affirmations).

After this critique, Brueggemann proposes a process of advancing from the Old to the New marked by four "maneuvers":[14]

1. Recognizing the insuperable and unavoidable polyphony of testimony in the Old Testament, whose affirmations always remain surprisingly open.

2. Going beyond a distinction between a "past meaning" and a "present meaning" in order to go deep into a kind of imaginative interpretation that in no way implies an abuse of the text.

3. Recognizing the legitimacy of an ecclesial interpretation that, being amazed before the person of Jesus, adapts this polyphonic text to its own situation; always keeping in mind that "the connections between the two Testaments are made, as surely they must be, from the side of the New Testament and not from the side of the Old Testament."[15]

4. Consequently, from this Brueggemann concludes with a negative evaluation of every interpretation that intends to reduce "the polyphonic, elusive testimony of the Old Testament to one single, exclusivist construal, namely, the New Testament–Christological construal" (and here Brueggemann includes that of Childs).[16]

For Brueggemann, the Christian exegete who does theology of the Old Testament can evaluate and admit the connections that the New Testament

---

point in chapter 7 of this volume, and in Augustín Giménez González, *"Si el justo es hijo de Dios le socorrerá": Acercamiento canónico a la filiación divina del justo perseguido en Sab 1–6*, ABE 48 (Estella: Verbo Divino, 2009), 30–31.

13. Cf. Brueggemann, *Theology*, 731–732.

14. Brueggemann, *Theology*, 731.

15. Brueggemann, *Theology*, 732.

16. Brueggemann, *Theology*, 732. The consequences of this approach for dialoguing with the Jewish people are, according to Brueggemann, disastrous, for (729): "Jewish religious claims are overridden in the triumph of Christian claims." "The Old Testament, for the most part, disappears as Childs seeks to do 'biblical theology' under the aegis of christological claims" (729n13).

establishes with the Old, but the exegete should not strive to establish such connections through his or her theological labor, because they are not in the testimony of Israel, but in a posterior activity that transcends the text.

c) Evaluation of the controversy

There is in the first place a common point of departure for both authors. The two recognize the "open" and "expansive" character of the Old Testament. Childs refers to the inalienable character of its own voice and to its "mysterious" and "obscure" dimension, while Brueggemann speaks about its openness and its elusive character.[17]

What radically differentiates the two is the question of the "witness to Christ" in the Old Testament. How can we adequately formulate and resolve this divergence?

1. In reality, the question that is at the heart of the controversy could be formulated in this way: can or should the Christian interpreter be situated before the Old Testament *ut si Novum non daretur* ("as if there were not the New")?

It is evident, in the first place, that the Christian reader is in fact informed by reading the New Testament in his or her approach to the Old, and that, "in spite of generations of scholarly denial, few Christians can read Isaiah 53 without sensing the amazing morphological fit with the passion of Jesus Christ."[18] The decisive question, however, is whether this prejudice (accepted and recognized) should illuminate in some sense one's reading of the Old Testament or whether the Christian exegete of the Old Testament should rather, to the extent possible, abstract from it and bracket it.

We think, on the one hand, that a certain exercise of distancing oneself is necessary in order to recognize the processes through which particular connections are realized within the Old Testament fabric. In this sense, Brueggemann's observations are beneficial and warn us against the danger of thinking that the link between the Old and the New is immediate and accessible through an immediate synthesis.

This "exercise of distancing oneself" is necessary in order to recognize other possible realizations of the Old Testament and thus to understand better

17. Childs, "Does the Old Testament Witness?," 63; Brueggemann, *Theology*, 731–732. On the "open" character of the Old Testament, see Ignacio Carbajosa, "El Antiguo Testamento, realidad abierta," 21–50 in *Entrar en lo Antiguo: Acerca de la relación entre Antiguo y Nuevo Testamento*, ed. Ignacio Carbajosa and Luis Sánchez Navarro, PreDi 16 (Madrid: Universidad Eclesiástica San Dámaso, 2007).

18. Childs, "Does the Old Testament Witness?," 63.

that the Christological event is a radical act of freedom, not constrained or required by a previous stringent logic. This exercise is also necessary so that the affirmation of fulfillment is not hardened and made insensible to reality, to the detriment of the Christological principle itself.

2. This precaution, however, should not cause us to forget the radical Christian claim that we find in the New Testament: Jesus "fulfills" the Scriptures.[19] Brueggemann, as a Christian reader, accepts this terminology and points out that "it is completely appropriate, to say in an act of bold, imaginative construal, as the New Testament frequently does, 'the Scriptures were fulfilled'"; but then he adds that this affirmation *cannot* be realized from the side of the Old Testament, that is to say, that this "fulfillment" should not influence the interpretation that the Christian exegete makes of the Old Testament.[20]

We have to say, however, that this affirmation of Brueggemann does not reflect the real claim to "fulfillment" in precisely the way that it occurs in the writings of the New Testament. The fulfillment consists here in saying, with the fourth Gospel, that Moses "wrote of me" (John 5:46) or that "Abraham rejoiced that he was to see my day" (8:56). These sayings imply that for the first Christians it was not possible to say that Jesus was the Word, the Son of God, without passing through a *new reading of the Old Testament*. Will it be the same way for us?[21] For the authors of the New Testament, the key to the new reading, which was encoded in Jesus, was not simply one among several possibilities (as it is for Brueggemann[22]), but rather the definitive and unifying one.

3. To read the Old Testament in the school of the New is not equivalent to reading immediately all of the New in the Old. We thus share with Brueggemann the yearning to respect the proper voice of the Old Testament. It seems to us, however, that the project of a "theology of the Old Testament" illuminated by the New is not only legitimate but also corresponds with creative obedience to the revealed Truth.

---

19. For a study focused on this theme, see *Vetus in Novo: El recurso a la Escritura en el Nuevo Testamento*, ed. Filippo Belli, Ignacio Carbajosa, Carlos Jódar Estrella, and Luis Sánchez Navarro, Ensayos 290 (Madrid: Encuentro, 2006).

20. Brueggemann, *Theology*, 732.

21. The claim of fulfillment was not a late reflection that was posterior to the redaction of the text, but rather it was anterior to (and decisive in) the formulation of the Christian Bible. In fact, thanks to this claim, the Christian Bible was made into a text in which the appearance of the New Testament "altered" the Scriptures of Israel; on this point, see Carlos Jódar Estrella, "La relación Antiguo-Nuevo Testamento y la configuración de la Biblia como texto," 69–84 in *Entrar en lo Antiguo: Acerca de la relación entre Antiguo y Nuevo Testamento*, ed. Ignacio Carbajosa and Luis Sánchez Navarro, PreDi 16 (Madrid: Universidad Eclesiástica San Dámaso, 2007).

22. Brueggemann, *Theology*, 733.

Here we are linked also with Paul Beauchamp's project of reading, which could well be called "canonical" but which is perhaps better defined as a "theological reading" of the two Testaments.[23] The "theology" to which he makes reference would go beyond an "archaeology of the New Testament," which is reduced to the explicit or implicit references to the Old. For Beauchamp "it is the entire structure of the Old that points toward the New, and not a list of isolated verses."[24] In reality, this theological correlation "displaces also the meaning within each text."[25] This "displacement of meaning" affects, therefore, the Old Testament also, and it is not only legitimate but also necessary (according to that necessity belonging to the Christological event) to keep in mind in our interpretation of the texts.

In reality, what is here at play is not an academic or formal question, but a true requirement of the very affirmation of New Testament faith in the divine identity of Jesus.[26] The practical criteria of this teleological rereading of the Old Testament is very simple: "the act [of rereading] continues if the facts nourish it, and it is discouraged in the contrary case."[27]

10.2. Critique of Childs's ontological claim

The second great critique that Brueggemann directs at Childs consists in wanting "more than the text."[28] The thesis that "the text references beyond itself" appears to Brueggemann as a temptation, in effect. In order to make this critique understandable to its fullest extent, it is necessary to begin with Childs's own position on this matter.

---

23. On our particular issue, see Paul Beauchamp, "Lecture christique de l'Ancien Testament," *Biblica* 81 (2000): 105–115. See also his two volumes: *L'un et l'autre Testament: I. Essai de lecture; II. Accomplir les Écritures* (Paris: Éditions du Seuil, 1976; 1990). In Spanish, the two French volumes bear the titles: *Ley, profetas, sabios: Lectura sincrónica del Antiguo Testamento* (Madrid: Cristiandad, 1977); *El uno y el otro Testamento: Cumplir las Escrituras*, BAC (Madrid: Biblioteca de Autores Cristianos, 2015).

24. See Paul Ricœur, "Comme si la Bible n'existait que lue," 21–28 in *"Ouvrir les Écritures": Mélanges offerts à Paul Beauchamp*, LeDiv 162 (Paris: Cerf, 1995), 28.

25. Beauchamp, *Ley, profetas, sabios*, 34.

26. "The Old Testament, in this perspective, is not only useful for understanding the New, nor is it only a preparation for it, but it should be seen as a path that is continually necessary to travel, as an ongoing condition for access to the mystery of Christ, in whose act all figures find their fulfillment." Carlos Granados, "Cumplimiento y exégesis figurativa en P. Beauchamp," *Estudios Bíblicos* 64 (2006): 19–29, at 19.

27. Beauchamp, *Ley, profetas, sabios*, 80.

28. Brueggemann, *Theology*, 721–722.

a) The "ontology" of Childs

In the same article that we cited earlier, Childs criticizes that "widespread reflex of biblical scholars to dismiss the term ontology as an illegitimate intrusion from the side of philosophy."[29] He then affirms that an adequate exegesis should not be reduced only to discovering the grammatical meaning of the text, but that through the text it tries to reach the very object (*res*) to which the text points.

Childs considers this affirmation to be decisive—so much so that in his biblical theology of the two Testaments, he comes to affirm:

> A major thesis of this book is that this basic problem in Biblical Theology can only be resolved by theological reflection which moves from a description of the biblical witnesses to the object toward which these witnesses point, that is, to their subject matter, substance, or *res*.[30]

For Childs, to remain at the textual level is to lose the key that unites the diverse and differentiated voices of the two Testaments. In confrontation with the position of David Kelsey, who "defends the position that the Bible's authority does not rest on any specific content or property of the text, but lies in the function to which biblical patterns have been assigned by the 'imaginative construals' of a community of faith," Childs reaffirms the necessity of putting oneself in relationship with the real content, that is, with the *res* to which the text refers.[31] He advocates in a certain way for a *Sachkritik* (a critique in terms of the content), but in such a way that this *Sache* (*res*) is defined in relation to the testimony of both Testaments. That is to say, this *res* is not the New Testament, but rather the living person who is the Lord Jesus, witnessed to by the New and the Old, in different ways, in different times, and by different people.

b) Brueggemann's critique

Brueggemann sees things very differently. For him everything that we have in the Bible is discourse and this should be enough for us.[32] By being centered on the language, Brueggemann brackets all questions about history; therefore he affirms:

29. Childs, "Does the Old Testament Witness?," 60.

30. Childs, *Biblical Theology*, 80.

31. Childs, *Biblical Theology*, 81–82. Childs directs at Brueggemann a critique centered on this point in his review: "Walter Brueggemann's *Theology of the Old Testament: Testimony, Dispute, Advocacy*," *Scottish Journal of Theology* 53 (2000): 228–233.

32. Brueggemann, *Theology*, 725: "Utterance as testimony is enough, as it was for the community of Israel."

We are not asking, "What happened?" but "What is said?"[33] But this "historical agnosticism" is accompanied by something else that is more profound,
which refers to the questions of ontology. "We have, however, few tools for
recovering "what happened" and even fewer for recovering "what is," and
therefore those issues must be held in abeyance, pending the credibility and
persuasiveness of Israel's testimony, on which everything depends.[34]

This is the motive according to which Brueggemann considers the temptation to look beyond the text, and here again we find him criticizing Childs:

> Brevard Childs writes, in his canonical approach, about "the reality of God"
> behind the text in itself. In terms of Old Testament theology, however, one
> must ask, What reality? Where behind? It is clear that such an approach as
> that of Childs derives its judgments from somewhere else, from an essential-
> ist tradition, claims about God not to be entertained in the Old Testament
> text itself.[35]

c) Evaluation of the controversy

Brueggemann has undoubtedly recognized a crucial question that in the exegetical field had remained obscure because of what was considered at times to
be a purely methodological difference. This author knows how to see percep-
tively the essential question that separates his approach from that of Childs.
He does so in a particular paragraph where he shows his intellectual honesty:
"I have found the issue of speech/reality among the most problematic for my
current study. . . . This is an exceedingly important and dense issue, one I am
not able to resolve clearly."[36]

The path from language to reality, which is drawn with clear strokes in
Childs, has totally disappeared in Brueggemann, because the language constitutes the reality, and the one who ends up being God in Israel will depend,
according to him, on the discourse of the Israelites or, secondarily, on the discourse of the text.

This position of Brueggemann, however, leads to unresolvable contradictions. We thus share Barr's astonishment at the way in which Brueggemann
deforms the judicial image that is in the background of his *Theology*. According to Brueggemann, in the courtroom the testimony becomes the "original"
thing and the court can only and exclusively judge from the testimony, without

33. Brueggemann, *Theology*, 118.
34. Brueggemann, *Theology*, 118.
35. Brueggemann, *Theology*, 65.
36. Brueggemann, *Theology*, 65n11.

any possibility of speculating about "actual event."[37] To this presentation Barr responds by affirming: "Surely this is absurd! How would this work in an accusation of murder or fraud? What sort of 'court,' whether in ancient Israel or in the metaphor-world of this volume, is *bound* to accept the testimony that it hears and cannot decide whether person A killed person B, because that would be 'speculation'?"[38]

Effectively, a testimony goes back to (or at least has the intent of going back to) a reality. This reality is the *original* thing and on it depends the truth of the testimony. Brueggemann, for his part, would express his persistent difficulty: what if arriving at the "reality," at the original thing, is a hopeless undertaking? Would it not be better for us to stick with the language of the testimony? Certainly, the attempt to access the original event through a reading of the biblical text as "an index of facts" has given us unsatisfactory results. But there also exists the possibility of reading the text as a "testimonial monument" and thereby reading it in a unitary way, receiving its testimony "in the heart of the Church, with the guarantee that the world-view that the reading is able to open up for me does justice to the original event. And, therefore, it reveals it."[39]

Childs arrives at comparing Brueggemann's claim to that of Gnosticism, insofar as both are opposed by the existence of a *regula fidei* founded in the truth of the Israelite faith, incarnated in the person of Jesus Christ, and established as the ultimate interpretive criterion. "Such a confessional interpretation of Scripture Brueggemann now characterises as 'oppressive, hegemonic, and reductionist.'"[40] Perhaps Brueggemann himself, who openly declares his preference for the sophist presuppositions as opposed to the Socratic vision of reality, would not reject this comparison.

10.3. Conclusion

Brueggemann's critique is directed precisely at the heart of canonical exegesis, and at that cornerstone which allows one to keep the Old and New Testaments united. And that cornerstone is the *res*, an extra-textual reality, the Christological event.

It is thus necessary for a canonical approach to defend the linking of language and reality or, in other words, of word and event. In another context,

---

37. Brueggemann, *Theology*, 120–121.
38. Barr, *Biblical Theology*, 548.
39. Jódar Estrella, "La relación," 84.
40. Childs, "Walter Brueggemann," 232.

some years back, then-Cardinal Joseph Ratzinger reclaimed the importance of recovering this link:

> If we wish to remain within the specific perspective of the Bible, we need to consider word and event as equi-primordial. The dualism between word and event, which banishes the event into the realm of the word-less, which is to say, into the realm of the sense-less, actually robs the word itself of its capacity to mediate sense, because the word then stands in a world from which all sense has been stripped. It leads to a docetic Christology, in which the reality, that is, the concrete bodily existence of Christ and of men in general, is removed from the domain of sense. But when this happens, the essence of the biblical witness is missed.[41]

If historical-critical exegesis (to which Ratzinger refers in these lines) was obligated, through fidelity to its principles, to remain with the Christ of the past, the postmodern exegesis of Brueggemann, staying faithful to its presuppositions, would always remain with the particular Christ and would be incapable of passing to the universal Christ and, therefore, it would be incapable of fully integrating the affirmations of the New Testament as a whole.

41. Joseph Ratzinger, "Biblical Interpretation in Conflict," trans. Adrian Walker, 1–29 in *Opening Up the Scriptures: Joseph Ratzinger and the Foundations of Biblical Interpretation*, ed. José Granados, Carlos Granados, and Luis Sánchez-Navarro (Grand Rapids: Eerdmans, 2008), 25.

PART III

The Teaching in Benedict XVI's *Verbum Domini*

11

Listening to the Word: On the Subject of *Verbum Domini*

Luis Sánchez-Navarro

In 2010, Pope Benedict XVI introduced his Post-Synodal Apostolic Exhortation *Verbum Domini*, on the Word of God in the life and mission of the Church; in it he put forward his authoritative teaching about that central reality in the Church's life, to which Sacred Scripture testifies in a special way.

It is a long document, divided into three parts: the first and most extensive, *"Verbum Dei"* ("The Word of God"), is dedicated to the theological study of the Word and its correct interpretation; the second, *"Verbum in Ecclesia"* ("The Word in the Church"), is centered on the ecclesial life of that Word, with a special emphasis on the sacred liturgy; finally the third, *"Verbum mundo"* ("The Word for the World"), deals with the meaning of the Word of God for the present world, to which the Church is called to proclaim it. The three parts are linked by the biblical text that constitutes the "thread" of the entire document, as the pope points out at the beginning of the document (§5): the prologue of the Gospel of John (John 1:1–18), that true hymn to the divine *Logos*, the preexisting and incarnate Word of God. This biblical passage expresses, in an unsurpassable synthesis, the mystery of faith and of Christian life.

In the pages that follow, through some introductory aspects, we will present the first part (*Verbum Dei*), which proposes anew the ecclesial teaching about the word of God and its adequate interpretation. Let us note from the beginning its relation to the other two parts; the word of God does not exist without that double "existential" (the Church) and "missional" (the world) link. In all of them is articulated the presentation of that Word to which human beings are called to listen. In Scripture, listening is synonymous with obedience to a prior love; it is at the center of Israel's religiosity, as one prays in the *Shema*: "Hear, O Israel: . . . you shall love the LORD your God . . . " (Deut 6:4–5). This receptive and efficacious listening is what makes the Church grow: "And today, too, the ecclesial community grows by hearing, celebrating and studying that word" (§3). This document is dedicated to encouraging this renewed listening.

11.1. Preliminary aspects

In the first place we will discuss some points that help us to approach *Verbum Domini*. By clarifying the theological significance of the expression "Word of God" we will briefly present the antecedents of this document: on the one hand, the principal ecclesial interventions dedicated to Sacred Scripture in the last decades; and on the other hand, the personal trajectory of Joseph Ratzinger/Benedict XVI.

a) What is the Word of God?

We begin by remembering that "the Word of God" is not simply identifiable with the "Bible" or "Sacred Scripture." Certainly, Scripture read in the Church is the Word of God, as we proclaim each day in the liturgy; but it does not exhaust the Word. For the Word of God is a reality "living and active, sharper than any two-edged sword" (Heb 4:12); in fact, at the beginning of the new exhortation we find a section dedicated precisely to detailing the analogical character of the expression "Word of God," whose variety of meanings is such that it allows us to speak about a "symphony of the Word" (§7). The Word of God is quintessentially Jesus Christ, the incarnate *Logos*; but the Word of God is also creation (the *liber naturae*), the primordial revelation. And that Word has resonated in a particular way in the mouth of the prophets, as well as in the apostolic announcement that continues in the Church; that announcement which, transmitted in its heart orally and so to speak "vitally," acquires a stable form in Sacred Scripture. "Apostolic Tradition occurs in two ways: through the living transmission of the word of God (also simply called Tradition) and through Sacred Scripture which is the same proclamation of salvation in written form."[1] Receiving this Word, we human beings open ourselves up to revelation, and we enter into dialogue with God; in this process Scripture has great importance, testimony written and inspired by the revelation of God.

---

1. *Compendium of the Catechism of the Catholic Church* (Vatican City: Libreria Editrice Vaticana, 2005), §13. Cf. Luis Sánchez Navarro, "La Escritura y el *Compendio* del *Catecismo de la Iglesia Católica*," *Teología y Catequesis*, 99 (2006): 11–24, at 12–15.

The Word of God is therefore a living reality that constitutes the nucleus of the Apostolic Tradition (this also being living reality); to the very dynamic of the Word of God belongs its written form: "The word of God, attested and divinely inspired, is sacred Scripture, the Old and New Testaments" (§7).

b) Ecclesial precedents of Verbum Domini

The Exhortation is preceded by a long and consistent ecclesial Magisterium, whose most recent authoritative expression is the constitution *Dei verbum*, from the Second Vatican Council. Among the ecclesial pronouncements that are not magisterial, the document of the Pontifical Biblical Commission in 1993 stands out.

Dogmatic Constitution Dei verbum *(1965)*
In this conciliar document dedicated to divine revelation, a point arrived at after almost a century of pontifical magisterial teaching about Sacred Scripture,[2] the Council strongly emphasizes the unity between Scripture and Tradition: they are not two fonts of divine revelation but rather two expressions, mutually implying each other, of the Gospel of Christ, the one and only font of that revelation. The two parts dedicated to inspiration and the truth of the Bible (*DV* §11), as well as its interpretation, have particular importance for biblical studies; and interpretation should attend to the double dimension (human and divine) belonging to Sacred Scripture (§12). With all this, the Council offers some precious elements that illuminate the task of the Christian exegete. To this are united the instructions contained in the final part, which is dedicated to Sacred Scripture in the life of the Church; there we read in particular how "the study of the sacred page should be, as it were, the very soul of theology" (§24), thus emphasizing the necessity for exegesis to be theological, and for theology to be profoundly rooted in Scripture. This document, among the most profound and fruitful of the Council, has marked the reflection and the exegetical practice of the last forty years.

The Interpretation of the Bible in the Church (1993)
On the occasion of the hundredth anniversary of the encyclical *Providentissimus Deus* and the fiftieth anniversary of *Divino afflante Spiritu*, the Pontifical Biblical Commission published a long document about the ecclesial interpretation of Scripture. After first reviewing the methods and approaches for

2. In particular the encyclicals *Providentissimus Deus* (Leo XIII, 1893), *Spiritus Paraclitus* (Benedict XV, 1920), and *Divino afflante Spiritu* (Pius XII, 1943).

interpretation, it addresses questions of philosophical and theological herme-neutics, in order to present in a third part the dimensions characteristic of Cath-olic interpretation; the last part is dedicated to the interpretation of the Bible in the life of the Church.[3] Of notable interest as an attempt to unite historical exegesis and theological interpretation of Scripture, this document appears as a good synthesis of the general situation of biblical investigation in the final stretch of the twentieth century.

c) Joseph Ratzinger and reflection on Scripture

The intellectual trajectory of Joseph Ratzinger before his elevation to the seat of Peter shows his constant interest in the interpretation of the Bible and his notable scientific competency in this field, which took on a new dimension after his election as the bishop of Rome. The milestones that we could mention are numerous, but we will limit ourselves to two publications: one from before 2005, and the other more recent from the apostolic chair.

"Biblical Interpretation in Conflict" (1988)

In January of 1988, Ratzinger, then cardinal prefect of the Congregation for the Doctrine of the Faith, gave a lecture with the same title in New York; the complete version being published the following year in German, this essay about biblical hermeneutics has been translated into the principal European languages and has exercised a notable influence on the exegetical world.[4] In it, Ratzinger openly advocates, in the face of the already evident crisis of his-torical-critical methodology, for undertaking a "criticism of the criticism": an analysis that, employing the potential of scientific criticism, will bring to light the limits of that methodology (in order to avoid them) and its points of strength (in order to reinforce them); his proposal identified the ultimate

---

3. Cf. Peter S. Williamson, *Catholic Principles for Interpreting Scripture: A Study of the Pon-tifical Biblical Commission's "The Interpretation of the Bible in the Church"*, SubBi 22 (Rome: Pon-tifical Biblical Institute, 2001).

4. Joseph Ratzinger, "Biblical Interpretation in Conflict," trans. Adrian Walker, 1–29 in *Opening Up the Scriptures: Joseph Ratzinger and the Foundations of Biblical Interpretation*, ed. José Granados, Carlos Granados, and Luis Sánchez-Navarro (Grand Rapids: Eerdmans, 2008). Originally published in English as "Biblical Interpretation in Crisis: On the Question of the Foundations and Approaches of Exegesis Today," 1–23 in *Biblical Interpretation in Crisis: The Ratzinger Conference on Bible and Church*, ed. Richard John Neuhaus, Encounter Series 9 (Grand Rapids: Eerdmans, 1989). Complete text in German: "Schriftauslegung im Widerstreit. Zur Frage nach Grundlagen und Weg der Exegese heute," in *Schriftauslegung im Widerstreit*, ed. Joseph Ratzinger, QD 117 (Freiburg: Herder, 1989), 15–44.

origin of the historical-critical method in its classical form in Kantian reason (it is therefore a philosophical origin). We need to dispossess historical analysis of its philosophical illuminist presuppositions—says Ratzinger—properties of a reason that renounces the transcendent, in order therefore to recuperate the true history that reflects biblical writings: paying attention to the narrative techniques then in use, without the previous limitations of a philosophical nature that question the possibility of God intervening in human history. Only thus can one achieve a reading that, as *Dei verbum* calls for, keeps in mind the double character, human and divine, of Scripture, and is therefore capable of receiving it as what it is: the Word of God in human language.

Jesus of Nazareth (2007–2012)

In 2007, Pope Benedict XVI published the first part of his *magnum opus, Jesus of Nazareth*, in which he discusses Jesus from his Baptism to his Transfiguration; the second volume, edited in March of 2011, covers the entrance into Jerusalem up to the Resurrection; and the next year he published a shorter volume dedicated to the origins of the Lord.[5] In the first volume, he explicitly affirms that its character is not magisterial;[6] but this fact does not deprive it of the intellectual and moral *authority* that it deservedly enjoys. His reading of the Gospels, which is attentive to history and at the same time profoundly spiritual, makes his work similar to the genre of the "mysteries of the life of Jesus"; he shows how, in order to know the true "Jesus of history," it is necessary to begin with the deepest aspect of his identity: his identity as the Son.[7] Jesus appears as the prophet like Moses (cf. Deut 18:15–18); but he is at the same time radically superior, since as the only-begotten Son he is the definitive revealer of the Father (cf. John 1:18), who thus brings about the complete fulfilment of the Scriptures.

In the prologue to his first volume, the pope makes explicit the motives that have carried him toward this publication, which "has had a long gestation"[8]

---

5. Benedict XVI, *Jesus of Nazareth, I: From the Baptism in the Jordan to the Transfiguration*, trans. Adrian Walker (New York: Doubleday, 2007); *Jesus of Nazareth, II: Holy Week: From the Entrance into Jerusalem to the Resurrection*, trans. Philip J. Whitmore (San Francisco: Ignatius Press, 2011); *Jesus of Nazareth: The Infancy Narratives*, trans. Philip J. Whitmore (New York: Bloomsbury, 2012).

6. "Everyone is free, then, to contradict me. I would only ask my readers for that initial good will without which there can be no understanding." Benedict XVI, *Jesus of Nazareth, I*, xxiv.

7. "In the foreword to Part One, I stated that my concern was to present 'the figure and the message of Jesus.' Perhaps it would have been good to assign these two words—figure and message—as a subtitle to the book, in order to clarify its underlying intention." Benedict XVI, *Jesus of Nazareth, II*, xvi.

8. Benedict XVI, *Jesus of Nazareth, I*, xi.

springing from his years of theological formation. The separation between the "Jesus of history" and the "Christ of faith," disseminated throughout the academic environment in recent times, has dramatic consequences for the faith:

> All these attempts have produced a common result: the impression that we have very little certain knowledge of Jesus and that only at a later stage did faith in his divinity shape the image we have of him. This impression has by now penetrated deeply into the minds of the Christian people at large. This is a dramatic situation for faith, because its point of reference is being placed in doubt: Intimate friendship with Jesus, on which everything depends, is in danger of clutching at thin air.[9]

In response to this conception, he affirms: "I wanted to try to portray the Jesus of the Gospels as the real, 'historical' Jesus in the strict sense of the word. . . . I believe that this Jesus—the Jesus of the Gospels—is a historically plausible and convincing figure."[10] He therefore turns to "canonical exegesis," which, developed in the last decades of the twentieth century, emerges as a necessary perspective, because of its capacity to combine critical study and theology of Scripture;[11] no wonder that in the prologue to the second volume he considers it obvious that "in two hundred years of exegetical work, historical-critical exegesis has already yielded its essential fruit."[12] In order to continue to bear fruit, biblical exegesis must adopt a "hermeneutic of faith";[13] a theme of capital importance, as we will see, in the exhortation *Verbum Domini*.

11.2. *Verbum Dei*: a comprehensive look

Pope Benedict XVI's exhortation is the most important magisterial document that refers to the Word of God and Sacred Scripture since the Second Vatican Council's Dogmatic Constitution on Divine Revelation *Dei verbum*. In the exhortation, the pope again proposes that ecclesial teaching which was ruminated upon throughout the previous decades, making it possible to outline some questions relative to biblical hermeneutics.

---

9. Benedict XVI, *Jesus of Nazareth, I*, xiii. This concern led him to publish the first volume of his work before the second had been prepared (xxiv).

10. Benedict XVI, *Jesus of Nazareth, I*, xxii.

11. Cf. Augustín Giménez González and Luis Sánchez Navarro, eds., *Canon, Biblia, Iglesia: El canon de la Escritura y la exégesis bíblica*, PreDi 30 (Madrid: Universidad Eclesiástica San Dámaso, 2010), 14–16.

12. Benedict XVI, *Jesus of Nazareth, II*, xiii.

13. Benedict XVI, *Jesus of Nazareth, II*, xiv.

In its first part, *Verbum Domini* presents divine revelation in its dialogical character, following the conciliar approach; in this way its structure can be deduced: revelation of God ("The God Who Speaks": §§6–21) and reception of this revelation ("Our Response to the God Who Speaks": §§22–28). And it is the case that, as then-Cardinal Ratzinger taught years earlier, "revelation is a dynamic event between God and man, which again and again becomes reality only in the encounter."[14] Sacred Scripture is therefore a *testimony to revelation,* which always remains as something that transcends Scripture: "The biblical Word attests to Revelation, but does not contain it in the sense of absorbing it and turning it into a sort of thing that one could stick in one's pocket. The Bible attests to Revelation, but the concept of Revelation as such is broader."[15] In this way the human response pertains to revelation itself; it is not something that happens afterward.

We then find in this first part of the exhortation a long development of "The Interpretation of Sacred Scripture in the Church" (§§29–49), which undoubtedly represents the most significant portion of the entire document; we will center our attention on this part in particular.

11.3. The God Who Speaks (§§6–21)

"The God Who Speaks" (§§6–21) has, from all eternity, a Word, a *Logos* with whom he lives in intimate communion; since the creation of humanity, a creation *by* the Word (cf. John 1:3), God is desiring to communicate with his creatures. The great novelty of revelation is precisely this: God goes out to meet human beings in their searching, and he desires to speak with them. He wants to communicate the "logic of love": "The Word . . . reveals God himself in the dialogue of love between the divine persons, and invites us to share in that love"; in this way he desires to illuminate humanity's existence, to make clear "the enigma of the human condition" (§6). This "logic" God speaks to us in diverse ways; the word of God is therefore an analogous reality, which in its diverse dimensions constitutes a veritable "symphony."

a) Symphony of the Word of God

Given that God is communicative in his essence, his acting *ad extra* is also an expression of himself. The greatest realization of this is the incarnation of the Logos, the Word that is consubstantial with the Father. But the manifestation

14. Ratzinger, "Biblical Interpretation in Conflict," 26.
15. Ratzinger, "Biblical Interpretation in Conflict," 26.

of God begins with the work of creation, realized through his word: "And God said . . ."[16] As the Psalmist prays, commenting on this biblical passage: "By the word of the LORD the heavens were made, and all their host by the breath of his mouth. . . . For he spoke, and it came to be; he commanded, and it stood forth" (Ps 33:6, 9). In this way, the "book of nature," *liber naturae*, is a loving word from this God to human beings (§7); moreover, Benedict XVI recalls—citing St. Bonaventure—that "every creature is a word of God, since it proclaims God" (§8). Even more so, every image of God (Gen 1:27) resounds the loving word of its creator.

But, furthermore, the hidden God "has spoken his word in salvation history" (§7), entering into dialogue with human beings; thus begins the revelation of the face of God, first to Abraham and the patriarchs, then to Moses. These great friends of God have heard his voice; a mysterious but very real voice, so much so that it has brought them to carry out unexpected actions: to leave one's fatherland for an unknown land (Abraham), to take one's people out of Egypt against the will of Pharaoh (Moses); all of this was unthinkable without an intervention of God in history.

God's intervention, however, did not stop there: the Lord has spoken to all of Israel through the prophets (§7). The voice of the eternal God has resonated in this way in human throats, which can truly say: "Thus says the LORD," "the word of the LORD." Israel has been able to hear the word of God in a human language, with human words, adapted to their ear and their mind, capable, therefore, of entering into their heart. Similarly, the wise ones of Israel have communicated the deep wisdom that is enclosed in the word of YHWH: the sapiential books attest to the closeness of that Word to Israel, which gives light to Israel in all its paths: "Thy word is a lamp to my feet, and a light to my path" (Ps 119:105). In this manner, Benedict XVI says, one reaches complete realism: "Those who know God's word know fully the significance of each creature," its true reality, in such a way that the "word of God makes us change our concept of realism: the realist is the one who recognizes in the word of God the foundation of all things" (§10).

b) The fullness of the Word

We thus arrive at the mystery of the Incarnation, the definitive communication of God to human beings: "In many and various ways God spoke of old to our

---

16. The expression appears 10 times in Genesis 1 (Gen 1:3, 6, 9, 11, 14, 20, 24, 26, 28, 29); the first chapter of the Bible presents to us, therefore, the "creative decalogue" of God, a true anticipation of the decalogue of the Covenant that will be proclaimed on Sinai.

fathers by the prophets; but in these last days he has spoken to us by a Son" (Heb 1:1–2). The symphony thus arrives at its culminating moment:

> In this symphony one finds, at a certain point, what would be called in musical terms a "solo," a theme entrusted to a single instrument or voice which is so important that the meaning of the entire work depends on it. This "solo" is Jesus. . . . The Son of Man recapitulates in himself earth and heaven, creation and the Creator, flesh and Spirit. He is the center of the cosmos and of history, for in him converge without confusion the author and his work. (§13)

Now the Word not only resounds in human language, but acquires a concrete and visible shape: "Now the word is not simply audible; not only does it have a *voice*, now the word has a *face*, one which we can see: that of Jesus of Nazareth" (§12). In effect,

> The eternal Word, expressed in creation and communicated in salvation history, in Christ became a man, "born of woman" (Gal 4:4). Here the word finds expression not primarily in discourse, concepts or rules. Here we are set before the very person of Jesus. His unique and singular history is the definitive word which God speaks to humanity. (§11)

The Gospel of St. John clearly shows the radical newness that this event contains: "No one has ever seen God; the only Son, who is in the bosom of the Father, he has made him known" (John 1:18). As Benedict XVI has explained in the first volume of his book about Jesus, in these words of the evangelist the Son made man is presented as the eschatological prophet that God promised to Moses (Deut 18:15–18): "It is in Jesus that the promise of the new prophet is fulfilled. What was true of Moses only in fragmentary form has now been fully realized in the person of Jesus: He lives before the face of God, not just as a friend, but as a Son; he lives in the most intimate unity with the Father."[17] The word of Jesus is not his own, but the Father's: "What I say, therefore, I say as the Father has bidden me" (John 12:50); neither do his works belong exclusively to him: "The Son can do nothing of his own accord, but only what he sees the Father doing" (5:19). Therefore he can affirm with audacity: "He who has seen me has seen the Father" (14:9). If every human being, by the fact of being so, is the image of God (Gen 1:27), how much more will be the only Son of God made man, the incarnate Word! This occurs in such a way that in Jesus' humanity the face of the Father is manifested. This image will reach all of its splendor on the morning of Easter: "In the resurrection the Son of God

---

17. Benedict XVI, *Jesus of Nazareth*, I, 6.

truly emerged as the light of the world. Now, by living with him and in him, we can live in the light" (§12).

c) The transmission of the Word

That Word will never be silent: "The same Spirit who spoke through the prophets sustains and inspires the Church in her task of proclaiming the word of God and in the preaching of the Apostles; finally, it is this Spirit who inspires the authors of sacred Scripture" (§15). The word continues to resonate therefore in the apostolic preaching, is transmitted in the living Tradition of the Church, and is expressed in a singular way in Scripture, which the pope defines as "the word of God, attested and divinely inspired" (§7).

> The Church lives in the certainty that her Lord, who spoke in the past, continues today to communicate his word in her living Tradition and in sacred Scripture. Indeed, the word of God is given to us in sacred Scripture as an inspired testimony to revelation; together with the Church's living Tradition, it constitutes the supreme rule of faith. (§18)

But this Scripture, the work of the Holy Spirit, can only be understood under the guidance of the Spirit (cf. §16); just as the Second Vatican Council will solemnly affirm: "Holy Scripture must be read and interpreted in the same Spirit in which it was written" (*DV* §12).[18] The mission of the Church will consist in transmitting the word of God to all human beings, interiorly moved by the Spirit. In this consists the Apostolic Tradition, the living reality "which makes us adequately understand sacred Scripture as the word of God" (§17). For the Tradition, the inspired Word is a living and present-day reality.

11.4. The human response: faith in the Word (§§22–28)

Next we are presented with "Our Response to the God Who Speaks" (§§22–28), and it is nothing other than faith in the God who hears us and responds to our questions. The word of God awaits the response of human beings, in order to be able, therefore, to enter into a covenant with them. And he invites every human being, at the same time that he opens the doors of salvation: "Each of us is thus enabled by God to *hear and respond* to his word" (§22). But furthermore, it is true that we encounter in this response the key for understanding our own existence, because "we were created in the word and we live in the word; we cannot understand ourselves unless we are open to this dialogue"

18. Translator's note: I have rendered the Latin *eodem Spiritu* as "same Spirit," a more exact translation than "sacred spirit" in the Gonzalez edition.

(§22); "God alone responds to the yearning present in the heart of every man and woman" (§23). It is not a word of the past, but rather it is wholly present now, and it is capable of dialoguing with the problems and the situations that confront human beings today. In that word, God speaks with clarity to everyone who desires to hear him and open oneself up to him out of faith. Particularly illuminating is the book of Psalms (§24), in which God himself offers us the words with which we can direct ourselves to him, aligning our life with his will, whatever our concrete situation may be; the Psalms are thus a true school of living faith.

In this context, sin is not without deliberate deafness to the Word of God (§26). Just as Jesus himself shows in the parable of the sower, the powerful seed of the Word can remain untouched, and therefore sterile, if it is not received cordially. The Word of God not only reveals the will of God, but also human sin: the ancient sins attested by Sacred Scripture, and the actual sin of those who close themselves to that Word, hindering its germination. Sin consists in not knowing how, and in not wanting, to *listen to the Word*: "It is important that the faithful be taught to acknowledge that the root of sin lies in the refusal to hear the word of the Lord, and to accept in Jesus, the Word of God, the forgiveness which opens us to salvation" (§26).

In contrast with the people of Israel—who so many times showed their "stiff neck"—as well as all the generations that have been closed to the Word and have thus obscured human dignity, the Virgin Mary—*mater Verbi*—shines as the *mater fidei*, that perfect figure in whom we discover the icon of our Christian vocation to listen to the Word and at the same time to give a cheerful and bold response. In her is fulfilled, in a simple and also joyful way, our vocation: "From the Annunciation to Pentecost she appears as a woman completely open to the will of God"; she who meditated on the words and actions of Jesus, pondering them in her heart (cf. Luke 2:19, 51), is the "Virgin ever attentive to God's word . . . ; she treasures in her heart the events of her Son, piecing them together as if in a single mosaic" (§27). She is capable, therefore, of discovering the profound harmony of the will of God, as it was manifested in the events of her life. In Mary, as Benedict XVI beautifully indicates, "the word becomes a way of life" (§27): it totally molds her existence. In the *Magnificat*, Mary's familiarity with the Word of God is revealed, and it is something that made her capable of receiving and realizing her own mission. "Since Mary is completely imbued with the word of God, she is able to become the Mother of the Word Incarnate."[19] All of us, as believers in Christ, are called to that same familiarity.

---

19. *VD* §28, quoting Benedict XVI, *Deus caritas est* (December 25, 2005), §41.

11.5. Biblical hermeneutics and interpretation (§§29–49)

The third section of this first part is dedicated to "The Interpretation of Sacred Scripture in the Church" (§§29–49). It is undoubtedly of vital importance for Pope Benedict, as indicated by its greater length, but also its contents; we will dedicate a specific part to showing its principal lines of thought. But at this point let us note the title: "The Interpretation . . . *in the Church*": the final words have a fundamental, programmatic importance. For, as he establishes in the first parts, the Church (her faith and her life) is the only place where one can hear the Word of God, in its totality, testified to by Scripture, and it is therefore the home of all true interpretation.

a) Interpretation in the Church

"*The primary setting for scriptural interpretation is the life of the Church*" (§29). In this way justice is done to its origins, since the Bible was born *in* the community of faith and *from* the community of faith; its pages are an expression of the faith of the sacred authors, and they are intended to nourish and to make mature the faith of its addressees. "The Bible was written by the People of God for the People of God, under the inspiration of the Holy Spirit" (§30). Therefore, to detach biblical interpretation from the community of faith—the Church—presumes to uproot it; and whatever lacks roots lacks life.

Therefore, outside the ecclesial community, the Bible is composed of elements that are more or less unconnected, distinguished examples of ancient literature but without internal cohesion and without any significance for the present. "Approaches to the sacred text that prescind from faith might suggest interesting elements on the level of textual structure and form, but would inevitably prove merely preliminary and structurally incomplete efforts" (§30). Only ecclesial faith is capable of discovering in these writings a vital unity, which makes them capable of communicating the Word of God to people of all times, and thus also [to people of] today. "The Bible is the Church's book, and its essential place in the Church's life gives rise to its genuine interpretation" (§29). This ecclesial character of biblical interpretation, as the great St. Jerome teaches us, "is not a requirement imposed from without: the Book is the very voice of the pilgrim People of God, and only within the faith of this People are we, so to speak, attuned to understand sacred Scripture" (§30). Therefore, the teaching of the Magisterium of the Church about Scripture (cf. §§32–33) does not deform it or impose violence upon it, as neither does it inhibit biblical investigation, but completely the opposite: it is at the service of Scripture in order to allow it to express, in a true form, the faith that has generated it; in order to allow it to resound as what it is: the Word of God.

To put it another way: Scripture requires the plural; "we can never read Scripture simply on our own" (§30). Nothing is further from the intention of the sacred authors than to write for an individual: faith in Christ is precisely to the contrary: it engenders plurality; it engenders community. Equally it is said, with reason, that the Gospel cannot be understood if it is not put into practice—it has not been put down in writing in order to be read, but in order to be lived—and so also it must be said that Sacred Scripture remains closed if we intend to make a particularist use of it: if I look for it to speak *to me* and not *to us*. The community of faith—the Church—assures us that personal reading, which nourishes the soul and illuminates the concrete situations of life, is not an individualist reading, valid only *for me*. The truth—including the truth of Scripture—is discovered only in communion. And at the same time, it nourishes communion: "Listening to the word of God introduces and increases ecclesial communion with all those who walk by faith" (§30).

b) Exegesis and theology

From the essentially ecclesial character of the Word of God, the theological character of biblical exegesis follows necessarily. A merely descriptive exegesis, which is centered on preliminary aspects but which is incapable of arriving at affirmations of faith, becomes an academic exercise without any relevance for theology. Because of this, and taking up again a classical expression in the Magisterium, Benedict XVI insists that "the study of the sacred page should be, as it were, the very soul of theology" (§31).[20] And it is the case that "where exegesis is not theology, Scripture cannot be the soul of theology, and conversely, where theology is not essentially the interpretation of the Church's Scripture, such a theology no longer has a foundation" (§35). Similarly, many years earlier, then-Cardinal Ratzinger affirmed, if exegesis

> wishes to be theology, it must take a further step: acknowledge that the faith of the Church is the sort of sym-pathy without which the text remains closed. It must acknowledge this faith as the hermeneutic, as the locus of understanding, which does not dogmatically force itself upon the Bible, but is the only way of letting it be itself.[21]

20. This quotation is taken from *DV* §24; cf. Leo XIII, *Providentissimus Deus* (November 18, 1893), §2; Benedict XV, *Spiritus Paraclitus* (September 15, 1920), §3.
21. Ratzinger, "Biblical Interpretation in Conflict," 29.

And recently the pope affirmed, returning to the question again: "If scholarly exegesis is not to exhaust itself in constantly new hypotheses, becoming theologically irrelevant, it must take a methodological step forward and see itself once again as a theological discipline, without abandoning its historical character."[22] This must necessarily be reflected in the academic study of theology, just as Benedict XVI solemnly expresses: "It is my hope that, in fidelity to the teaching of the Second Vatican Council, the study of sacred Scripture, read within the communion of the universal Church, will truly be the soul of theological studies" (§47).

The affirmation that biblical exegesis should be theological does not, however, make this exegesis detached from Christian life and spirituality; the reality is totally the opposite. Theology is a science that turns on the reality of God, and of human beings and the world in light of God; therefore, the *theological* reading of the Bible will be interested in penetrating into the *reality* to which Scripture testifies in a true way. Reading the Bible with the eyes of a theologian means reading it with attention to its current significance for life in the present day; thus is discovered its teaching about the truth of the world and of human beings (and not only about historical events that pertain to the past); about the path of goodness that we are called to travel (and not only about the customs or the ethics of extinct civilizations); about the truth that moves us (and not only about the beliefs of generations that have died); about the action of the Spirit in our hearts (and not only about the religious experience of a culture irretrievably lost). The exegete that prescinds from faith, and therefore from theology, will remain in the description of the past. The theological exegete—that is to say, the Christian exegete—reads with eyes of the present, in such a way that the Scripture of the past unexpectedly becomes living and eloquent.

c) The hermeneutic of faith

An aspect on which Pope Benedict insists in a special way is the hermeneutic that guides interpretation: a hermeneutic that must be illuminated by the faith of the Church. This hermeneutic follows from *Dei verbum* §12, a crucial passage of the Second Vatican Council, whose fundamental principle is that "Holy Scripture must be read and interpreted in the sacred spirit in which it was written." In this conciliar text we find, as the title of §34 of Benedict's exhortation significantly reads, "a directive to be appropriated." We must note that these paragraphs (*VD* §§34–35) have a special importance within the exhortation, since they synthesize the address that Benedict XVI made on October 14, 2008

22. Benedict XVI, *Jesus of Nazareth, II*, xiv.

in the Synod Hall, an address totally oriented to the question of hermeneutics.[23] The paragraphs in *Verbum Domini* respond, therefore, to his deepest interest.

In the interpretation of Scripture, one must attend to all of its human elements, to this end employing the scientific methods that are appropriate; but the task of the exegete does not stop there, for he must also have in mind what the divine author has wanted to reveal in the words of the human authors (*DV* §12). Therefore "the Dogmatic Constitution indicates three fundamental criteria for an appreciation of the divine dimension of the Bible: 1) the text must be interpreted with attention to *the unity of the whole of Scripture*; nowadays this is called canonical exegesis; 2) account is be taken of the *living Tradition of the whole Church*; and, finally, 3) respect must be shown for *the analogy of faith* (§34).

The pope calls attention to this point, in a long part of the exhortation about "the danger of dualism and a secularized hermeneutic" (§35). The question is simple: if an interpreter prescinds from the hermeneutic of faith, he does not remain in mere objectivity, something that is otherwise impossible. To the contrary, in place of the ecclesial hermeneutic "there inevitably enters another hermeneutic, a positivistic and *secularized hermeneutic* ultimately based on the conviction that the Divine does not intervene in human history. According to this hermeneutic, whenever a divine element seems present, it has to be explained in some other way, reducing everything to the human element. This leads to interpretations that deny the historicity of the divine elements" (§35b).[24] The adoption of this hermeneutic makes theology, pastoral work, and, finally, Christian life impossible. This hermeneutic "is the product of reason's attempt structurally to exclude any possibility that God might enter into our lives and speak to us in human words" (§36). Therefore—as Benedict XVI has indicated in the second volume of his work about Jesus—it needs to mature, by being transformed: "The positivistic hermeneutic . . . does not constitute the only valid and definitively evolved rational approach; rather, it constitutes a specific and historically conditioned form of rationality that is both open to correction and completion and in need of it."[25] This perfecting of the historical method comes, precisely, from the vision of faith: "A properly developed

23. Benedict XVI, Address during the 14th General Congregation of the Synod of Bishops (October 14, 2008); English trans. "Modern Exegesis Necessary for a Living Faith Today," *L'Osservatore Romano* 41, no. 43 (October 22, 2008): 13.

24. Later on, speaking about the consequences for the approach of theological studies, the pope adds: "A notion of scholarly research that would consider itself neutral with regard to Scripture should not be encouraged" (§47).

25. Benedict XVI, *Jesus of Nazareth, II*, xiv–xv.

faith-hermeneutic is appropriate to the text and can be combined with a historical hermeneutic, aware of its limits, so as to form a methodological whole."[26]
It is necessary, therefore, to open up our reason to the reality of God:

> Here too, we need to urge a *broadening of the scope of reason*. In applying methods of historical analysis, no criteria should be adopted which would rule out in advance God's self-disclosure in human history. The unity of the two levels at work in the interpretation of sacred Scripture presupposes, in a word, *the harmony of faith and reason*. (§36)

d) The unity of Scripture: the Old in the New

The hermeneutic of faith allows us to spontaneously grasp the profound unity that binds together the biblical writings, both the Old and the New Testaments.[27] The fact, purely linguistic, that the word "Bible," originally plural ("books"), has become a singular word, is significant and reflects something constitutive of the biblical books: their unity is stronger than their diversity (which is also evident) and, without eliminating the diversity, the unity confers on the Bible the singular character of a grand work, with a grand argument: Christ, pre-announced and proclaimed. So states the pope, citing Hugh of St. Victor: "All divine Scripture is one book, and this one book is Christ, speaks of Christ and finds its fulfilment in Christ" (§39). This fundamental intuition is basically from canonical exegesis.[28]

The relationship with the writings of the Old Covenant is constitutive for the faith of the Church; just as Benedict XVI luminously shows when referring to the accounts of the Passion of Jesus, "the facts are, so to speak, permeated with the word—with meaning; and the converse is also true: what previously had been merely word—often beyond our capacity to understand—now becomes reality, its meaning unlocked."[29] The mystery of Christ leads to a new and innovative reading of the Scriptures of Israel, which is demanding because it implies tensions that it must necessarily welcome in all the profundity of their meaning: "The Old Testament is itself replete with tensions between its institutional and its prophetic aspects. The paschal mystery of Christ is in complete

26. Benedict XVI, *Jesus of Nazareth, II*, xv.

27. On this question, see *Vetus in Novo: El recurso a la Escritura en el Nuevo Testamento*, ed. Filippo Belli, Ignacio Carbajosa, Carlos Jódar Estrella, and Luis Sánchez Navarro, Ensayos 290 (Madrid: Encuentro, 2006); *Entrar en lo Antiguo: Acerca de la relación entre Antiguo y Nuevo Testamento*, ed. Ignacio Carbajosa and Luis Sánchez Navarro, PreDi 16 (Madrid: Universidad Eclesiástica San Dámaso, 2007).

28. *VD* §34, §57. See González and Sánchez Navarro, *Canon, Biblia, Iglesia*.

29. Benedict XVI, *Jesus of Nazareth, II*, 202.

conformity—albeit in a way that could not have been anticipated—with the prophecies and the foreshadowings of the Scriptures; yet it presents clear aspects of discontinuity with regard to the institutions of the Old Testament" (§40). Here appears the originality of the Christological reading of Scripture, a new font of unity for that great monument of faith that represents the Old Testament, and which allows us to discover an unexpected coherence and conformity with the event of Christ, as the blessed Augustinian saying reads: *Novum in Vetere latet, et in Novo Vetus patet,* "The New Testament is hidden in the Old, and the Old is made manifest in the New" (§41).[30]

e) The Bible and the saints

The pope closes this dense hermeneutical section by pointing out the role that the saints of yesterday and today play in the correct understanding of the Scriptures (§§48–49). To this end, he follows the principle expounded by St. Gregory the Great: *viva lectio est vita bonorum,* "the life of the saints is a living reading of Scripture" (§48). The list enumerated, although necessarily incomplete, is very extensive: Abbot Anthony, Basil the Great, Benedict, Francis and Clare of Assisi, Dominic of Guzmán, Teresa of Jesus, Thérèse of the Child Jesus, Ignatius of Loyola, John Vianney, Pio of Pietrelcina, Josemaría Escrivá, Teresa of Calcutta, Teresa Benedicta of the Cross (Edith Stein), and Blessed Aloysius Stepinac, archbishop-martyr of Zagreb. "Every saint is like a ray of light streaming forth from the word of God" (§48). And it is the case that men and women who have lived the Gospel in its radicality show a vital understanding of that very Gospel, which connects with its profound strength, thus showing its internal rationality and beauty.

> Holiness inspired by the word of God thus belongs in a way to the prophetic tradition, wherein the word of God sets the prophet's very life at its service. In this sense, holiness in the Church constitutes an interpretation of Scripture which cannot be overlooked. The Holy Spirit who inspired the sacred authors is the same Spirit who impels the saints to offer their lives for the Gospel. In striving to learn from their example, we set out on the sure way towards a living and effective hermeneutic of the word of God. (§49)

---

30. Regarding the conformity of the New Testament with the Old, cf. the Pontifical Biblical Commission, *The Jewish People and Their Sacred Scriptures in the Christian Bible* (Vatican City: Libreria Editrice Vaticana, 2001), §7. "The Christian faith, then, is not based solely on events, but on the conformity of these events to the revelation contained in the Jewish Scriptures."

The evangelists wrote the Gospels, as we said earlier, not to be read, but to be lived; therefore, those who have lived it in an eminent way have something to say about its true meaning.

The saints are, then, teachers of the interpretation of the Word of God. This does not mean that the academic study of Scripture has to have methodological recourse to the testimony of the saints, as if it were necessary in order to prove its conclusions; although on occasion it can be pertinent and even recommended to illuminate the texts with that living experience, to do it in a systematic way could become problematic. But if the results of scientific exegesis were not capable of keeping in mind the experience of the saints throughout time, illuminating it and showing its roots in Scripture, that exegesis would have to question seriously its own process, because most surely it would be far from the understanding of the texts that it aims to interpret.

f) Mary and the interpretation of Scripture

The Mother of Jesus is the cornerstone of the authentic interpretation of Scripture; the Mother of the *Logos* is at the same time the Mother of faith (§27): the listening virgin (§27: *Virgo audiens*) who thus teaches us to make of the Word of God a pattern for our daily existence. "Mary is the image of the Church in attentive hearing of the word of God, which took flesh in her. Mary also symbolizes openness to God and others; an active listening which interiorizes and assimilates, one in which the word becomes a way of life" (§27). Citing his first encyclical, Benedict XVI adds: "Here we see how completely at home Mary is with the word of God, with ease she moves in and out of it. She speaks and thinks with the word of God; the word of God becomes her word, and her word issues from the word of God. Here we see how her thoughts are attuned to the thoughts of God, how her will is one with the will of God" (§28). Therefore the study of the Word of God in Scripture cannot prescind from the Mother of Jesus; to the point that the pope exhorts scholars "to study the relationship between *Mariology and the theology of the word.* This could prove most beneficial both for the spiritual life and for theological and biblical studies. Indeed, what the understanding of the faith has enabled us to know about Mary stands at the heart of Christian truth" (§27). The theology of the Word is inseparable from the Mother of the Word; and at the same time, reflection on the Mother of God leads to the very heart of Scripture.

11.6. Conclusion: a fascinating challenge

With his apostolic exhortation *Verbum Domini*, Benedict XVI has wanted to point out to the Church of the third millennium a challenge and a path. The challenge: to recuperate the freshness of the Gospel, loved and lived. The path: to return to the fountains of our faith, those fountains that inexhaustibly emerge in the pages of Sacred Scripture, thus renewing the existence of those who approach it in faith; to return to *hearing the Word* in a new way. Our world can thus rediscover God, that great treasure that, revealed in Christ, the Church carries through the ages. As the pope indicates at the beginning of the document,

> In a world which often feels that God is superfluous or extraneous, we confess with Peter that he alone has "the words of eternal life" (Jn 6:68). There is no greater priority than this: to enable the people of our time once more to encounter God, the God who speaks to us and shares his love so that we might have life in abundance (cf. Jn 10:10). (§2)

12

The Fulfillment of the Scriptures according to *Verbum Domini*

Carlos Granados

The theme of the relationship between the Old and New Testaments is discussed in *Verbum Domini* under the fundamental category of "fulfillment of the Scriptures." This concept puts in tension three dimensions that should be correctly integrated

> It must be observed, however, that the concept of the fulfilment of the Scriptures is a complex one, since it has three dimensions: a basic aspect of *continuity* with the Old Testament revelation, an aspect of *discontinuity*, and an aspect of *fulfilment and transcendence.* (VD §40)

In reality, this tension, affirms Benedict XVI, is nourished by another earlier one, which affects the Old Testament itself. "The Old Testament is itself replete with tensions between its institutional and its prophetic aspects" (§40). *Verbum Domini* thus tends to identify continuity with the "prophetic" side of Scripture, while it localizes the elements of discontinuity in the "institutional" side of Scripture. We have here a primary path that we will try to travel in order to study in depth the relationship between the Old and New Testaments: the polarity between the institutional and the prophetic (part 1).

Verbum Domini situates the theme of the fulfillment of the Scriptures, however, within a broader framework for taking up again the concept of "typology" (cf. §41). We will dedicate, therefore, a second part of our study to demonstrating the hermeneutical possibilities that open up this point of view for understanding the relationship between the Old and New Testaments (part 2).

Given that the magisterial document also invites scholars and pastors, in this context, "to help all the faithful to approach these [obscure Old Testament] passages through an interpretation which enables their meaning to emerge in the light of the mystery of Christ" (§42), we will propose a reading (illuminated by the principles of typology) of a difficult passage of the Old Testament: the sacrifice of Isaac in Genesis 22 (part 3).

12.1. The polarity between the institutional and the prophetic

We want to understand how the institutional and prophetic aspects of the Old Testament have found their fulfillment in Christ, particularly how the prophetic dimension has served as a means for the institutional elements to reach a form of fulfillment that also implies transcendence.

By speaking about a polarity between these two dimensions we are not evoking a contradiction. "Transcending" the institutional is not here equivalent to "transgressing it," but rather to manifesting the ultimate and definitive meaning to which all of the cultic worship was oriented.[1] In this sense we read the words of Norbert Lohfink:

> The prophets were not the founders of the Old Testament religion. They are not the innovators but rather the defenders of what is old. Therefore, they are, in reality, in an authentic sense, conservators. It is possible that this affirmation will not excite us too much, because today we like the revolutionaries more. But perhaps we can learn from the prophets something about revolutionary truths. Precisely through their connection to the ancient dispositions, they ended up becoming, definitively, men who introduced something completely new.[2]

This apparently paradoxical status of a revolutionary anchored in the old is proper to the prophet. He announces a form of transcendence of the law that is at the same time a fulfillment. Therefore, the tension between the prophetic and the institutional is poorly expressed when one speaks of a "subversive

1. We employ the terminology that Benedict XVI applies to the relationship between the Old and New Testaments: he speaks of a "transcendence [*Überschreitung*]" that is not a "transgression [*Übertretung*]"; see Benedict XVI, *Jesús de Nazaret, I: Desde el Bautismo a la Transfiguración*, trans. Carmen Bas Álvarez (Madrid: La Esfera de los Libros, 2007), 152–153; cf. Benedict XVI, *Jesus of Nazareth, I: From the Baptism in the Jordan to the Transfiguration*, trans. Adrian Walker (New York: Doubleday, 2007), 120.

2. Norbert Lohfink, "Los profetas ayer y hoy," 97–144 in *Profetas verdaderos, profetas falsos*, ed. Angel González, Norbert Lohfink, and Gerhard von Rad, BEB 16 (Salamanca: Sígueme, 1976), 110.

intention" in the prophets, that is, an aim to dismantle the institutional and to oppose the figure of the legislator (Moses).[3] It is important, rather, to situate the prophets in continuity with the figure of Moses. The prophet is, according to Deuteronomy 18:15-18, the "heir" of the legislator (Moses) and, as such, his legitimate interpreter. Prophecy is, in some way, the inheritance that Moses leaves to Israel.[4]

It would be, however, one-sided for us to stop here. We would falsify the prophetic announcement if we insisted exclusively on pointing out the continuity between Moses and the prophets. Walther Zimmerli speaks in this sense about the prophet as that person enabled by God to "reinterpret" the tradition in light of a new principle of understanding.[5] The prophetic oracles manifest in many cases a certain tension with the written word of the law. Why? Above all, because the prophet has to announce something new with respect to the exigencies of the law, an unconditional and gratuitous liberation that goes beyond what is expected in the legislation and makes possible a new beginning.

Verbum Domini applies this "tension" between the institutional and the prophetic in the case of sacrifices: "The mystery of Christ stands in continuity of intent with the sacrificial cult of the Old Testament, but it came to pass in a very different way, corresponding to a number of prophetic statements and thus reaching a perfection never previously obtained" (§40).

According to *Verbum Domini*, institutional sacrifice is fulfilled and transcended by Christ following the logic already present in the prophetic oracles. If we consider, however, the prophetic critique of sacrifice, it seems difficult to speak of fulfillment. Let us remember, for example, Hosea 6:6: "For I desire steadfast love and not sacrifice, the knowledge of God, rather than burnt offerings" (cf. Matt 9:13; 12:7).

What does this rejection imply? In order to understand it, we must

---

3. Horacio Simian-Yofre, "I profeti di fronte a Mosè (alla Torah)," *Ricerche Storico Bibliche* 16 (2004): 25–45, assumes the existence of a serious confrontation between Moses and the prophets. The allusions that link them with Moses in some prophetic texts are later insertions, but "the prophets themselves would have felt betrayed by this interpretation" (43).

4. There is effectively a line of succession that goes from Moses to Joshua, and from the latter to the whole series of prophets in Israel. Sir 46:1 points this out when the author affirms that Joshua was "mighty in war, and was the successor of Moses in prophesying," stating later that Samuel, "a prophet of the Lord, established the kingdom" (Sir 46:13), and immediately afterwards (according to this line of succession) that Nathan "rose up to prophesy in the days of David" (Sir 47:1).

5. See Walther Zimmerli, "Proclamation prophétique et réinterprétation," 79–109 in *Tradition et Théologie dans l'ancien Testament*, ed. Douglas A. Knight, LeDiv 108 (Paris: Cerf, 1982), 79–80.

consider the wider context of the prophetic critique of the sacrifices. It occurs in many texts of controversy between YHWH and his people, as is the case in Hosea 6:6, where reference is made to the fact that YHWH does not accept the gifts that the people present to him (cf. Isa 1:11–15; 43:22–24; Jer 6:20; Amos 5:21–23; Mic 6:6–7; Ps 50:8–13).[6] Israel looks to placate their God by offering a sacrifice as symbolic reparation. This mode of proceeding is, in principle, legitimate: it expresses the humble attitude with which the accused, showing his own culpability, looks to make reparation and ask for pardon. Let us remember that Jacob managed to placate his brother Esau, who came in fury to exterminate him (cf. Gen 33:8ss).[7] The offering of gifts is, therefore, a pertinent way in a litigation for the offender to express his culpability and manage to pacify the one offended. This honorable intention is translated to the sphere of relationships with God through the cultic (institutional) gesture of sacrifice. Why, then, do the prophets insist on the fact that God disapproves of this gesture?

It is necessary to exclude right away the interpretation according to which an exterior cult would be condemned in the name of a purely moral, interior religion. God does not reject gifts because he desires "spiritual worship." This interpretation devalues the corporal dimension and the symbolic character that exterior gestures have in the life of the spirit. What the prophet denounces is an ambiguity that derives from the very fact that the sacrifices are signs that do not immediately coincide with reality. These signs can be perverted, and end up becoming a mask for what is truly hidden in the heart. For this reason, the prophetic critique intervenes.

The fact that God asks for "mercy" (Hos 6:6), "obedience" (1 Sam 15:22), "a contrite heart" (Ps 51:19), or "justice" (cf. Isa 1:17; Amos 5:24) should not be understood as a substitution for sacrifice, but rather as the "irreplaceable" condition for the liturgical act to return to having meaning and being true; but the exterior act is not abolished by the prophetic tradition.

What *Verbum Domini* affirms also must be understood in this sense. Benedict XVI does not advocate here for a purely interior fulfillment that eliminates all the exterior (institutional) aspects. Rather, he treats of a form of fulfillment in which a new reality that breaks in (that of Jesus) uncovers the authentic and profound meaning (the "intention") of the institutional, of the sacrifices and

---

6. See a complete list with a bibliography in Pietro Bovati, *Ristabilire la giustizia: Procedure, vocabulario, orientamenti*, AnBib 110 (Rome: Pontifical Biblical Institute, 1986), 179–180.

7. Pietro Bovati, *"Così parla il Signore": Studi sul profetismo biblico* (Bologna: EDB, 2008), 141, also points out as a paradigmatic case Abigail's offering of gifts in 1 Sam 25, which manage to calm the fury of David.

the rites of the Old Testament, and is thus capable of renewing the exterior forms. The sacramental economy is the mature fruit of this logic.

12.2. The line of typology[8]

Alongside this criterion of differentiation between the "institutional" and the "prophetic," *Verbum Domini* offers us a broader context in which to situate the relationship between the Old and New Testament: typology.[9] The document gives us some paths for understanding the meaning of this concept:

- Biblical typology does not have an arbitrary character; that is to say, it does not consist in a game of similarities whose only criterion would be the subjectivity of the interpreter and his greater or lesser imagination.[10]
- Biblical typology is realized within the narrated events. That is to say, the typology is applied to the "account," the narration; it does not affect prophecy (an oracle) or the legal institutions only. Type or figure is above all a "stage or phase that the whole account passes through before its fulfillment."[11] This affirmation implies also that the figure is realized in the event and not outside of it (in the imagination of the interpreter) or parallel to it (in the more or less skillful comparison with another text). An immediate corollary is that typology affects all of Scripture, which is to say, it is not reduced only to certain cited verses in the New Testament.
- Typology is profoundly rooted in history. This aspect corresponds with what Paul Beauchamp denominates as the "mark" of figure, in other

8. Translator's note: The author's discussion of typology here closely follows chapter 5, section 2.b); see the note on "Original Publications" at the end of this volume.

9. Regarding the concept in general, see the interesting contributions in the work published under the direction of Raymond Kuntzmann on *lectio divina*: *Typologie biblique: De quelques figures vives* (Paris: Cerf, 2002).

10. Paul Beauchamp, "Exégèse typologique, exégèse d'aujourd'hui?," 407–412 in *Pages exégétiques*, ed. Yves Simoens, LeDiv 202 (Paris: Cerf, 2005), 411–412, discovers on the anthropological side of contemporary theology a salutary tendency "to admit that the writer is led beyond what he knows." This transcendence of Scripture is the condition of possibility for a typological exegesis. Its intention "would be sluggish or reckless if it were without rules" but at the same time "the process would be blocked if it were to expect from science its whole guarantee."

11. See Carlos Granados, "Cumplimiento y exégesis figurativa en P. Beauchamp," *Estudios Bíblicos* 64 (2006): 19–29, at 20. He also adds in that article that the figure is not "an inanimate thing, or a simple mental image of the fact, but rather a dynamic moment of the narrative collection."

words, its unrepeatable nature or unique concretization. Each figure is identified with a concrete time and a particular name.[12]

- Typology is understood within the framework of a Christological reading of the biblical text.[13] We can evoke in this respect the discussion between Brevard Childs and Rolf Rendtorff regarding the legitimacy of reading the Old Testament as a "testimony of Christ" (*Christuszeugnis*).[14] The typological reading is certainly oriented toward a *Christuszeugnis*. But not in an artificial way, straining the testimony of the Old Testament, but rather understanding that what the ancient authors "were conscious of saying" does not coincide with what "they say" and that it is therefore necessary to recognize a transcendence by the inspired word. Thus the possibility is opened up that a new reality (the paschal mystery of Christ, the Messiah) is at the same time old, and is made present in figures of the Old Testament.

- Exegesis according to figures, *Verbum Domini* points out at last, has a progressive character. This point means, in the first place, that the figure is "deficient" (for this reason it can progress). The episodes of Abraham's life, for example, clearly demonstrate this progression. Leon Kass states in this regard:

  It is not exactly traditional to speak about the education of Abraham. Pious tales of the patriarch regard him as a precocious monotheist even before God calls him, a man who smashed his father's idols, a man who sprang forth fully obedient and knowledgeable about the ways of the Lord. But a careful reading of the biblical text shows otherwise: Abraham indeed goes to school, God Himself is his major teacher, and Abraham's adventures constitute his education, right up to his final exam, the binding of Isaac.[15]

How is progress made in the biblical figures? By a sort of repetitive "insistence" that basically consists in the fact that figures "repeat themes, symbols, semantic structures, typical scenarios, opposition of terms, key concepts, and

12. See Paul Beauchamp, *L'un et l'autre Testament: II. Accomplir les Écritures* (Paris: Éditions du Seuil, 1990): 223–224.

13. In this sense, see also the observations of Paul Beauchamp in "Lecture christique de l'Ancien Testament," *Biblica* 81 (2000): 105–115.

14. Brevard S. Childs, "Does the Old Testament Witness to Jesus Christ?," 57–64 in *Evangelium, Schriftauslegung, Kirche: Festschrift für Peter Stuhlmacher zum 65*, ed. Jostein Ådna et al. (Göttingen: Vandenhoeck und Ruprecht, 1997).

15. Leon Kass, *The Beginning of Wisdom: Reading Genesis* (Chicago: University of Chicago Press, 2003), 251.

other series of significant elements that make it possible to connect them so that they speak together."[16] Typology, then, rests on the following fundamental postulate: the ultimate truth of the "figure" is given only in its capacity to dialogue with other similar figures that disclose what it is.

Is there some criteria that allows us to discern the proximity of a figure to its fulfillment? We can refer here to a fundamental one that Paul Beauchamp denominates as "concentration."[17] As the figures get closer to their fulfillment they become concentrated, which is to say, they cause more elements of the whole account to coincide within them. This concentration tries to gather all the symbols in a single point. An example is Revelation 21–22. The spousal and food symbolism is concentrated: Jerusalem will be the "bride adorned for her husband" (21:2) and in her is the "tree of life" (22:14). The nuptial union and the consummation of the fruit of the tree are a single thing: they satisfy a single and unique desire. The figures are concentrated in order to point out the One who will be the Messiah, Prophet, and Priest. This concentration also implies an "excess": the figure accumulates and unites within itself so many elements that it is overflowing. The path toward fulfillment implies a logic of superabundance, a sort of increasing paroxysm according to figurative logic.

12.3. Difficult pages of the Old in light of the New: the sacrifice of Isaac

In order to illustrate the utility and importance of everything that has been said, we focus now, following the indications of *Verbum Domini* §42, on the explanation of an obscure passage of the Old Testament: the sacrifice of Isaac (Gen 22). Two witnesses confirm for us its difficulty. In the first place, Walter Brueggemann, who points out the "immediate aversion experienced before a God who commands the murder of one's own son."[18] In the second place, André Lacoque, who states: "Abraham becomes by divine order a child-murderer, an assassin, and he contradicts the express commandment not to kill, thus pitting God against God. The fact that the story of Genesis 22 'ends well' does not change in any way the fact that Abraham is an assassin and figures as such."[19] How do we explain this biblical passage? How do we shed light on it without falling into the intolerable image of a capricious and arbitrary God? How do we "discover its meaning in light of the mystery of Christ"?

16. See Granados, "Cumplimiento y exégesis figurativa," 22.
17. Granados, "Cumplimiento y exégesis figurativa," 26–27.
18. Walter Brueggemann, *Genesis* (Atlanta: John Knox, 1982), 185.
19. André LaCocque, "No matarás," 89–126 in *Pensar la Biblia: Estudios exegéticos y hermenéuticos*, ed. André LaCocque and Paul Ricœur (Barcelona: Herder, 2001), 118.

A first kind of interpretation, common in Jewish literature, is that which tries to refine the harsh things in the account in order to make it morally acceptable. Thus, for example, Joseph H. Gumbiner affirms that Genesis 22 is the demonstration that God does not require the sacrifice of a son.[20] The account would, on the contrary, intend to criticize this false conception (cf. Lev 20:1–5). Still, the narration in this case would have to end with a criticism of Abraham for his mode of acting ("And YHWH said: 'I am not pleased with the sacrifice of your son'"), but what we find is instead the contrary: a blessing that approves of his proceeding in this way.

André LaCocque, after criticizing the interpretation just summarized, assumes a Kierkegaardian reading of the passage.[21] What Genesis 22 lays out is, in his opinion, a "teleological suspension of the ethical." The Akedah seems to him to be a paradigmatic account that aims to show the limits of the law. "The rule, the ethical thing, the Law, have to be transcended. To follow the rule is only the minimum that is required. But of Abraham, because he is the "man of faith," it is said that he is . . . above and beyond the line of obligation."[22] LaCocque sees Genesis 22 as an "exception to the law" that would ultimately intend to show the secondary value of the legislation within the economy of salvation. Now, this radical dialectic defended by LaCocque, even though it contains interesting elements, leads to the insoluble aporia of postmodernity, to the figure of a God who stops being "faithful," who goes against himself. But, in our understanding, the drama proposed in the text does not lead to contradiction; the text is given, rather, for us to think, allowing for other paths of understanding. Armed with the tools offered by *Verbum Domini*, we will try to inspect one [of these paths].

"Typology" provides here an effectively irreplaceable aid. We have insisted on the necessity of situating each figure in the series of figures that make it understandable. We will try to situate Genesis 22 in two series that touch on two essential aspects of the passage: first, that which makes reference to the character of "trial" that the episode has; second, that which evokes the "sacrificial" element of the episode.

---

20. Joseph H. Gumbiner, "Existentialism and Father Abraham," *Commentary* 5 (1948): 143–148.

21. Concerning Søren Kierkegaard's reading of Genesis 22 in *Fear and Trembling*, we would refer to the interesting article of Ronald M. Green, "'Developing' Fear and Trembling," in *The Cambridge Companion to Kierkegaard*, ed. Alastair Hannay and Gordon Daniel Marino (Cambridge, UK: Cambridge University Press, 1998), 257–281.

22. LaCocque, "No matarás," 118.

a) The test of life and death in Abraham

The test to which Abraham is subjected (cf. Gen 22:1) is defined by two elements. In the first place, it has a purpose of making known or uncovering something (cognitive purpose): YHWH aims to know whether Abraham fears God (v. 12). In the second place, there is a reward that will be given (or not) depending on the success of the test; in our case, the reward is the "blessing" which Abraham receives in verses 16–18. To these two elements must be added also what constitutes the very contents of the test, that is, the life of Abraham's most precious son (the son of the promise) being put into play. The test affects, then, in its ultimate substance, the tension between life (offspring) and death.

Claus Westermann has shown with particular insistence the relationship between this figure and that of "Israel tested in the desert":

> The expression [testing] is typical of the Deuteronomic instruction (above all Deut 8:2: "and you shall remember all the way . . . these forty years . . . that he might humble you, testing you . . ."). With it is described the sojourning in the desert and particularly the hard events of the road as a test of God. This representation is presupposed in Genesis 22.[23]

The presupposition for understanding the test in Genesis 22 is, therefore, what Israel underwent in the desert. We will try to describe briefly this other figure. The test of Israel in the desert is about vital sustenance, the manna. Fundamentally a common theme persists (there is an "insistence" on it): to accept that life (offspring, food) comes from God.[24] The purpose that YHWH pursues in this case is, as in the case of Abraham, to be able "to know what is in your [Israel's] heart" (Deut 8:2). The perspective of a reward, of a "blessing," such as the one that is expressed in verse 1, accompanies this purpose.

In Deuteronomy 8:2–16, we encounter, however, an interesting expansion of the cognitive reach of the test: thanks to this test, Israel will also reach a new knowledge (v. 3: "that he might make you know that . . . "). Thus is seen clearly its "pedagogical" dimension: being nourished by God, Israel will come to understand that "man does not live by bread alone, but that man lives by everything that proceeds out of the mouth of God" (v. 3: he lives by obedience). Did Abraham also have to learn, with the sacrifice of Isaac, something with regard to life? Something with regard to what links life to obedience?

---

23. Claus Westermann, *Genesis*, vol. 1, *Kapitel 1–11*, BKAT I/1 (Neukirchen-Vluyn: Neukirchener Verl, 1983), 436.

24. See in this sense the observations of Pietro Bovati, *Il libro del Deuteronomio (1–11)* (Rome: Città Nuova, 1994), 112–118.

Another figure, entering into dialogue with the two foregoing figures, allows us to extend this reflection. This time it is about the Servant of YHWH.

Marta García points out the closeness of both figures, above all on the part of two features: 1) the Servant is a "covenant of the people" (Isa 42:6; 49:8), an expression that must refer to Abraham; 2) the Servant will "see his offspring" and will obtain a "portion with the great," thanks to his obedience (Isa 53: 10, 12), a theme that also evokes the figure of Abraham.[25]

For us it is important to note that the Servant is also subjected to a test. The conditional expression "when he makes himself an offering for sin" (Isa 53:10) clearly evokes this aspect. Again we have to say that everything hinges on that line that separates life from death: overcoming the test of death, the Servant will reach true life ("he shall see his offspring, he shall prolong his days"). In this case the perspective of a reward, of a "blessing," is also expressed (formulated with terminology similar to that of Abraham: Isa 53:10, 12). Finally, the test of the Servant also has a cognitive purpose: the Servant will learn, will be satisfied with knowledge, through his sufferings (53:11).

Was Abraham also called to be filled with a new knowledge? Was the sacrifice of Isaac a way of making him see that there is a life (obedience to God) that is worth more than life (cf. Ps 63:4)? The series of figures that, as we have just seen, have prolonged in the biblical narration this "test of Abraham" serves to clarify potentialities that were enclosed in it. The "test of Abraham" was called to be linked to a teaching about the authentic meaning of life, with a pedagogy about the concept of living that human beings form for themselves. We can thus better evaluate the interpretation that Hebrews 11:17–19 gives of Genesis 22. Exegetical science habitually presupposes that this Christian interpretation is based on a superimposition or on an equivocation. Westermann emphatically points out that "the time of the Patriarchs did not know this meaning."[26] But, even while accepting the hypothesis that "the time of the Patriarchs" did not know it, we are not obligated to conclude that "the text" ignores it also. Just as the test of Israel in the desert and the test of the Servant have a pedagogical purpose—they look to teach, and to teach something about what "living"

---

25. See Marta García, *Consolad, consolad a mi pueblo: El tema de la consolación en el Deuteroisaías*, AnBib 181 (Rome: Gregorian & Biblical Press, 2010), 273–274: in Isa 53:12 the justified sons are the wages of the Servant of YHWH, just as offspring was Abraham's reward for his obedience; on p. 289: the Servant of YHWH is put forth as a covenant, that is to say, as mediation of the same, thus making an allusion to the figure of Abraham, for only in this case is it said, "by you all the families of the earth shall bless themselves" (Gen 12:3).

26. Westermann, *Genesis*, 440: "It is evident that it is the Christian theologian [of Heb 11] who has thus presented things; the time of the Patriarchs did not know this meaning."

means—so also Abraham is tested in order for his concept of life to mature, so that he will learn to link life with obedience to God. This Genesis text does not say what Abraham hoped for; we do not know whether he believed that Isaac would be able to be resurrected once he had died.[27] But it begins to work on the revelation of a mystery: the resurrection of the just Servant. The maturation of the concept of life, which begins here, prepares the believer for receiving the aforesaid mystery. To read about the figure of Abraham with this "teleological" perspective is much more enriching than to read about the figure only in light of the restrictions that are defined by a (hypothetical) reconstruction of the ideological world in which it germinated.

b) The sacrifice-redemption of Isaac as a figure

The "sacrificial" theme is key in our text. More concretely, the text seems to allude to the institution of the "sacrifice of redemption."[28] For Israel, the first-born sons belonged to YHWH (for he had redeemed them in Egypt from extermination) and they should be redeemed in a symbolic way through the offering of an animal (see Exod 13:12–15; 22:29; Num 3:13; 18:15). In the account of Genesis 22 something similar occurs: the first-born is substituted with an animal. LaCocque affirms in this respect:

> The account [of Gen 22] establishes in totally clear terms that the first-born son belongs to God, who possesses him as his own private property; the prescriptive repeatedly constitutes this divine property in a legal privilege and consequently prescribes the means by which the natural parents should redeem their first-born son from certain death, which is the way in which God reclaims what is his. The first-born is mysteriously a son of death (cf. Job 18:13) and, if he lives, is a survivor, a resurrected one (Exod 13:12, 13, 15; 22:29; Num 3:13; 18:15; see Luke 2:13).[29]

---

27. In this sense, see the affirmations of Brueggemann, *Genesis*, 193: "It is the word of resurrection which leads us through this text to the God who surprises us with life. That is not to say simply that Isaac would be raised had he been killed. For that is speculation and is not the claim of the text. Heb. 11:17–19 links Isaac to the power of the resurrection, but not in terms of raising a dead man. Resurrection concerns the keeping of a promise when there is no ground for it."

28. See Westermann, *Genesis*, 433; but, as Gordon J. Wenham, *Genesis 16–50*, WBC 2 (Dallas: Word, 1994), 105, points out, the text of Genesis 22 is not fully understood by affirming that it is a simple etiology for explaining why human sacrifices are not agreeable to God. A polemic purpose is not perceived in the text, nor is there evidence that such sacrifices were common in Israel.

29. LaCocque, "No matarás," 114.

Two narrative figures are thus related to each other: the redemption of Isaac and the redemption of the first-born sons of Israel during the flight from Egypt. Let us focus on an interesting aspect that unites the two narrative moments. In Egypt, YHWH manifested himself first as Exterminator and then as Redeemer. On the mountain of Moriah, something similar occurs; there is an internal tension in the presentation of God: at first he appears as the one who asks for the life of the son, and then later as the one who saves Isaac from the hand of Abraham.

Gordon J. Wenham arrives at the point of wanting to see this duality expressed in the diverse denominations with which the narrator presents God at the beginning and at the end of the story of Genesis 22: Elohim (vv. 1, 3, 8, 9, 12) and YHWH (vv. 11, 14[x2], 15,16).[30] It is not that there is a contradiction between the God who threatens and the God who redeems (as one exegete thinks).[31] The narrative progress separates precisely both aspects, and shows that the ultimate revelation of the face of YHWH is that of the God who blesses and redeems. His other side, that of the Exterminator who claims the life of the son, is part of his manifestation in a story stamped with death and sin. There is not a contradiction but rather a beneficial tension, capable of saving.

In Egypt, the first-born sons of Israel were redeemed, that is to say, liberated from the "condemnation to death" that weighs on every human person sold into slavery. This figure helps us to understand better what occurs on Mount Moriah. Genesis 22 is understood in a more complete way when to the title "sacrifice of Isaac" is added its final meaning: "redemption of Isaac." Redemption from that obstacle (introduced through sin) which makes flesh and blood opposed to the gift of God. In this sense we can understand the affirmation of Gianfranco Ravasi: "The son of flesh and blood disappears in an ideal way on Mount Moriah; Abraham should renounce him. . . . The one who is now before him is no longer simply an heir and a son of Sarah; he is now the gift-son, the "promised" son."[32] Isaac is born again on Mount Moriah; he returns to life as "gift-son," just as the first-born sons of Israel are redeemed.

But there is yet another aspect of this sacrificial dimension of the episode of Genesis 22 that we have to illuminate. We should thus refer to the figure of the Servant, which we evoked earlier. The action of the Servant is described in

30. See Wenham, *Genesis 16–50*, 103: "In the first half of the story where God is acting in a strange, remote, and inexplicable way, he is called *'elohîm*, but when he is revealed as savior and renews the covenant promises, his personal name, 'the Lord,' is appropriate and is reintroduced."

31. Thus Brueggemann, *Genesis*, 188.

32. Gianfranco Ravasi, *Il libro della Genesi (12–50)* (Rome: Città Nuova, 1993), 122.

Isaiah 53:10 with sacrificial terminology: "when he makes himself an offering for sin."[33] We know that the Midrashic collections and the Talmud tend to link closely the figure of the Servant in Isaiah 53 with that of Isaac in Genesis 22 (see also John 1:29).[34] Certainly, in Genesis 22 we find ourselves before an enigmatic silence regarding Isaac's understanding of the gesture that his father enacts and the meaning of his offering. But this silence becomes precisely the hermeneutical locus, with the possibility that other figures can make explicit the potential dimensions of this account.

To this end, it is necessary to consider an "intermediate" figure that has contributed "to the formation of the picture of the Servant of YHWH who bears the guilt of many"[35] and that repeats the symbolism of the cords and "being bound" in preparation for his sacrifice (demonstrating a repetitive "insistence") with respect to what we encounter in Genesis 22. We refer to the prophet Ezekiel and, in particular, to Ezekiel 4:4–8:

> Then lie upon your left side, and I will lay the punishment of the house of Israel upon you; for the number of the days that you lie upon it, you shall bear their punishment. For I assign to you a number of days, three hundred and ninety days, equal to the number of the years of their punishment; so long shall you bear the punishment of the house of Israel. And when you have completed these, you shall lie down a second time, but on your right side, and bear the punishment of the house of Judah; forty days I assign you, a day for each year. And you shall set your face toward the siege of Jerusalem, with your arm bared; and you shall prophesy against the city. And behold, I will put cords upon you, so that you cannot turn from one side to the other, till you have completed the days of your siege.

"I will put cords upon you": the prophet is bound as a symbolic gesture that expresses the "passion of Ezekiel" for the city of Jerusalem. They [Jerusalem's enemies] will also besiege him (like the city), but he will survive in order

33. See the discussion in García, *Consolad*, 262–264.

34. See Frédéric Manns, "The Targum of Gen 22," 69–80 in *The Sacrifice of Isaac in the Three Monotheistic Religions: Proceedings of a Symposium on the Interpretation of the Scriptures Held in Jerusalem, March 16–17, 1995*, ed. Frédéric Manns (Jerusalem: Franciscan Printing Press, 1995), 71; and at 75: "The leading idea of Is 53 is parallel in *leitmotif* to the targumic tradition on Gen 22. . . . These common features of the two stories are on the scriptural level. In the Targum, the resemblances are plainly realized and the nature and effect of the Servant's passion are applied to the sacrifice of Isaac so that Gen 22 becomes the story of a just man who offered himself for the benefit of sinners." And at 76: "It could be assumed that the targumic interpretation of the Akedah resulted from the association of Gen 22 and Is 53."

35. See Walther Zimmerli, *Ezekiel 1* (Philadelphia: Fortress, 1979), 165.

to be a figure of hope put before the people.[36] Ezekiel thus becomes a figure similar to that of the Servant, who offers atonement with his suffering and lives in order to manifest a horizon of hope.

In this light, the gesture of "the binding of Isaac" (from this we get the name of *Akedah*, which in the Hebrew tradition identifies this passage) acquires a new coloring. Why is so much relevance given in Genesis 22 to the fact that Abraham binds his victim? It is not a detail that makes reference to the sacrifice, for it is mentioned nowhere else that the sacrificial victim had to be bound.[37] Neither does the text evoke an act of violence that makes us think that Isaac was bound by force (in order to prevent him escaping). For this reason Wenham thinks that this particular situation is described in order to demonstrate that Isaac participates voluntarily in the sacrifice:

> And there was plenty of time for Isaac to realize, if he had not before, what was going to happen and to run away. But he did not. In fact, he allowed himself to be bound before Abraham cut his throat. This action above anything else indicates his consent . . . he was tied, indicating his own willing submission to God's command revealed to his father.[38]

Perhaps Wenham goes too far here and it would be better for him to respect the silence of the text. In any case, that silence implies an identification and an opening. This opening leads us precisely to the figure of Ezekiel and that of the Servant. In them is offered to us the development and the manifestation of that which is present in a germinal way in Genesis 22. The silence in which Isaac assumes his own sacrifice is a prelude to the actions of Ezekiel and the expiatory work of the Servant.

There still remains an objection to resolve, because earlier we linked the figure of Abraham with that of the Servant and now we are doing the same with that of Isaac; does this not create a species of schizophrenia in the figure of the Servant? Absolutely not, for, as we have indicated, the criteria of "concentration" is precisely the sign of proximity to the fulfillment. The Servant assumes in himself diverse figures in order to show that in his flesh he approaches closer to the final hour.

36. We should read the expression of verse 8, "the days of your siege (*matsôr*)," in parallel with that of verse 7, "the siege (*matsôr*) of Jerusalem." The "passion" of the prophet in his body corresponds to the "passion" of the city; on this matter see Mario Cucca, *Il Corpo e la città: Studio del rapporto di significazione paradigmatica tra la vicenda di Geremia e il destino di Gerusalemme* (Assisi: Cittadella, 2010).

37. Westermann, *Genesis*, 433, effectively points out that the background of this action is not cultic.

38. Wenham, *Genesis 16–50*, 115.

12.4. Conclusion and perspectives

Typology, proposed by *Verbum Domini* as an instrument for the interpretation of the biblical text, does not intend to reach historical certainties about the text or to recognize the footprints that diverse literary traditions have left on it. Typology is a project of teleological reading: it opens up the text to its future. Therefore, as we have said, it is a Christological reading. We have had the occasion to show, in our interpretation of Genesis 22, how the trajectories that are germinally present in the text become clear, remaining in tension in order to develop in dialogue with other figures.

Typology helps us to understand that a mode of the prophetic has carried out a "transcendence" of the institutional that is, in reality, a fulfillment. The preliminary figure of the Servant brings to fulfillment the sacrificial figure of Isaac, and they found their institutional form in the sacrifices of the Old Testament. These sacrifices are transcended precisely when their ultimate intention is brought to its end.

We have limited our application of typology in Genesis 22 to the trajectories that the Old Testament reveals, arriving at the figure of the Servant. We would thus want to insist on the truth of this affirmation of *Verbum Domini*, according to which the tension around fulfillment already exists in the Old Testament. In any case, the New Testament gives us interpretive keys for understanding the account typologically. Texts like Romans 8:32 or John 3:16, but also James 2:21–23 and Hebrews 11:17–19 (which we have mentioned in the course of this exposition), help us to catch sight of diverse trajectories of fulfillment. These trajectories cannot immediately be harmonized. They do not always read the Old Testament figure in the same way. But this variety, this lack of uniformity, becomes precisely the principle that makes the figurative exegesis fertile.

The language of typology that we have employed here has a heuristic function of first order; it produces progress in the true understanding of the text, which one would not obtain through a more conceptual, abstract, or generic methodology. The pertinence of figurative discourse will always be justified by testing precisely the fruit or hermeneutical progress that results in the understanding of the text.[39]

---

39. See the interesting observations of Antoine Vergote, "Psychanalyse et interpretation biblique," col. 252–260 in *Supplément au dictionnaire de la Bible*, vol. 9, ed. Henri Cazelles et André Feuillet, (Paris: Letouzey & Ané, 1979), col. 257, in this respect. This author points out that "the sole criterion of truth remains the power that the diverse anticipatory theories have to render an account of the full text, of its motifs and its structure. A minimalist interpretation is certainly not more objective in this regard: by a subjective decision it declares certain elements to be random, which another reading reveals as essential."

13

Verbum Domini:
A Logocentric Vision of the Christian Faith

Luis Sánchez-Navarro

The post-synodal apostolic exhortation *Verbum Domini* represents, as we have already pointed out in chapter 11, the most recent proposal of the contemporary Magisterium about the importance and the function of the Word of God in the life and mission of the Church. In it are offered important directives about the criteria that must preside over the interpretation of Sacred Scripture so that it can be, truly, faithful to its proper mission of testifying to the Word of God and making access to it possible; the ecclesial character of these criteria stands out, as an indispensable and foundational dimension. But the reading of this document alone reveals that its reach is broader and extends over all aspects of the Christian faith, as they are seen in their relationship with the divine Logos. In these pages we will show the originality of the magisterial teaching of Pope Benedict; something that—since it cannot be any other way in a thinking so firmly anchored in Scripture—emerges from the Gospel itself.

13.1. The prologue of John, synthesis of the Christian faith

To start off, Benedict XVI shows what has to be the "interior guide," as we could call it, of his proposal, its true backbone: the beginning of the Gospel of John, generally known as its "prologue" (John 1:1–18: *VD* §5). The influence of Johannine theology, and of this passage in particular, on the exhortation is decisive, for it constitutes the foundation of a nuclear doctrine in *Verbum Domini*: the analogous character of the expression "Word of God," which has its *princeps analogatum* [principal analogous counterpart] in the eternal Word and which allows us to speak, therefore, of a true "symphony of the Word" (*VD* §7–16).[1] Only in the Johannine writings is Jesus spoken of as the Word: besides the beginning of the Gospel we should also cite the prologue of the First Letter of John (which speaks of "the Word of life": 1 John 1:1) and the Book of Revelation, which, in its final chapters, refers to the mysterious rider of the white horse—Jesus resurrected—as "the Word of God" (Rev 19:13).[2]

The Gospel of John begins by affirming the eternity and divinity of the Word; not only did he exist "in the beginning," but he "was with God" and "was God" (John 1:1). This one verse contains the nucleus of Christian revelation: in God there is a plurality, given that there exists a subject (the Word) who "is with God" from the beginning. The Spirit is not yet spoken of in the prologue: only later, when Jesus goes to consummate his earthly existence, will the Spirit acquire a consistent relevance (John 14–16). But already in the beginning of the Gospel, the "plural" condition of the one God is uncovered, which thus develops Jewish monotheism in a surprising direction. Moreover, the raison d'être of this Logos is a communicative reason; his proper name (Word) indicates it, and the evangelist will make it explicit in the conclusion of the prologue: "No one has ever seen God; the only Son . . . *has made him known*" (John 1:18). "Jesus of Nazareth is, so to speak, the 'exegete' of the God whom 'no one has ever seen'" (*VD* §90). This means that, in the very reality of the eternal God, there exists a person who expresses him and can reveal him: the eternal Word. The Christian faith is therefore faith in the revelation of this Word.

After expressing in a simple and unfathomable way the eternal mystery of God, the prologue of John details the action *ad extra* of the Logos. The affirmation is also impressive in its simplicity: "All things were made through him" (1:3). This eternal Word of God mediates all creative work; John thus interprets with a Trinitarian key the foundational account of Israel, that of creation (Genesis 1), in which God creates by means of his word: "And God said . . ."; the ten times in which the expression appears allow us to understand this narrative as the "creative Decalogue" of God.[3] He creates by means of "ten words"; in effect,

---

1. See Augustín Giménez González, "La sinfonía de la Palabra," 31–46 in *Escudriñar las Escrituras: Verbum Domini y la interpretación bíblica*, PreDi 32, ed. Luis Sánchez Navarro (Madrid: Universidad Eclesiástica San Dámaso, 2012).

2. To these writings can be added the Letter to the Hebrews, which in its beginning implicitly presents Jesus as the definitive, eschatological word of the Father: "in these last days he has spoken to us by a Son" (*ep'eschatou tōn hēmerōn toutōn elalēsen hēmin en huiō*: Heb 1:2).

3. Gen 1: 3, 6, 9, 11, 14, 20, 24, 26, 28, 29. "Ten times the word 'said' appears. And the thought of the creative word is completed with the actions of 'calling.' The Word of God is

the creative work of God does not appear there—for example—under the simile of an architect (cf. Prov 8:27–31) or of the potter (cf. Gen 2:7). God does not work to accomplish something; he only speaks, and his word is efficacious. Just as the Psalm proclaims: "By the word of the Lord the heavens were made, and all their host by the breath of his mouth" (Ps 33:6). This teaching reappears in the Letter to the Hebrews: "By faith we understand that the world was created by the word of God" (*rhēmati theou*: Heb 11:3). The amazing new thing proclaimed by John is rooted, therefore, in the genuine tradition of Israel received by the New Testament.

In the center of the prologue we find the raison d'être of the Gospel: that Logos "became flesh." It is impossible to comment even roughly on the depth of this affirmation. But let us limit ourselves to the obvious: Jesus of Nazareth is the divine Logos who became *sarx*, in such a way that "we have beheld his glory" (John 1:14). In his humanity, Jesus is the Word of God: "now the Word has a *face*, one which we can see: that of Jesus of Nazareth" (*VD* §12). His works cause us to know the Father; his speaking is speaking about the Father. And it is the case that *his very being is the word of the Father*: "His unique and singular history is the definitive word which God speaks to humanity" (*VD* §11). His flesh communicates God; Jesus is the revelation of the God whom "no one has ever seen" (John 1:18). The being of Jesus is revelatory; his mission is to reveal, to communicate the truth (*alētheia*). His human existence is existence as *the human word of God*. Therefore his mission consists in disseminating the Word, just as he affirms in a veiled way in the parable of the sower, the "parable of parables": "The sower sows the word" (Mark 4:14).[4]

In Jesus the Word, God is revealed *exhaustively*; in order to know the Transcendent, it will be enough to look upon Jesus with faith: "He who has seen me, has seen the Father" (John 14:9). The Christian faith therefore has at its center the Word; it is essentially "logocentric."

13.2. A God who knows how to speak

The true newness of the Christian faith is this: that God speaks. Human reason can indeed know with certainty the existence of God, the ultimate cause of

---

the dominant element of this marvelous picture." Domingo Muñoz León, *Palabra y Gloria: Excursus en la Biblia y en la Literatura Intertestamentaria* (Madrid: Consejo Superior de Investigaciones Científicas, 1983), 64.

4. The version in Luke says even more plainly: "The seed is the word of God" (*ho logos tou theou*: Luke 8:11).

reality and the one who rewards;[5] but it is incapable of arriving beyond that, to the point of contemplating God's face, of entering into intimate union with him. The history of revelation, on the contrary, shows us that God is a God who speaks, who expresses himself and thus makes himself close to us and understandable—that he descends to us. And that in Jesus Christ he has uttered his ultimate and definitive Word, as the pope recalls in developing the *eschatological dimension* of the Word (cf. *VD* §14). In the comparative history of religions, the discontinuity of the Christian vision of God with that which other religious traditions present stands out: dogmas like the divine Trinity or the Incarnation of the Son of God are unimaginable for any human mind, even as elevated as its religious sensibility may be; the similar phenomena that can be adduced in other religions, as for example the adoption of human forms on the part of divinities in the Greek pantheon, keep such a vast distance from the Christian Creed that it amply transcends whatever isolated similitude that one can point out. The Christian faith, which took centuries to find an adequate doctrinal formulation for expressing these realities, affirms them not because it has invented them, but rather because it has received them. It is the originality of God, who speaks and thus makes himself really present in the life of human beings, without limiting himself to the role of a Transcendent One who is always absent.

The Bible, Old and New Testament, is a speaking of God by means of Jesus Christ; "Christ is the living word of God and explains himself using the words of Sacred Scripture."[6] But the speaking of God is not a simple monologue; rather it awaits man's response. In reality, *he knows how to dialogue*. The history of salvation attested in Scripture presents to us a God who looks for man, who waits for his response, who respects his freedom. "In this vision every man and woman appears as someone to whom the word speaks, challenges and calls to enter this dialogue of love through a free response. Each of us is thus enabled by God to *hear and respond* to his word" (*VD* §22). The Word of God thus implies the word of man; God speaks to man, so that man can learn to speak to God. This is confirmed in a singular way in the book of Psalms and in the many prayers that we find throughout the biblical canon (*VD* §24).

In this way, man also learns how to understand himself.

---

5. Cf. Heb 11:6b: "For whoever would draw near to God must believe that he exists and that he rewards those who seek him."

6. Kurt Koch, "L'annuncio di un Dio che parla: Riflessioni sul rapporto tra Rivelazione, Parola di Dio e Sacra Scrittura," 61–75 in *Ascoltare, rispondere, vivere: Atti del Congresso Internazionale "La Sacra Scrittura nella vita e nella missione della Chiesa" (1–4 dicembre 2010)*, ed. Ernesto Borghi (Milan: Terra Santa, 2011), 74.

13.3. The Word of God and the human person

"We were created in the word and we live in the word; we cannot understand ourselves unless we are open to dialogue" (*VD* §22). We touch here on a central element of the Christian faith; as Vatican II affirms with concise terms, "only in the mystery of the incarnate Word does the mystery of man take on light" (*GS* §22). Anthropology belongs to revelation: human beings do not understand themselves if they are not revealed to themselves by God through his Word, the Logos. The pope specifies two fundamental aspects of this revelation: "The word of God discloses the *filial and relational* nature of human existence" (*VD* §22: emphasis added). From its first pages, Sacred Scripture presents the human person as a creature, but as an absolutely singular creature, distinct from all the rest, since the human person is created in the image and likeness of God (Gen 1:27). Human beings are, therefore, in their very being, in relationship with the Transcendent: they cannot prescind from this basic dimension of their existence. Human beings, who are present throughout all the pages of the Bible, are in relationship with God: a relationship that is serene or stormy, accepted or rejected, but a relationship that is constant until the end. Therefore, every human being is also a "word of God" and speaks, with his or her very existence, about God; if—as Pope Benedict teaches, following Bonaventure's words—"every creature is a word of God, since it proclaims God" (*VD* §8), how much more are human beings, man and woman, created in his image and likeness (cf. Gen 1:26)?

The human person's relationship with God, as *Verbum Domini* tells us, is "filial": the Word of God reveals to us that every human being is called to be a son or daughter of God. The filial relationship with God confers on human beings a very high dignity which they are called, on their part, to express and deepen in all of their actions. The true nature of the human person, a nature revealed by God, thus contains a call. From this point of view, again, all Scripture taken together offers an irreplaceable light: "Your word is a lamp to my feet and a light to my path" (Ps 119:105). For the Israelites, the Torah, deepened by the Prophets and the Writings, is the light that allows them to walk with security in all moments of existence. In a special way, the Decalogue, whose solemnity and singular character is emphasized by the Torah, signals the necessary conditions not only for being faithful to the Covenant but also for being human. But this Scripture passage reaches its summit in the mystery of Christ; in fact, the only time that *Verbum Domini* cites this verse of Psalm 119, it does so by referring to the resurrection of Jesus along with it:

> Christ is thus "the light of the world" (Jn 8:12), the light which "shines in the darkness" (Jn 1:5) and which the darkness has not overcome (cf. Jn 1:5).

> Here we come to understand fully the meaning of the words of Psalm 119: "Your word is a lamp to my feet and a light to my path" (v. 105); the risen Word is this definitive light to our path (*VD* §12).

Jesus reveals in his resurrection the call of every human being to follow the path of God, the path which he has traveled first. The Word Incarnate "coming into the world" is thus "the true light that enlightens every man" (John 1:9).

13.4. The Word of God and the Church

If anything is firmly established in *Verbum Domini*, it is the mutual implication between the Church and the Word of God; it would be sufficient, therefore, to recall its second part, dedicated precisely to "The Word in the Church" (*Verbum in Ecclesia*: §§50–89).[7] But already, from its introduction, it is established that the pope's objective in this magisterial act is the following: "I wish to point out certain fundamental approaches to a rediscovery of God's word in the life of the Church as a wellspring of constant renewal. At the same time I express my hope that *the word will be ever more fully at the heart of every ecclesial activity*" (*VD* §1: emphasis added). From this we come away with a double affirmation:

a) The Word of God must be present, not in some activities or moments of the life of the Church, but rather *in all her activities*. Its presence must be, simply put, all-encompassing. The liturgy is certainly the privileged setting for reading and interpreting the Word, the place in which its potentiality develops to the greatest degree: "Every liturgical action is by its very nature steeped in sacred Scripture" (*VD* §52).[8] But the fecundity of the Word of God is not limited to the liturgy: it is meant to characterize all ecclesial acts, from transmission of the faith and formation of disciples, to works of the apostolate and works of charity. No aspect of the life of the Church can perdure and bear fruit without constant reference to the Word of God transmitted in the Church and attested in Scripture.

b) This presence of the Word in the Church, moreover, is not marginal, secondary, or added. It is "her heart": something central in every ecclesial activity, which does not see in the Word of God simply a theological justification or a concrete illumination regarding what she lives out; on the contrary, she discovers in that Word the root out of which her entire life grows.

---

7. Cf. chapter 2 of this volume, "The Word of God and the Church in the New Testament."
8. See Manuel Aroztegi, "Una Palabra eficaz: Palabra y sacramento," 65–83 in *Escudriñar las Escrituras*, ed. Luis Sánchez Navarro.

The origin of all ecclesial life is the Holy Spirit, always living and efficacious; but that Spirit speaks and inspires through the inspired Scripture (cf. 2 Tim 3:16); not without cause is the Word of God, just as Sacred Scripture testifies, described in the Letter to the Hebrews with those very words: "living and efficacious" (Heb 4:12).[9]

It does not seem exaggerated, therefore, to affirm that Benedict XVI proposes what we could denominate as a "logocentric ecclesiology."[10] If John Paul II affirmed in the title of his last encyclical that the Church is born of the Eucharist, we can deduce something analogous in the present document, which even from its first page points out the irreplaceable function of "the Word of God in the life and mission of the Church." Certainly, the Church has been born of that Word; therefore "this people cannot exist without Sacred Scripture, since in it this people finds the foundation of its existence, vocation, and identity."[11]

13.5. The Word of God and Christian morality

As we have already seen, the Bible is presented to man as a light that is capable of illuminating his paths: "Your word is a lamp to my feet and a light to my path" (Ps 119:105). The metaphor of the "path" is perhaps one of the most characteristic in Scripture for speaking about man's moral life. Let us remember that decisive passage of Deuteronomy in which, at the doors of the promised land, Moses puts before the people their own responsibility; the great prophet-legislator of Israel will equip them for walking in the path of YHWH by obeying his Word and thus being able to have life: "If you obey the commandments of the LORD your God which I command you this day, by loving the LORD your God, by walking in his ways, and by keeping his commandments and his statutes and his ordinances, then you shall live and multiply" (Deut 30:16). Throughout history, the Word of God to which Scripture testifies has been for Christians the guide that orients our steps in the pursuit of true happiness, that happiness which comes out of the promise of full life, which God makes possible in Jesus Christ.

That same Word is efficacious as a reminder, as Benedict XVI points out: "Listening to the word of God leads us first and foremost to value the need to

9. Translator's note: I depart from the RSVCE translation of "living and active" here.

10. "The sweeping 'Word-centeredness' of Benedict's ecclesiology is truly remarkable and unparalleled among theologians of his generation, Catholic or otherwise." Scott Hahn, *Covenant and Communion: The Biblical Theology of Pope Benedict XVI* (Grand Rapids: Brazos Press, 2009), 48–49.

11. Koch, "L'annuncio di un Dio che parla," 66.

live in accordance with this law 'written on human hearts' (cf. *Rom* 2:15; 7:23)" (*VD* §9). These words express the newness of the New Covenant. Christians, strictly speaking, do not learn from Scripture how we ought to live: we have an interior teacher, the Holy Spirit given by the Resurrected One, who effectively teaches us how to follow Christ, inscribing the "New Law" in our hearts. But the Spirit is validated in this regard by the Sacred Scriptures, the treasury of revelation inspired by him; and moreover, the Word to which Scripture testifies remains the authority, external and intimate at the same time, that allows man to hear ever anew that law that has been written on his heart, and to orient his life according to this light.

From this perspective we understand how, by speaking about man's response to the God who speaks, the pope presents sin as "a *refusal to hear the word*" (*VD* §26). To sin is to close the ears of the heart; the exhortation is thus deeply rooted in Scripture, which describes Israel's distancing itself from God in these terms. It is enough to recall such important passages as Isaiah 6:10 ("Make the heart of this people fat, and their ears heavy, and shut their eyes; lest they see with their eyes, and hear with their ears, and understand with their hearts, and turn and be healed"), the text to which Jesus returns in his "discourse on the parables" in Matthew 13 and Mark 4; or also Psalm 95 ("O that today you would hearken to his voice! Harden not your hearts, as at Meribah"), on which the Letter to the Hebrews comments extensively (Heb 3–4). Every sin is, at its very root, a failure to receive the Word, that is, the presence of God. On the contrary, the loving listening to the Word, made possible by the action of the Spirit, is the point of departure for a life that is agreeable to God, for a "worship according to the Word" (*logikē latreia*: Rom 12:1). This explains how, as Pope Benedict teaches, the life of the saints—the most mature fruit of the Spirit—is an unavoidable criterion for the correct interpretation of the Bible: *viva lectio est vita bonorum* (*VD* §48).

13.6. The Word of God and the Holy Spirit: a biblical spirituality

Scripture is a spiritual reality, in the strong sense: it is the work of the Spirit, who has inspired it (cf. 2 Tim 3:16). "The word of God is thus expressed in human words thanks to the working of the Holy Spirit" (*VD* §15). And furthermore, as the "Spirit of truth," he makes it possible to understand the Word and thus leads us to the fullness of truth (cf. John 16:13). "In fact there can be no authentic understanding of Christian revelation apart from the activity of the Paraclete" (*VD* §15). This understanding is not merely intellectual, but rather vital: it consists in grasping not only the internal harmony of revelation (which is expressed in the analogy of faith[12]), but also the profound attunement that exists among the most noble desires of the human heart and that revelation to which Sacred Scripture attests. The work of the Spirit, as YHWH affirms through the mouth of the prophet ("I will put my law within them, and I will write it upon their hearts": Jer 31:33), is the full interiorization of the Word.

This being so, we understand the solemn declaration that the conclusion of *Verbum Domini* contains: "We must never forget that all authentic and living Christian spirituality is based on *the word of God proclaimed, accepted, celebrated and meditated upon in the Church*" (§121). Sacred Scripture is for the Christian "spiritual reading" par excellence, as Vatican II opportunely recalls (*DV* §25). The following has recently been written in this regard, comparing the current situation of Scripture in the Church with what the resurgence of the Eucharistic practice for young children implied, exactly a century ago:[13]

> In sum, would we not need to begin a new *devotio*? A true "devotion" to the Sacred Scriptures so that they can become the daily book of the entire Christian world?[14]

These words adequately reflect Benedict XVI's proposal in the present moment about ecclesial history. Evidently it is not about an absolutely new thing, since the biblical foundation of theology and the Christian experience are obvious in the ecclesial tradition; on the subject of *lectio divina* the pope has already affirmed: "The word of God is at the basis of all authentic Christian spirituality" (*VD* §86). Not in vain does he also recall how "it is certainly not by chance that the great currents of spirituality in the Church's history originated with an explicit reference to Scripture" (*VD* §48). But the insistence and originality of this "return to the Scriptures" evoked and practiced by Pope Benedict, something that has been able to be verified in every homily, every discourse, every public speech, and every book, leads us to look at the Book of books with new eyes, capable of discovering in its pages the Word of God always in the present, which illuminates definitively the questions and the desires that move twenty-first century man. Moreover, the attitude toward Scripture defines in a particular way the attitude of man toward God.

12. Cf. Klemens von Stock, "La hermenéutica de la Sagrada Escritura en *Verbum Domini*: Perspectivas y reflexiones," 15–30 in *Palabra encarnada: La Palabra de Dios en la Iglesia*, ed. Ignacio Carbajosa and Luis Sánchez Navarro, PreDi 20 (Madrid: Universidad Eclesiástica San Dámaso, 2008), 22–23.

13. Translator's note: The author alludes to the effects of Pope Pius X's decree *Quam singulari*, which instructed the Church that children should receive First Communion around the age of seven, the age of reason, rather than being delayed.

14. Vincenzo Paglia, "Introduzione," 9–14 in *Ascoltare, rispondere, vivere*, ed. Borghi, at 13.

This has a close relationship with the significant importance that one recognizes in *lectio divina* as a central element in Christian spirituality. Following the urgent recommendation of the Second Vatican Council (*DV* §25), Benedict XVI picks up the insistence of the Synod on "the need for a prayerful approach to the sacred text as *a fundamental element in the spiritual life* of every believer" (*VD* §86, emphasis added); and illustrates it with the doctrine of two greats, Augustine and Origen (*VD* §86). Prayerful reading of Scripture is a foundation, a bedrock, of the spiritual life of the Christian; the challenge that is proposed both to pastors and exegetes and to the faithful is demanding and fascinating at the same time.

One cannot conceive of a "Christian spirituality," that is, an authentic living out of the faith, without constant recourse to the Sacred Scriptures, the Old and the New Testament. For only the Word of God to which they testify can be the foundation of this spirituality. The Scriptures are therefore called to generate a "devotion" in the proper sense of the word, which speaks to us about a religious dedication, about a style of life oriented toward God, who manifests himself in all his dimensions. The true Christian *devotion* is an intrinsically biblical devotion; in it the revelation of God, his Word, occupies a central place.

13.7. The Marian dimension of the Word of God

In the Christian faith, as the Church lives it out and Sacred Scripture testifies to it, the function of the Virgin Mary is central and inalienable, something which the exegesis of the Gospel account of the infancy in Luke, or of the Gospel of John, openly demonstrates.[15] Therefore, recourse to the Mother of Jesus could not be lacking in Benedict XVI's proposal; as we read in the document, "what the understanding of the faith has enabled us to know about Mary stands at the heart of Christian truth" (*VD* §27). This is shown particularly in the three parts that are explicitly dedicated to her, and that characterize the entire document:

a) In the first part of the exhortation (*Verbum Dei*), in developing the response of man to the God who speaks, the figure of Mary, who in her faithful hearing of the Word of God appears as *Mater Verbi Dei* and *Mater fidei* (§§27–28), is presented as a preeminent model. In her "the reciprocity between the Word of God and faith" is accomplished completely (§27);[16] the attunement

15. Cf. Ignace de la Potterie, *María en el misterio de la Alianza*, BAC 533 (Madrid: Biblioteca de Autores Cristianos, 1993); Klemens von Stock, *María, la madre del Señor, en el Nuevo Testamento*, Vida y Misión 34 (Madrid: EDIBESA, 1999).
16. Translator's note: Here I follow the Spanish translation and depart from the English

between the heart of Mary and the heart of Scripture—the Holy Spirit—is total. This brings the pope to suggest, for theological studies, a close relationship between Mariology and the theology of the Word, for mutual benefit (§27); and it is the case that "the Incarnation of the Word cannot be conceived apart from the freedom of this young woman who by her assent decisively cooperated with the entrance of the Eternal into time" (§27). Mary appears, in the end, as the human person who has lived out to the highest degree the familiarity that one can have with the Word of God (§28). A singular demonstration of her familiarity is the Magnificat, in which "we see how completely at home Mary is with the word of God" (§27). The pope proposes the "Marian way" of relating to the Word as a model for the spiritual life of believers: "As we contemplate in the Mother of God a life totally shaped by the word, we realize that we too are called to enter into the mystery of faith, whereby Christ comes to dwell in our lives" (§27).[17]

b) The second part (*Verbum in Ecclesia*) deals, in its final section, with "the word of God and Marian prayer" (§88). The Marian prayers (among which are mentioned the Rosary and the Angelus, and also the principal Eastern prayers: the Akáthistos and Paráklesis) represent a recourse that is very valuable as "an aid to meditating on the holy mysteries found in Scriptures" (§88). But Marian prayer carries out another important function in the spiritual life of the faithful: to ask God that "through Mary's intercession, we may imitate her in doing his will and in welcoming his word into our lives" (§88). The objective of Marian prayer is for the faithful to interiorize and reproduce in their lives the welcoming of the Word of God on the part of the Mother of Jesus.

c) The concluding paragraph of *Verbum Domini* has as its title "*Mater Verbi et Mater laetitiae*" (§124). In it, Benedict XVI, inspired by the words of Elizabeth—"blessed is she who believed" (Luke 1:45)—takes up again the figure of Mary under the sign of happiness. She has lived the joy that comes from her loving hearing of the Word of God (cf. Luke 11:28); she thus appears as an encouragement for every believer, in a time in which the principal testimony that the Church can offer to the world is that of true happiness.

Mary and Scripture form, therefore, a binomial in which they mutually require each other. The heart of Mary is that new heart in which is written, engraved in fire, the Word of God (cf. Jer 31 and Ezek 36); Sacred Scripture,

translation.

17. In this respect, then-Cardinal Ratzinger affirmed in 1983: "In order to reflect truly the beam of light [of the Word], or in order to return it to its original splendor, it is not enough to study its historical genesis . . ." Cited in Koch, "L'annuncio di un Dio che parla," 75.

which was the nourishment of her faith, appears also for us as that living Word, capable of feeding, filling, vivifying, and opening ever new horizons.

13.8. Conclusion: faith in the Word

"'The obedience of faith' (Rom. 16:26; see 1:5; 2 Cor 10:5–6) 'is to be given to God who reveals'" (*DV* §5): with this declaration, Vatican II placed faith in the Word of God in the center of Christian existence. Faithfully following the track of the Council and going deeper into it, Benedict XVI has demonstrated in *Verbum Domini* the profound present necessity of opening the ears of the heart to this Word. The Christian is the person who puts his faith and hope in the Word of God Incarnate, the Resurrected Jesus Christ. The Word of God, transmitted in the Church, witnessed to by Scripture, celebrated and welcomed in the liturgical celebration, and incarnated in the life of the Christian, thus appears as an element that is capable of fruitfully integrating all the aspects of the Christian faith; this thus appears to us, in its deepest sense, as a *logocentric* reality.

Original Publications

Most of the published texts in this book are updated versions of previously published essays, which have appeared in various journals or collaborative works. The following are the previous texts of both authors which have served as the basis of this volume.

Granados, Carlos. "El cumplimiento de las Escrituras según *Verbum Domini.*" *Teología y Catequesis* 109 (2011): 31–48.

Granados, Carlos. "Pablo y el buey que trilla (1 Cor 9,9)." In *Pablo y Cristo: La centralidad de Cristo en el pensamiento de san Pablo*, proceedings of the international conference "Pablo y Cristo," Madrid, February 26–27, 2009, pp. 227–238. Collectanea Mattritensia 5. Madrid: Publicaciones San Dámaso, 2009.

Granados, Carlos. "Walter Brueggemann: Una crítica posmoderna a la exégesis canónica de Childs." In *Canon, Biblia, Iglesia: El canon de la Escritura y la exegesis bíblica*, edited by Augustín Giménez González and Luis Sánchez Navarro, 117–130. Presencia y Diálogo 30. Madrid: Universidad Eclesiástica San Dámaso, 2010.

Sánchez Navarro, Luis. "Antiguo y Nuevo: ¿Conflicto o plenitud?" *Unum Sint-Communio* 10 (Autumn 2008): 24–37.

Sánchez Navarro, Luis. "Carácter testimonial de la Sagrada Escritura." *Revista Augustiniana* 43 (2002): 349–369.

Sánchez Navarro, Luis. "Los cristianos y el Antiguo Testamento: Enseñanza del Vaticano II (DV 15–16)." In *Fuente de agua viva: Homenaje al Profesor*

D. Enrique Farfán Navarro, edited by Joaquín Pascual Torró and Juan Miguel Díaz Rodelas, 95–110. Series Valentina 55. Valencia: Facultad de Teología, San Vicente Ferrer, 2007.

Sánchez Navarro, Luis. "Escuchar la Palabra: A propósito de *Verbum Domini.*" *Tabor* 13 (2011): 15–30.

Sánchez Navarro, Luis. "La lectura eclesial de la Escritura." In *Jesucristo en el pensamiento de Joseph Ratzinger*, edited by Gabriel Richi Alberti, 21–38. Collectanea Mattritensia 9. Madrid: Universidad Eclesiástica San Dámaso, 2011.

Sánchez Navarro, Luis. "Palabra de Dios e Iglesia en el Nuevo Testamento." In *Palabra encarnada: La Palabra de Dios en la Iglesia*, edited by Ignacio Carbajosa and Luis Sánchez Navarro, 67–96. Presencia y Diálogo 20. Madrid: Universidad Eclesiástica San Dámaso, 2008.

Sánchez Navarro, Luis. "La relación Antiguo-Nuevo, clave hermenéutica de la Escritura." In *Entrar en lo Antiguo: Acerca de la relación entre Antiguo y Nuevo Testamento*, edited by Ignacio Carbajosa and Luis Sánchez Navarro, 51–67. Presencia y Diálogo 16. Madrid: Universidad Eclesiástica San Dámaso, 2007.

Sánchez Navarro, Luis. "*Verbum Domini*: Una visión logocéntrica de la fe Cristiana." In *Escudriñar las Escrituras: Verbum Domini y la interpretación bíblica*, edited by Luis Sánchez Navarro, 85–100. Presencia y Diálogo 32. Madrid: Universidad Eclesiástica San Dámaso, 2012.

Contributors

Carlos Granados, DCJM, is a priest of the Disciples of the Hearts of Jesus and Mary and a doctor in Sacred Scripture from the Pontifical Biblical Institute in Rome (2010). He is currently a professor of Old Testament at San Dámaso Ecclesiastical University in Madrid. Granados is a member of the Spanish Biblical Association (ABE) and the alumni association of the Pontifical Biblical Institute of Rome. His publications include: *Deuteronomio* (Madrid: Biblioteca de Autores Cristianos, 2017); *El camino del hombre por la mujer. El matrimonio en el Antiguo Testamento [The way of man through woman. Marriage in the Old Testament]* (Estella, Spain: Verbo Divino, 2014); and *El camino de la ley. Del Antiguo al Nuevo Testamento [The way of the Law. From the Old to the New Testament]* (Salamanca: Sígueme, 2011). Granados also coedited two books with Fr. Sánchez-Navarro: *Enquiridion bíblico. Documentos de la Iglesia sobre la Sagrada Escritura [Enchiridion Biblicum: Documents of the Church on Sacred Scripture]* (Madrid: Biblioteca de Autores Cristianos, 2010); and *Opening Up the Scriptures: Joseph Ratzinger and the Foundations of Biblical Interpretation* (Grand Rapids, MI: Eerdmans, 2008).

Luis Sánchez-Navarro, DCJM, is a priest of the Disciples of the Hearts of Jesus and Mary, and a doctor in Greek Philology from the Complutense University of Madrid (1995) and in Sacred Scripture from the Pontifical Biblical Institute of Rome (2004). He is currently a professor of New Testament at San Dámaso Ecclesiastical University in Madrid. Sánchez-Navarro is a member of the Spanish Biblical Association (ABE), the alumni association of the Pontifical Biblical Institute of Rome, and the Catholic Biblical Association of America. His publications include: *Un cuerpo pleno. Cristo y la personalidad corporativa en la Escritura [A Full Body. Christ and the Corporate Personality in Scripture]* (Madrid: Ediciones Universidad San Dámaso, 2021); and *El logos del reino. Las diez parábolas de Mateo [The Logos of the Kingdom. The Ten Parables of*

Matthew] (Estella, Spain: Verbo Divino, 2013). Sánchez-Navarro also coedited two books with Fr. Carlos Granados, as listed above.

Kristin Towle has taught for many years as an adjunct professor of Theology at The Saint Paul Seminary School of Divinity, of the University of St. Thomas (St. Paul, MN), as well as other institutions. She holds a bachelor's degree in Catholic Studies and Spanish from the same university, and a Ph.D. in Theology from Ave Maria University. Towle focuses her teaching and speaking on Thomistic moral theology, the Church's spiritual traditions, and Christian political philosophy, but she loves to branch out into other areas of theology, including biblical studies. She has simultaneously raises her big family as she continues to remain engaged as a scholar.

Kevin Zilverberg earned his Doctorate in Sacred Scripture from the Pontifical Biblical Institute in Rome and currently serves as an assistant professor of Sacred Scripture at The Saint Paul Seminary School of Divinity, of the University of St. Thomas (St. Paul, MN). Beyond the classroom, his responsibilities include the direction of Saint Paul Seminary Press, the general editorship of the Catholic Theological Formation Series, and the direction of the Institute for Catholic Theological Formation. Zilverberg has authored *The Textual History of Old Latin Daniel from Tertullian to Lucifer* (Madrid: Consejo Superior de Investigaciones Científicas, forthcoming). Besides having coedited *Approaches to Greek and Latin Language, Literature and History: Κατὰ Σχολήν* (Newcastle upon Tyne, UK: Cambridge Scholars Publishing, 2019), Zilverberg is the lead editor of *The Revelation of Your Words: The New Evangelization and the Role of the Seminary Professor of Sacred Scripture* (St. Paul, MN: Saint Paul Seminary Press, 2021), and *Piercing the Clouds:* Lectio Divina *and Preparation for Ministry* (St. Paul, MN: Saint Paul Seminary Press, 2021).

Index of Names and Subjects

Index of Scripture References

Genesis

1:1	127
1	100, 176n16, 204, 204n3
1-2	112, 150n8
1-3	127
1:22	47n54
1:26	207
1:26-28	150n8
1:27	176, 177, 207
1:28	47n54
1:29-30	150n8
2:7	205
2:22	49
2:24	93
3:15	109
3:24	128
6-9	100
8:17	47n54
9:1	47n54
9:2-3	150
9:6	150
9:7	47n54
9:9-17	108
12:3	197n25
15:18	108
17:2	108
17:20	47n54
22	5, 114, 189, 194-202
28:3	47n54
28:10-22	108
33:8	191
35:11	47n54
47:27	47n54
48:4	47n54
49	109

Exodus

1:7	47n54
13:12-15	198
14	99, 100
19:2	108
19:4	103?
20:10	149
20:12	93
22:29	198
23:4-5	149, 150, 151
23:13	149
23:19	148
24:8	78, 122n18
34:26	148
34:29-35	116
34:34	116, 122n16, 142n44

Leviticus

20:1-5	195
26:9	47n54

Numbers

3:13	198
18:15	198

Deuteronomy

5:14	149
5:16	93
6:4-5	170
8:2-16	196
11:18	60
11:20	60
14:21	148
15:4	77
15:11	77n12
17:18	60
18:15-18	127n40, 173, 177, 190
19:15	37
22:1-4	149, 151
22:6-7	148
23:2	44n47
23:3	44n47
23:4	44n47
23:9	44n47
23:25	151
24-25	151
24:10-13	151
24:14-15	151, 152
24:19-22	151, 152
25:4	4, 147, 150-155
30:16	209

Joshua

3	99
3:14-17	100